THE NINE TRANSFORM[ATIONS]

REGENERATION, LONGEVITY, AND IMMORTALITY IN CHINESE ALCHEMY

DR. MARK T. HOLMES, O.M.D., L.AC
Dipl. Acupuncture (NCCAOM) and Dipl. Chinese Herbs (NCCAOM)

CAULDRON
PRESS

COPYRIGHT © 2020 MARK T. HOLMES

This work is licensed under a Creative Commons Attribution-Noncommercial-No Derivative Works 4.0 International License.

Attribution — You must attribute the work in the manner specified by the author or licensor (but not in any way that suggests that they endorse you or your use of the work).
Noncommercial — You may not use this work for commercial purposes.
No Derivative Works — You may not alter, transform, or build upon this work.

Inquiries about additional permissions should be directed to: drmarkholmes@yahoo.com

Cover Design by Pixel Studios
Edited by Kathryn F. Galán, Wynnpix Productions
Published by Cauldron Press
www.DrMarkHolmes.com
Acupuncture points diagrams from www.acupuncture.com. Copyright © 1996-2017 Cyber Legend Ltd.
Title page image: "Physicists at the Large Hadron Collider at the CERN in Switzerland announced the discovery of a new sub-atomic particle they named, 'pentaquark.'"

DISCLAIMER: The information provided in this book is designed to provide information and motivation and is not meant to be used, nor should it be used, to diagnose or treat any medical condition. The author and publisher are not responsible for any specific health needs that may require medical supervision and are not liable for any damages or negative consequences from any action to any person reading or following the information in this book. Or, in other words, this book is meant to give you a framework and method for introspection and self-discovery, and you are responsible for whatever it is that you discover and what actions you take afterward. Readers should be aware that the websites listed in this book may change.

ISBN 979-8-6323-8305-9

The Nine Transformations *is a product of fifty years of personal alchemical work and attending patients. I hold in deep respect my primary way-showing mentors and all doctors who represent an eclectic world approach:*
John-Roger, USA, Masaru Toguch, Japan, Dr. Lee-Shing Sheng, Taiwan, Se Han Kim, Korea, Reinhold Voll, Helmut Schimmel, Germany, and Jeffrey Yuen, China.

I also dedicate this workbook to people everywhere who express from their True Self.

ALSO BY DR. MARK HOLMES

Original Innocence, The Nature of the Soul

Across the Golden Bridge

CONTENTS

Also by Dr. Mark Holmes _____ 4

PROLOGUE _____ 9

ALCHEMY'S FIRST CONCEPT _____ 14

    From Where Did I Come? _____ 14

    Who Am I and What is My Curriculum? _____ 14

    The Cycles of 7 and 8 _____ 17

    The Cause of Disease _____ 18

    A Firm Foundation Upon Which to Stand _____ 20

    Why Are We Here and Where Are We Going? _____ 21

    The Order in which Spirit Enters the Body _____ 22

    E-motions Have Status and Direction _____ 23

    Notes _____ 26

FIVE PHASES _____ 27

    Wood _____ 28

    Fire _____ 29

    Earth _____ 30

    Metal _____ 30

    Water _____ 31

    Forgiveness _____ 33

    Preparing the Cauldron _____ 34

    Jin Bian/The Nine Transformations _____ 36

    Important Alchemical Formulas _____ 38

    Notes _____ 39

1. HEALTH PALACE — 40
- There Are No Incurable Diseases, Only Incurable People — 41
- Spirit Does the Healing — 43
- Using Herbs as Teachers — 47
- Theory and Treatment of Aging and Senility — 48
- Zhuyou/The Power of Words — 55
- Important Alchemical Formulas and Homework — 57
- Notes — 58

2. WEALTH-AMBITION PALACE — 59
- Exercise and Movement — 62
- Sexual Practice — 63
- Circulating Qi/the Microcosmic Spirit — 63
- Unwillingness or Inability to Change Is a Major Cause of Disease — 64
- What is Natural? — 65
- Wealth and Longevity — 66
- Notes — 67

3. PROSPERITY-HONOR PALACE — 68
- The Big Picture — 70
- Life Can Depend on How We Process Information — 73
- Changing the Mind to Change the Condition — 74
- The Five Taxations — 76
- Personality Temperament — 78
- Personality Temperament and Choices — 84
- The Three Worms/Karma — 88
- Moxibustion — 91
- Notes — 95

4. RELATIONSHIP PALACE — 96
- Three Treasures, Three Selves — 97

High Self-Wisdom and Beyond 99
The Basic Self—Survival 101
Conscious Self—Having Experiences 104
Working with the Three Treasures/Three Selves to Balance the Five Phases ... 105
Aligning the Three Treasures/Three Selves 112
Notes 116

5. CREATIVITY-CHILDREN-FRIENDSHIP PALACE 117
True Self—False Self 118
Opening the Portals Further 119
Exercises 121
Notes 122

6. GLOBAL ADVENTURE-JOY-HAPPINESS PALACE 123
Boundless Breathing 127
Notes 136

7. CAREER-KNOWLEDGE PALACE 137
The Eight Extraordinary Vessels 139
Aligning the Three Treasures/Three Selves 148
Thread Breathing for Daily Microcosmic Orbit Balancing and Extraordinary
    Vessel Treatment 150
Clearing the lower Portals 155
Seeing the Perfection and Being a Sage 156
Notes 158

8. WISDOM PALACE 159
Toning and Chanting 160
Using Trees to Tonify the Body and Assist Ascension 162
Anti-Aging 164
Co-Creating 165
The Hun/Basic Self and Po/Conscious Self 165

Yi/Intention and Zhi/Will 168
Cheng Xian/The Art of Prolonging Life and Achieving Immortality 171
Observing, Accepting, and Cooperating with What Is 172
The Cauldron, the Furnace, and the Firing Process 173
I Ching Meditation 175
Notes 179

9. COMING HOME TO THE SPIRITUAL FULFILLMENT PALACE 180
Chanting the Names of God 182
The Golden Bridge 184
Alchemical formulas 186
Notes 187

10. LIBERATION-IMMORTALITY 188
Respect, Caring, and Support 189
Ho'oponopono 191
How to Practice Ho'oponopono in Four Simple Steps 192
Notes 196

APPENDIXES 197
Forgiveness Process 197
Eight-Foot Cube of Light 199
Calling in the Light 200
Planting a Light Column 201
Sound Current 203
Using Herbs as Teachers 204
Notes 213

REFERENCES 214
ACKNOWLEDGMENTS 217
ABOUT THE AUTHOR 218

PROLOGUE

THE GOAL OF NEIDAN, or internal alchemy, is to redeem one's spirit from materiality by changing base personality traits, referred to as the false self, into the golden elixir of the true self. Chang Po-tuan (Tzu-yang) 983-1082, the Southern School Complete Reality Taoism founder called this becoming a real human being. In the west we define this as running the splits between the celestial and earthly domains, going back and forth quickly between the two. The aim is having the celestial spiritual mind run the terrestrial human mind as we know the human mind is a great servant but a poor master. We quiet the human mind and watch for the return of our original celestial mind, open our consciousness, access Spirit and ride the sound current into the ocean of divine love.

Waidan, or external alchemy, refers to chemical sciences, the changing of base metals into gold and/or the production of physical longevity. Early alchemists reasoned that, since metals could not be dissolved by soaking them in water, or spoiled when buried in earth, or chemically changed by melting in fire, they were the most incorruptible of substances and by swallowing them the body would respond with longevity. Early Chinese emperors and many adepts discovered their error after swallowing mostly poisonous metallic substances like cinnabar and realgar; they suffered strokes or died attempting to change their genetics and force open their consciousness.

Around the 4th century AD, the Chinese developed the Neidan/internal alchemy format presented in this book. The Nine Transformations model is attributed to Ge Hong (283-343 AD), an Eastern Jin Dynasty Taoist scholar who lived during a time of Chinese political upheaval. Ge's teacher had been a student of Ge's uncle, who attained immortality, it is said, through Taoist internal alchemical practices. In addition to compiling the Nine Transformations, Ge Hong wrote *The Inner Chapters of the Master Who Embraces Simplicity*, *The Outer Chapters of the Master Who Embraces Simplicity*, and *A Handbook of Formulas for Emergencies*. He also compiled *Traditions of Divine Transcendents*, in which is presented about eighty-five transcendents who lived for 125-200 years of age between 200 BC and 200 AD by utilizing meditation, breathing exercises, physical exercises, diet, and herbalism.

I received the framework of the Nine Transformations from Jeffrey Yuen, an 88th-generation Taoist priest with whom I have studied many topics in seminar format since 1993. After three separate seminars specifically on the Nine Transformations, I have taken thirteen-plus years to format this Workbook after satisfactorily putting myself, my seminar participants, and various patients through aspects or in its entirety multiple times.

My great joy is teaching people to take care of themselves. As such, I am not a fan of the *Doctor, heal me* model, as it often underemphasizes patient responsibility and puts unrealistic emphasis on the doctor and whatever technique he/she utilizes.

Yuen has joked that the only thing a doctor can cure is ham, as a way to illustrate that healing is not done by the doctor; the herbs/acupuncture treat the disease while the patient heals themselves with doctor's and Spirit's assistance.

We realize that Earth is a school for learning and growth and once we have learned the lesson provided by the illness or dis-ease, we no longer need to experience that which provided the lesson, and we heal. My goal for this Workbook is to assist you in understanding who you are, so you can gracefully overcome difficulties/illness and discover and complete whatever you are here to accomplish.

***

Traders traveling the Silk Road between China and Persia, where alchemy is translated as *elixir*, reintroduced alchemy to Europe in the thirteenth century after centuries of persecution. The Italian di Medici family commissioned Marsilio Ficino to translate the *Corpus Hermeticum* from Greek into Latin and after its printing in 1471, a focus on Hermetic literature is believed to have assisted the Renaissance to emerge from the Dark Ages.

Hermes, the recognized founder of alchemy, is to have said, *The furnace or cauldron used by alchemists to maintain a uniform temperature of the human body contains within it all that is needed to produce the great circulation of oxygen and blood. The fire of Spirit and the vessel of our gross and subtle bodies are One. Nothing needs to be added. Just remove the impurities that surround it.*

Hermetic followers operate under the philosophy that impurities and unhealthy attitudes and actions deplete a person's vital energies, overtaxing the organs and nerves which leads to disease. They taught that doctors should be cognizant of a person's karma, so the treatment does not get in the way of learning and growth. These same basic tenets have been adopted or discovered independently by subsequent Eastern and Western alchemical practitioners.

Alchemy, whether Eastern or Western, has three important questions to explore:

> ➢ Who am I and from where did I come?
>
> ➢ What is my curriculum I am to learn in this life?
>
> ➢ Where am I going?

According to the Chinese Nine Transformation model, all people have in common nine aspects (herein called Palaces) through which we explore these three questions in depth, both by engaging in the world and through self-introspection:

1. Health
2. Wealth
3. Prosperity-Honor
4. Relationship
5. Creativity-Children-Friendship
6. Global Adventure-Joy-Happiness
7. Career-Knowledge
8. Wisdom
9. Going Home

And, classically, there is a tenth one, referred to as the Hero's Journey, which involves sharing what we have learned with others. The Palaces can be sources of joy or a lifelong challenge, depending upon one's viewpoint.

It is interesting to note that modern science has found that having a relaxed mental state and getting adequate sleep are the two most important anti-aging factors we can utilize. This approach is the same as the ancient Chinese dictum that a *quiet mind* is the most beneficial technique for longevity.

Also, extensive contemporary research into the gut's microbiome has demonstrated the importance of gut health in all areas of health, disease, and aging. Similarly, from an Oriental medical perspective, the process of digestion is the most important physical attribute linked to thriving into old age.

***

As we explore our Zhen Ren/authentic self through the Nine Transformation method, we start with techniques to nourish the physical body so the material world does not sap our Qi/life force and diminish our efforts.

In China, the approach to nourishing life to enhance spiritual cultivation (the terms, like *cultivation* come from an agrarian society where life and death depended upon growing enough food and protecting oneself from inclement weather and enemies) unfortunately shifted during Tang Dynasty (618-907 AD) toward a focus on treating disease rather than nourishing life to prevent illness which is where we often find ourselves today, in both the East and West.

A Taoist definition of health, which maintains the pre-Tang awareness, is not *absence from disease,* but rather *we are healthy if we are content with ourselves.* This does not refer to our being content with our immediate environment or the world at large; it means being content with our inner environment, who we perceive ourselves to be. By this definition, one could have a life-threatening disease and still be healthy. The point to a long, healthy life is to give us enough time to complete our karma/curriculum and to use experiences as a springboard into higher consciousness. The alchemist realizes the opportunity for oneness in every experience.

The Old Testament tells stories of Patriarchs and others who lived many hundreds of years, led by Methuselah's 969 years. After the Flood, many men are depicted with life spans over 120 years.

The East has a similar historical record. In *The Mystery of Longevity,* Liu Zhengcai writes that many ancient Chinese scholars enjoyed long life spans like Peng Zu who was noted for his cooking skills, dao-yin exercises, and qigong breathing; he lived to 767 in the time of Yao of Tang. The mysterious Gui Gu Zi, Master of Ghost Valley, was said to live several hundred years during the Warring States Period (475-221 BC).

During the Eastern Han Dynasty (25-200 AD), the famous physician Li Changzai, who wrote *Prescriptions of Li,* was commonly believed to have lived for hundreds of years, as did the Three Kingdoms (220-265 BC) scholar, Xi Jian, who ate the mushroom **Fuling/Poria Cocos/Hoelen/Guiding my Soul's Destiny** to release what is no longer working so we are not stuck in the past.

Wang Lie, during the Jin Dynasty, ate mostly **Huang Jing/Polygonatum/Solomon's Seal—Will Strengthener** to experience longevity. It has been said that will, will power and willingness is the fourth treasure in the Three Treasures system, being a necessary ingredient to breaking habits and holding through until *this too will pass*. Polygonum also connects the sexual Kidney energy with the loving heart, linking sexual function with good feelings to bring new levels of happiness.

The blind court musician Grandpa Dou of the Western Han Dynasty lived 180 years without taking any special tonics or foods or doing any particular exercises other than obtaining tranquility through a lifetime of lute playing. Each transcendent had their own unique way that best suited them, in their environment and during their time period, though between them we see common threads.

* * *

Throughout this Workbook we explore how to matriculate the Palaces wherein we have karma/attachments by applying time-tested longevity techniques such as:

- Meditations
- Visualizations
- Philosophy
- Understanding emotions
- Reframing beliefs
- Transforming Five Thieves into Five Virtues
- Balancing the Three Treasures/Three Selves
- Tonifying organs and meridians
- Adjusting diet
- Taking herbs
- Stimulating acupuncture points
- And more!

I am using the Nine Transformation model as a structural basis for internal alchemy. In the process of explaining my understanding of alchemy, I relate some of my experiences, realizations, and states of being. As such, this Workbook has gone beyond the Nine Transformations model; hopefully, it assists you to complete your curriculum/karma and offers you the opportunity to realize the aspect of you that is immortal. Join me in self-discovery while discerning what specifically works for you.

In contentment,

Dr. Mark T. Holmes

ALCHEMY'S FIRST CONCEPT

1) From where did I come?
2) Who am I what is my curriculum to learn?
3) Why are we here and where am I going?

From Where Did I Come?

WE KNOW WE CAME from our parents' sperm and egg. Contemplate however, the amount of Spirit/cosmic energy that was used to bring you forth into inception/incarnation and has assisted you to who you are today.

Deeply dive into your heart-sense and bring forward an inner knowing regarding your origin, whether evolved or created, or a combination of both. Record your awareness in your alchemical journal or in the space at the end of this section.

**

Who Am I and What is My Curriculum?

All humans have the same Nine Palaces in common through which we uniquely express ourselves. Two or three of the Nine Palaces will appear as primary lifelong opportunities for learning and growth. We tend to judge opportunities as good or bad, but alchemists realize there is opportunity for learning and growth in every experience and the blessing is what we learn about ourselves. Ultimately, we cooperate and complete without us having to exert excessive effort. This concept is explained in Palaces Seven, Eight, and Nine.

Chinese alchemists enumerated steps to reunite with our True Selves. They associated the nine acupuncture points of the Pericardium Channel with the energetics of each Palace, in perfect order, as a blueprint to transform dramas and traumas.

Because directly accessing the sanctity of the heart and altering one's destiny was deemed too invasive before 1500 AD, the heart meridian originally was not assigned points and so the Pericardium Channel, known as the Heart Protector, was the entryway used for this transformational process. In modern times we take advantage of both the pericardium and the heart channel points to probe a patient's personality temperament and behavior but to avoid confusion, this Workbook only deals with the Pericardium Channel points.

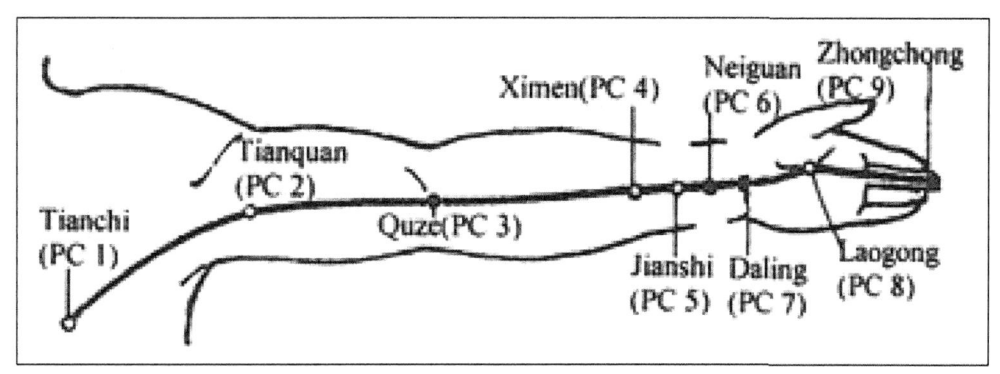

Pericardium Channel points. They are bi-lateral. Notice it starts in the heart area.

The Nine Transformation model is not about adding more abilities, becoming more learned, or accomplishing more in the world, mirroring Hermetic literature. An analogy during the Renaissance is how Michelangelo carved away all the marble that was *not David* to reveal what was already present in the raw stone. This model supports dropping false-self pretenses of an I/me/mine self-identification and embraces the true self's we/us/thou approach.

***

The Nine Palaces and their corresponding Pericardium channel points are:

1. **Health Palace:** Affecting all Palaces, good health means our attention is not drawn to health issues; poor health impacts our ability to plan, initiate, and complete in any palace. Under domain of the gall bladder/making decisions.

    Tian Chi/PC-1/Heavenly Pool opens the chest to allow us to more easily collect the Grace that comes from heaven reaching into our physical, mental and spiritual depths.

2. **Wealth Palace:** Do we have enough resources to survive, feed our families and have protection from heat, cold, danger and death? Under domain of the liver/choices.

   Tian Quan/PC-2 Heavenly Spring of the Kidney/Fountain of Life assists us to be grateful by understanding that challenges are not against us but designed to teach us about loving, caring and sharing.

3. **Prosperity-Honor Palace**: Do we have enough resources to share with others? Are people jealous, betraying, or stealing from us, and if they are, how does that affect us? Under domain of the small intestine/assimilation.

   Qu Ze/PC-3/Crooked Marsh is a reservoir of clear non-salty water/vital Qi that brings stability to what we manifest.

4. **Relationship Palace**: Relationships with spouses, family, and intimates as a heartfelt response. Under domain of the heart/loving.

   Xi Men/PC-4/Gate of Accumulation/Path of the Spirit heals emotional pain and suffering. It is interesting that this point is tonified with moxibustion to keep someone alive until they are transported to a hospital during a heart attack.

5. **Creativity-Children-Friendship Palace**: It is a basic belief that creativity comes from relationships and interacting with our children, acquaintances, and colleagues. We do not have as many children as the ancients did, but we have many avenues of creativity. What do we want our testimony of life to be? Under domain of the large intestine/letting go of what is no longer needed, a natural process of creativity.

   Jian Shi/PC-5/The Intermediary/The Passenger is the pericardial minister point that protects the heart under duress.

6. **Global Adventure-Joy-Happiness Palace**: In ancient days this was a small Palace as one could not travel quickly or far. Today we have planes, trains, and autos and we spend/waste time on the Internet/social media so this Palace has become more important in our time. Under domain of the lung/breath of life.

   Nei Guan/PC-6/Inner Gate/Perfect Love Point/Gate to Success opens the chest, regulates Heart Qi to calm the Shen/spirit, and is the best point for restoring balance between the body and the mind.

7. **Career-Knowledge Palace**: What is our chosen work? What do we do with the knowledge we gain in our endeavors? Under domain of the bladder, which has the most acupuncture points of any meridian channel, affecting every system, relationship, and interaction.

    Da Ling/PC-7/Big Mound/Spirit Gate is used when we do not know which way to go, or what to do in our career.

8. **Wisdom Palace:** Turning relationships, experiences, and knowledge into wisdom. Under domain of the kidney, which rules DNA, bones, spinal fluid, and brain, relating to our deepest physical aspects.

    Lao Gong/PC-8/Palace of Toil and Weariness is used for mental fatigue/Taxation Syndrome.

9. **Home Palace:** We follow the inner path to bring ourselves to the true self, whereby we achieve spiritual fulfillment. Under domain of the spleen-pancreas/stomach/our physical center.

    Zhong Chong/PC-9/Balanced Friendliness opens the eyes, ears, nose and mouth allowing us to perceive ourselves, others, and the world for what it is.

10. **The Hero's Journey**: Classically, there is this tenth aspect, the sharing with others what we have learned. We tune into Spirit to dictate how and what we share, not allowing the ego to dictate we *must* share with the less enlightened. We share what emanates from the heart. Since there are only nine points on the pericardium channel, there is no point associated with this aspect.

The Cycles of 7 and 8

Huangdi Neijing/The Inner Canon of the Yellow Emperor has been the fundamental Chinese medical source for more than two thousand years. This work is composed of two texts in a question-and-answer format between the Yellow Emperor and six legendary ministers, one of whom is the chief physician.

The first text, the *Su Wen/Basic Questions,* covers the theoretical foundation of Chinese medicine and diagnosis. It discusses an authentic human who thrives by nourishing his/her physical, emotional, mental and spiritual aspects and walks a spiritual path which is viewed as a path of peace. The text describes the natural cycles of women and men as being loosely assigned to seven and eight chronological years. The cycles of seven and eight fit into the Nine Transformations by indicating what ages we have more emphasis in certain Palaces. The first cycle corresponds to the First Palace, followed sequentially in order, with the second cycle associated with the Second Palace, third with the Third, etc.

The Health Palace affects our entire life, as this first cycle (for females, from gestation to seven years, and gestation until eight years for men) are formational years, physically and emotionally. Were we breast fed and bonded with mom or put on a grain or milk formula that precipitated food allergies? How does bonding or lack thereof affect our adult relationships? What real or perceived traumas that we experienced during these early years still affect us as adults?

Our ability to survive and our coping skills formulated during these early years greatly determine our default decision-making temperament that we carry throughout life. The Cycles of 7 and 8 are included in each of the Palace descriptions.

THE CAUSE OF DISEASE

Laozi, the purported author of the *Tao Te Ching* around 500 BC, noted, *I don't know what to call it, so I call it Tao/The Way*. Tao is *that which is*, the giver of life, both universal and specific, in everything and everyone. There is one Qi/Spirit with many manifestations and differentiations.

A planet has Qi. The physical elements have Qi, as do our bodies, and even invisible thoughts—everything is composed of Qi. A liver is not a kidney because the quality of the Qi differs.

Chinese medicine and philosophy determined that all disease comes either from a blockage of Qi/energy or a lack of efficient utilization of optimum Qi. The Chinese posit that if we have enough Qi we remain healthy, while insufficient Qi allows pestilent energies (e.g., climate, bacteria, poisons, beliefs, opinions, emotions) to insult us, ultimately causing disease and even death.

Yuan Qi/Original energy is what the Chinese call genetics. Yuan Qi plus our lifestyle/acquired Qi make up the totality of our Qi. The West has realized that our hygiene/lifestyle contributes about seventy-five percent of factors influencing longevity, while genetics are only twenty-five percent.

I was taught as a neophyte acupuncturist to understand how Qi manifests and operates in our bodies. In the spring, mountain streams are full of ice melt and rivers are a torrent of vibrant energy. In late summer when the streams are down to a trickle, moss, fungus, and bacteria grow in response to the lack of Qi of flowing water. These late-summer waters are from the same source as the spring torrents, but instead of being life-giving, they are now sources of turbidity and death. Once we are not able to eliminate ever-present pestilent energies because of blocked or deficient Qi, the body adapts an inferior metabolic function and, over time, adopts a position of ill-health.

The Chinese meridian channel identifies Five Antique Points, located from fingers to elbows and toes to knees, to describe the quality and effect of Qi.

The first antique point at the finger and toe tips have Qi/energy like water first emerging from a well. The Qi is scant because there is not much movement. Over time, the water accumulates and flows more forcefully into shallow pools, then to deeper pools, then becoming an unobstructed river, and finally emptying into a large lake or ocean that is vast and deep. The first points located on the fingers and toes are used for acute conditions, because of its changing quality going from the previous meridian vessel energetic to a new meridian. The points located at elbows and knees treat organ imbalances because the Qi is vast and deep.

We block Qi in three ways. Primarily, when we judge a situation or person, we are saying/acting like things should be different from the way they are. Hence, oriental medicine teaches emotions, which are choices stemming from our beliefs, are the number one cause of disease. Free-flowing Qi/energy is resumed when we accept and cooperate with what is and view situations without judgment. Secondly the external environment of wind, heat, cold, dryness, etc. can block Qi flow if we cannot adjust to its intricacies. The third cause is microbes, poisons, injuries, aging, etc.

To keep the meridian channels open and flowing throughout one's life, Koreans have utilized a technique of permanently inserting thin, two-centimeter-long gold wire needles into back Shu points for Lung, Heart, Liver, Pancreas and Kidney and the yang channels **Waiguan/TW-5/Outer Pass** and **Shenmai/Bl-62/Extending Vessel.** Silver wire needles are inserted into **Sanyinjiao/Sp-6/Three Yin Intersection.** The effect of this technique is similar to keeping a hose faucet in the open position.

Alchemy instructs us that we do not need to be in a hurry to take a pill or herb to get rid of symptoms, since our lessons are found within a symptom or situation. Alchemists *reframe* viewpoints by asking, *What is good about this situation?* This puts us in touch with the concept that *we* create, promote, or allow everything in our lives. Suffering can be a tool to show us what is not working and we pay special attention to chronic patterns or illnesses.

The Pericardium's role in the Nine Transformations process is to restore normalcy in accord with what is natural and congruent for us. Like a religious hymn to our own divinity, we use the Pericardium Channel to recognize that there are endless choices, and to honor what works for one may not work for another. We may feel limited due to definitions we self-prescribe, so we endeavor to remain open in consciousness and body.

A Firm Foundation Upon Which to Stand

To begin the process of self-revelation, we need a firm foundation. Those who have taken their lives in suicide likely decided they had nothing firm upon which to stand, or that there was no opportunity for change, or that whatever change possible was not tolerable. Establishing a firm foundation to feel safe is enormously important. The location of this foundational base in the body is **Pohu/Bl-42/ Door of the Corporeal Soul,** a point associated with the lungs. Spirit comes into the body first through the breath, and this point has deep access to the metaphysical function of breath and Qi/vitality.

Many of us are tight in the area under the scapula, indicating the free flow of Qi/life force is either blocked or deficient.

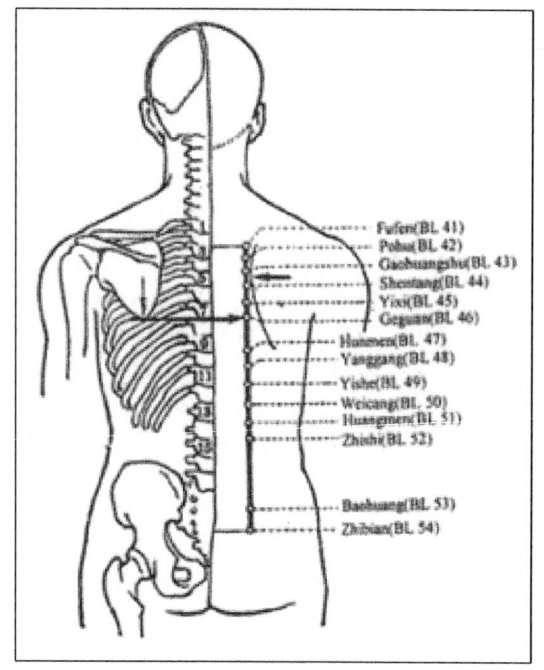

To establish a foundation, open the scapula by moving your arms across the front of your body and hug yourself. Opening the paravertebral muscles will also bring more space, elasticity, and fluids to the spinal nerve roots. Bend forward and provide space for the spinal discs. The yoga posture Plough is highly beneficial. (Caution is indicated if this pose is painful.)

Balance the movement by clasping your hands behind your back with straight arms and squeezing the scapulae toward each other.

From a physical standpoint, having a licensed practitioner apply acupuncture and/or moxibustion or having an osteopath or chiropractor adjust vertebrae and nerve flow can be beneficial for those who have lost their sense of purpose or suffered certain traumas, like loss of home, family, or deeply held beliefs.

Why Are We Here and Where Are We Going?

> People want to know why we are here. If the answer lay in the mind, engineers would have figured it out already and become our spiritual leaders. If having power in the world was the answer, then the politicians would be our enlightened guides. If the answer was found in fame and glamour, then our celebrities would offer us much more than publicity and good looks.
>
> Our true leaders are those who look at life in a radically different way. They know that love is the radical solution. It is radical because most of us don't approach life that way. For the most part, we approach life reactively, trying to control rather than letting go.
>
> It is said, "Out of God comes all things; God loves all of its creation, and not one Soul will be lost." This is the context for living a life without fear or worry. As you integrate these truths into yourself, you will let go and relax into the arms of the Beloved. (John-Roger, www.msia.org; subsequent references will be attributed with a simple J-R).

It is interesting how health issues direct us to explore for answers in avenues we normally would not entertain, either scientifically, energetically, philosophically, and even religiously. Wisdom teaches us to let go of what is not working and embrace what does work. We witness family members, friends, and acquaintances (and ourselves) continuing a belief and subsequent behavior when it is not yielding beneficial results. Possibly we stay with beliefs and behaviors because they are familiar, or we are afraid to let go of what control we think we have, as losing control is one of our five basic fears. Letting go can ultimately be described as dropping self-will to bring our will in alignment with the Creator's will for us. When we are sick and tired, hopefully we admit "I" cannot do this life by myself and we ask for guidance. However, ego-death and extinction are two other fears of the major five, so dropping self-will is not easy to do.

Many years ago, I learned a valuable lesson: the only way to get out of a dilemma (i.e., should I? shouldn't I?) is to physically remove myself from the situation.

I was in a long-term relationship that was wonderful for both of us but had deteriorated. I wanted more, while she was content flying at half-mast. I tried various strategies to drive the situation the way I wanted. One day, after being despondent for a number of months, I was mucking out my horse's manure from his stable at my house, and I realized I was putting my happiness/contentment on an external situation. It did not matter what someone else did or did not do, or said or did not say... It only mattered what I decided to think and feel, and subsequently do or not do.

We all make choices based on myriad reasons. I realized that other people's decision/actions do not have much to do with me. I learned not to take others' actions/non-actions personally. This awareness gave me the freedom I sought from my pain and suffering of living *out there*.

God is infinite and exists inside and outside of creation. We have finite bodies, so we cannot fully co-create with God in the infinite, but we can fulfill the destiny/purpose that God/Source has for us here. Everyone needs a sense of purpose to feel good about themselves, whether we believe in a higher power or not. Since the mind and emotions are not designed to understand the infinite, when we go deeper and access the part of consciousness that does understand life's meaning, we experience a peace that is beyond understanding to the mind and emotions. Each human journey is unique and precious. There is not just one way. Spirit provides perfect next steps for each of us, in perfect timing.

The Order in which Spirit Enters the Body

For over two millennia, the Chinese have referenced how altering the amount of oxygen coming into the lungs increases or decreases blood circulation. Since we live or die at the cellular level, blocked or stagnated Qi/oxygen leads to inefficient blood circulation/blood stasis, which diminishes metabolic function.

Chinese medicine details the order in which Spirit comes into the physical body, showing the importance of breathing, exercising, and removing blockages.

1. Breath
2. Nerves/meridian channels
3. Blood/blood vessels
4. Muscles
5. Bone marrow
6. Tendons and ligaments
7. Bones
8. Whole body

The body can go four minutes without air, approximately four to eight days without water, and about twenty days without food; hence we can view oxygen as more important than food. However, there is less financial gain in touting free air over selling certain diets or superfoods, so it is easy to see why our culture emphasizes what food and supplements we should eat or avoid.

The saying that we are what we eat is not accurate. We are who we are. We are souls with bodies, and when the soul no longer needs its container, it moves on, and the body goes to dust. During life, which is over very quickly, focusing on the soul's education is more important than what we eat or how we exercise. Of course, with proper intention, food and exercise support the soul's journey, but alchemists point out that excessive attention to the body takes Qi/life force that possibly can be used in a more enlightened manner.

In Chinese medicine, the cause of disease is threefold.

1. First, internal causes are most important: aberrant beliefs and excessive or deficient emotions.
2. Second are the external environment of climate, with its associated pathogenic factors of wind, cold, heat, damp, dryness, and summer heat.
3. Tertiary causes are accidents and injuries, external pathogens and toxins, toxic substances and poisons, inadequate nutrition, lack of or improper exercise, and lack of adequate rest and sleep.

E-MOTIONS HAVE STATUS AND DIRECTION

Chinese medicine posits emotions as the number-one cause of disease.

E-motions are self-directed and manifest as a choice from the mind. Notice in the discussion below, there are specific payoffs for choosing certain emotions. We are not victims to emotions over which we have no control. Since energy follows thought, it is important to think thoughts that propel us in a direction we want to go.

Negative or demeaning images of self and others block us from the loving, peace, harmony, resources, and ultimately the good health we all want.

Moods are less intense, as they come and go easily.

> **Anger/frustration/self-righteousness/individualism/irrationality/ frustration/aggression** makes us feel superior at a time when we feel inferior. Anger ascends Qi/energy and, in excess, causes headaches, dizziness, or eye trouble.
>
> **Cure**: Express our innocence and creativity through flexibility, receptivity, and

caring.

- **Excessive joy/pleasure** is a response when we are feeling lack. Excessive joy/pleasure disperses energy. An example would be a person who is in an over-the-top party mood.

    Cure: Drop the false self and embrace and live from the true self.

- **Anxiety/frightfully overjoyed/abnormal laughing/lack of emotion/ rapid mannerisms and speech** are responses we exhibit when we are not relaxed. Anxiety causes energy to become chaotic and affects the nervous system.

    Cure: Drop what is bothering us and let our Light and good deeds shine.

- **Worry/pensiveness/low self-esteem, lack of trust in self, in others, in God/living through others/over concern/hopelessness/lack of control over events** is a response when we do not trust, which causes energy to bind up and stagnate, affecting the stomach and digestion.

    Cure: Move into faith, trust, and sincerity, and have truthful intentions.

- **Sadness/grief/yearning/cloudy thinking/anguish** is a response when we feel separated/shamed/mistaken/bad. Sadness depletes energy and affects the lungs and breathing.

    Cure: See what is good regarding situation/choices, embrace positive self-feelings, and engage with the world.

- **Fear/dread/bad memory/contemplation** is a response when the ego pretends it doesn't know. Fear suspends energy and affects the kidneys, reproduction, and low back.

- **Cure**: Embrace knowing from the soul-self.

***

Emotions can affect life decisions in many ways. Suppose we worry excessively and overthink situations. This can bind the digestive organs, and we become sensitive or allergic to foods and the environment. Subsequently, we are tired and make decisions of exclusion:

e.g., I don't feel like enrolling into a class or going to a party to celebrate, or I don't feel like committing to XYZ, although, if I did, it would be fulfilling.

If beliefs and/or emotions are strong enough and held for a long enough time, they can become stored in the consciousness, the blood, an acupuncture channel, the connective tissue, or an organ, causing blockages and dis-ease. Oriental medicine details how excessive emotions are shunted into auxiliary reservoirs, so the five yin organs (liver, heart, spleen/pancreas, lung, and kidney), the most important aspect of our physiology for maintaining life, will not be adversely affected. However, this innate survival strategy cannot go on indefinitely. When these extra channels become full, the burden falls back on the five main organs. We refer to negative personality characteristics as Thieves, in that they steal our life force. (Reference the Five Phases and the chart below for Thieves and Virtues relating to specific organs and functions.)

Alchemists do not like unresolved situations. We release habituation and do not allow illness to take up residency in our consciousness or body. We change our thinking and release postures/sinews; we clear blockages with forgiveness and loving, thereby dropping who we are not, and embrace who we are.

* * *

Notes

FIVE PHASES

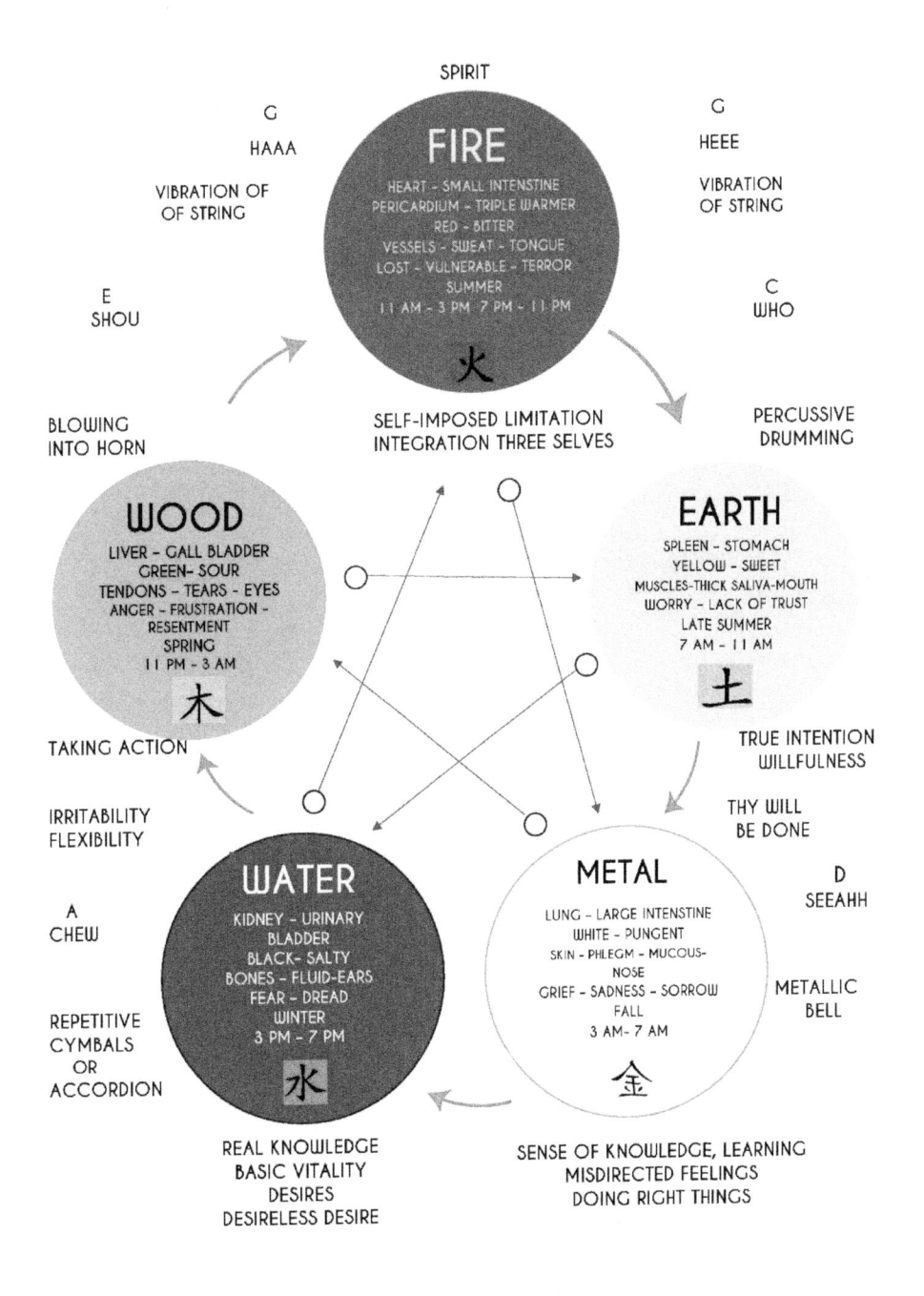

SPIRIT

FIRE
HEART - SMALL INTESTINE
PERICARDIUM - TRIPLE WARMER
RED - BITTER
VESSELS - SWEAT - TONGUE
LOST - VULNERABLE - TERROR
SUMMER
11 AM - 3 PM 7 PM - 11 PM
火

G
HAAA
VIBRATION OF
OF STRING

G
HEEE
VIBRATION
OF STRING

E
SHOU

C
WHO

BLOWING
INTO HORN

PERCUSSIVE
DRUMMING

WOOD
LIVER - GALL BLADDER
GREEN - SOUR
TENDONS - TEARS - EYES
ANGER - FRUSTRATION -
RESENTMENT
SPRING
11 PM - 3 AM
木

EARTH
SPLEEN - STOMACH
YELLOW - SWEET
MUSCLES-THICK SALIVA-MOUTH
WORRY - LACK OF TRUST
LATE SUMMER
7 AM - 11 AM
土

SELF-IMPOSED LIMITATION
INTEGRATION THREE SELVES

TAKING ACTION

TRUE INTENTION
WILLFULNESS

IRRITABILITY
FLEXIBILITY

THY WILL
BE DONE

WATER
KIDNEY - URINARY
BLADDER
BLACK - SALTY
BONES - FLUID - EARS
FEAR - DREAD
WINTER
3 PM - 7 PM
水

METAL
LUNG - LARGE INTESTINE
WHITE - PUNGENT
SKIN - PHLEGM - MUCOUS -
NOSE
GRIEF - SADNESS - SORROW
FALL
3 AM - 7 AM
金

A
CHEW

D
SEEAHH

REPETITIVE
CYMBALS
OR
ACCORDION

METALLIC
BELL

REAL KNOWLEDGE
BASIC VITALITY
DESIRES
DESIRELESS DESIRE

SENSE OF KNOWLEDGE, LEARNING
MISDIRECTED FEELINGS
DOING RIGHT THINGS

TO BETTER UNDERSTAND themselves and the world around them, the Chinese reduced everything in the universe into Five Phases and their correspondences. After fifty years of paying attention to these correspondences, I know the veracity and benefits of utilizing these practical groupings.

Wood

Organs: liver, gall bladder

Function: filtering blood, sinews/tendons/ligaments, producing tears, eyes

Color: green is partially a teaching action and partially a healing action, a balancer.

Flavor: sour

Season: spring

Time cycle: hours when these organs are predominant during the twenty-four-hour day and protect the body:
> 11 pm - 1 am Gall Bladder
>
> 1 am - 3 am Liver

Attribute: taking action

Emotions:
> Liver—anger, irrationality, frustration, aggression
>
> Gall Bladder—resentment, galled, stubborn, emotionally repressed, indecisive

Taxation: Walking too much is like preparing to reach an objective but never reaching it. This damages the liver because excessive movement damages the sinews, and then we cannot harmonize and maintain a smooth flow of energy.

Thief: irritability or impatient temperament

Virtue: receptivity and flexibility

Inner family: Basic Self

Spiritual family: following the Light

FIRE

Organs: heart, small intestine, pericardium, endocrine glands

Function: pumping blood through vessels, endocrine gland function, sweating, tongue

Color: red is full of energy and force, vitalizing the body. Use when energy is needed immediately. Orange creates a continual flow of energy and can be used to run several miles or if fatigued.

Flavor: bitter

Season: summer

Time cycle:

- 11 am - 1 pm Heart
- 1 pm - 3 pm Small Intestine
- 7 pm - 9 pm Pericardium
- 9 pm - 11 pm Triple Warmer/Endocrine system

Attribute: conscious thought

Emotions:

- Heart—frightfully overjoyed, abnormal laughing, lack of emotion, rapid mannerisms and speech
- Small intestine—lost, vulnerable, terror, abandoned, deserted, absent-mindedness, insecurity, deep unrequited love

Taxation: Looking too much at same events, ideas or emotions making the heart rigid by limiting possibilities

Thief: closed off/righteousness

Virtue: open consciousness/social courtesy/integration of Three Selves

Inner family: balance point, High Self

Spiritual family: Indwelling Christ

Earth

Organs: spleen, stomach, pancreas

Function: digestion, muscles, saliva, mouth, mental work

Color: yellow frequency as a mental process, intellect, quality of understanding or thinking.

Flavor: sweet

Season: late summer

Time cycle:

> 7 am – 9 am Stomach
>
> 9 am – 11 am Pancreas.

Attribute: true intention

Emotions:

> Spleen-pancreas—worry, low self-esteem, lack of trust in self, in others, in God; lives through others, over concern, hopelessness, lack of control over events
> Stomach—disgust, expanded importance of self, obsession, egotistic despair, nervousness.

Taxation: Sitting too much injures pancreas/spleen. Things in front of us are not worthy of our engagement.

Thief: arbitrary willfulness, my will be done

Virtue: true intent, truthfulness of true self, sincerity. Thy will be done

Inner family: mother

Spiritual family: mother Earth, Mother aspect of Father-Mother God

Metal

Organs: lung, large intestine, skin, immune

Function: breathing, immunity, mucous membranes, nose

Color: white is color of all colors combined, of Holy Spirit light above the soul and the magnetic light below the soul level.

Flavor: pungent

Season: autumn

Time cycle:

    3 am - 5 am Lung

    5am - 7am Large Intestine

Attribute: knowledge, learning

Emotions:

    Lung—grief, sadness, yearning, cloudy thinking, anguish

    Large intestine- dogmatically positioned, crying, compelled to neatness, defensive

Taxation: Lying too much injures lungs. Swallowing our pride, our good works, our breath, our life, or being too patient, too tolerant, feeling we cannot rebel weakens oxygen capacity and immunity.

Thief: misdirected feelings

Virtue: discriminating mind, justice, doing the right thing because it is the right thing to do.

Inner family: wise grandparent

Spiritual family: God breathing life into us, the lungs being the first location of spirit entering the body

WATER

Organs: kidney, bladder, adrenals, brain, bones

Function: filtering fluids, ears

Color: blue-black is part of a spiritualized intellect. Blue can assist to lift above some of the physical desire patterns of the Earth.
Purple is the highest vibration we can see. It transmutes.

Flavor: salty

Season: winter

Time cycle:

    3 pm - 5 pm Bladder/Adrenal

    5 pm - 7 pm Kidney

Attribute: basic vitality

Emotions:

    Kidney —fear, dread, bad memory, contemplation
    Bladder—paralyzed will, miffed, timid, inefficient, wishy-washy, comme ci, comme ça

Taxation: Standing too much consumes kidney/adrenal energy by putting pressure on the articulations of the spine. Excessive standing means there is something that stimulates and motivates us; our having things we want to accomplish.

Thief: desires/wants

Virtue: using pure wisdom to understand principles, sense of right and wrong, desire-less desire

Inner family: father, the will to act

Spiritual family: the father aspect of Father-Mother God, God supreme

    * * *

All diagnosis and treatment are rooted in Spirit. There are no incurable diseases, only incurable people. Relaxing, letting go, and trusting Spirit is part of transformation. One reason we do not transform or resolve disease is deciding we are unwilling or unable to change. Alchemists transform traumas and dramas into learning. Chinese practicality, based on centuries of human struggle, has shown that if we try to change our conditioning without accessing Shen/spirit, the Five Thieves attack and disaster ensues.

We go within and access the heart's knowledge of the True Self to know when to act and when to rest, when to speak and when to be silent. The most important virtue for our soul is being true to ourselves. The most important virtue for the human mind is sincerity of intent. The most important attribute for getting things done is having a powerful will. In the Chinese writing system, the bottom radical for both intent and will is the character depicting the heart, indicating the highest good is to look to the heart to define both intention and will.

Referencing the Five Phase chart, Intention is in the Earth Phase. Of the Five Thieves, the ancients taught the most disruptive Thief that steals our naturalness/True Self is arbitrary willfulness, found in this Earth Phase. From a Taoist viewpoint, having a true intention will gradually increase the other virtues and the Thieves will no longer be problematic.

FORGIVENESS

We choose to live *either* under the Law, which stipulates an eye for an eye, meaning, if we kill fifty times, then we must be killed fifty times; or we choose to live under Grace, which suggests there are other, more elegant ways to balance our actions and learn.

It is said that forgiveness is one of the keys to enter the Kingdom. The rationale is that God/Spirit does not judge us, but that we judge ourselves, based upon belief and conditioning, and this blocks us from self-awareness of our true nature. Judgments are not supported spiritually. Changes in action, however, are definitely supported.

> Forgiving yourself for your judgments usually releases the negative charge you have on yourself, on others, or on a situation. To begin the process, you can simply say, "I forgive myself for judging…," then add a reference to the person or issue in question. When you do this, you will often find, almost miraculously, that something lets go inside, and you feel as if a weight has lifted.
>
> Statements of forgiveness can be very general: "I forgive myself for judging my mother."
>
> However, if you do not experience a release of judgment, it might help to be more specific: "I forgive myself for judging my mother for not buying me the pair of shoes I wanted."
>
> * Perhaps you've hurt someone else—hurt their feelings, for example—but the other person isn't around, so you can't apologize directly. In that case, you might say, "I forgive myself for judging myself for anything I may have done to _____ [fill in the person's name] in _____ [fill in a descriptive word or phrase] situation."
>
> * How can you tell if you've released the judgment? You might spontaneously let out a sigh or take a deep breath. You might feel a surge of energy or warmth in your body or a feeling of relief. Whenever you make a judgment against another person, it is stored in your body. Forgiving yourself releases the other person from your energy field.

As you go through your day, give yourself forgiveness breaks. Take ten seconds to sit quietly and forgive yourself for judging yourself or others. (From J-R at www.msia.org.)

Preparing the Cauldron

In preparing the cauldron, we focus on continuing a discipline that is giving us positive results or begin one that we think/feel/intuit will redound positively for us.

Reframing from too many distractions and bringing awareness to choices regarding work, diet, relationships, all aspects of life, and taking quality time to foster life's meaning is recommended.

Buddha suggested we control the mind and have one overarching intention; what we do for work, who we associate with, what we do for relaxation and pleasure, what we eat, etcetera, can all support our intention.

* Following the Five Phase model, we start at the top with the Fire element's heartfelt alignment of the Three Treasures/Three Selves and proceed clockwise around the *generation cycle* and plant a yellow seed of sincere intention in the Earth Phase, where the mother principle resides.

* Next, we decide with the Conscious Self what knowledge in the Metal Phase we want to access and absorb. Then we live our intention in the Water Phase of will, location of the father principle within. Lastly, as the Wood Phase function of the Basic Self gets us involved in life, we enact what we intended and researched. We keep our mind focused on what we want more of to marshal resolve and resources, as the Basic Self cooperates well with focused mental images.

* After a suitable period of time we evaluate our results, beginning again with the heart's knowledge in the Fire Phase, and proceed again through the Phases. (The Basic Self, Conscious Self, and High Self have their own function in support of the soul and are defined elsewhere in this workbook.)

When we are drawn to an outside object, the mind leaves the body, and we are no longer *centered*. Since the mind is great servant and a poor master, it is better to evaluate our internal and external worlds neutrally, keeping the mind free of judgments and attachment. It is acknowledged that when we are careful where we put our attention, the celestial design is clearer, and we attract less tension and negativity. This leads us to the number-one key to longevity: *mental quietude.* Besides perceiving more clearly, neutrality frees us from having to balance/clear/forgive misconceptions at a later time.

In nature, things are birthed, mature, and die. Humans are part of a natural process, no matter how much we like to think of ourselves as wonderful, unique, or elite. Alchemy teaches us that *we cannot pick a flower without troubling a star*, meaning life has overarching relationships and one thought or action affects many aspects of our lives. An effective way of navigating our curriculum is to *be as steady as the North Star and as flexible as the wind*. We are steady in our focus to our intention and flexible as to how the Basic Self navigates situations and the dynamics of changes inherent within all action.

Softness and flexibility, whether in martial arts or life, overcome tension. We do not take deep-seated habits lightly, and we give up habituation as best we can. We acknowledge that *alchemy, redeeming our spirit from matter/materialism, requires loving, time, patience, focused attention, intention, and will*. According to Taoist precepts, it takes about six hundred days of meditation, relaxation, and focused breathing to regenerate the body after the age of sixty. (See the embryonic breathing section in Palace Six/Global Adventure.)

The concept of harmony and balance, a basic tenet of Asian culture, details how taking one's proper position in the universe, an intermediary between heaven and earth, permits an individual more health and contentment.

The heaven-man-earth hierarchy is used to decide acupuncture needle depth, from superficial to deep. Since spirit comes into the body first through the breath and because lungs control the function of the large intestine and skin, when dealing with disease in these categories we insert superficially to access the appropriate level of Qi. Since the kidney rules the bones, spinal fluid, brain, and fluid circulation, we insert deeply down to the bone when dealing with kidney-related issues. In the spring, we insert needles more superficially than in the winter since the seasonal Qi is more superficial and growing. We utilize different sets of points during different seasons for the same disease. We also follow the natural cycle of food flavors through the year: spicy in the spring, sweet in summer, pungent in the autumn, and salty in the winter. The only permanence is change, and so it behooves us cooperate with rather than resist change.

One technique to physically take our position in the universe is to ground ourselves terrestrially like tree roots growing into the earth by extending Qi/energy through visualization from the bottom of the foot at **Yongquan/Kidney-1/Gushing Spring**. The earth reciprocates, giving energy back such that we can feel the Earth's Qi in the lower Dantien/abdomen, approximately three finger widths below the naval. We can also be aware of our connection to celestial energies above.

* If you can, put your bare feet on soil, grass, or sand, and ground yourself. Feel the earth reciprocate. If you are inside, stand up and ground yourself through the floor. Extend your awareness to the celestial heavenly Qi, and accept your proper human position between the two. What awareness does this give you?

When dealing in dualities below the soul level, something is always referenced against something else. The head is closer to celestial Qi in man and is referred as yang and the location of spirit. The feet are yin and associated with terrestrial Qi or materiality. On a dog or cat, the lower back is yang and closer to celestial Qi because they walk on four paws. Scratch or rub a dog on its head. Then rub its lower back just above the hip bone and see which one gets the better response.

The right side of the body is yang compared to the left, as is the back of the body compared to the front. If there is a cold wind blowing, we instinctively turn our back to it, and cover our chest. During hurricanes, horses turn their rumps to the wind as a natural protective response. Oriental medicine is practical and developed by observing how Nature works and how we naturally respond.

The last step in preparing the cauldron is to accept who we are individually and what we contracted to accomplish. Most of us want things to be different from the way they are. Alchemists know it is wise to release ideas of how we think life should be and acknowledge how it is.

JIN BIAN/THE NINE TRANSFORMATIONS

China has an ancient history of Imperial consent for doctors to conduct autopsies on newly killed prisoners, so they were able to study the physical attributes of the pericardium and heart by looking directly at physical function. The pericardial sac around the heart is referred to as the heart protector, as it assures proper heart positioning, keeps the heart separate from the surrounding tissue, and protects against blood stasis.

The Chinese observed over centuries that illness is primarily caused by self-limiting beliefs; they realized transforming dramas and traumas into wisdom was a more elegant and purposeful way of being then disassociation and avoidance.

Looking at the idea that everything is to benefit us, we can see that suffering often pushes us toward a more enlightened approach. A friend of mine who is a professional drummer came to me for severe spasm of the teres minor muscle in back of his right shoulder. The acupuncture and herbal treatment helped, but he noticed, if he closed himself off to people and did not communicate his true thoughts and feelings, his shoulder ached so much that he could not drum. When he did communicate, his shoulder did not bother him, and so he used pain as feedback, and it became a steppingstone rather than an obstacle.

We can ask cells or tissues where a pain is located, *What do you want?*

- ★ Settle back, close your eyes, and ask questions of an area of pain or imbalance. An answer will come to mind. Maybe you are making up the answers, but a wise man once asked me why I was making up particular answers, rather than another answer. Consider how the answers you get could give you the freedom you are seeking. Check it out. See if they are accurate. Life is a process of enfoldment.

Once we find out what is causing pain (it could be emotional pain without yet a physical correlation), an effective approach is to re-frame negative thinking or a non-accepting attitude by asking, *What is good about this?* This frees us to accept what we are experiencing. Then we ask ourselves how we created the situation, taking full responsibility for our actions, even if awareness is unconscious and unknown to us. We then stop acting like a victim, regain power over the situation, and make decisions to move forward instead of choosing to be stuck.

Everyone is responsible for their total beingness. Victimhood is a contracted consciousness. We are responsible for our lives. If we do not like something, we can either change our attitude or change the situation. If we cannot change the situation to one we can live with, we can always walk away. Voting with our feet and moving streets, cities, states, or countries is a radical example that many people utilize.

The body is in a high state of cooperation, maintaining homeostasis/cellular balance and health. The body, coupled with the mind and emotions, gives us feedback as to how we are doing. Sometimes, taking a pill or herb so the feedback will go away is not the most enlightened approach. The more we understand ourselves, the more enthusiastically we can cooperate and participate in life. Seeing what is good about a situation allows us to relax diaphragmatic breathing, which is connected to the pericardium, allowing more circulation of oxygen and blood through the chest and throughout the body; this feels pleasurable and further improves our attitude, allowing us to more easily deal with and participate in life. When we fully participate, are happy with our choices, and feel comfortable with ourselves, there is no room for dis-harmony/dis-ease.

Chang Po-tuan (983-1082), founder of Southern School of Complete Reality Taoism stated:

Clearing the mind, dissolving preoccupations, purifying thoughts, forgetting feelings, minimizing self, lessening desire, seeing the basic, embracing the fundamental--- this is meditation of the Transformative Way.

Health, like life, is a continual process of education, adjusting one's attitude, and cooperating with what is. Your next step is that which is right in front of you. Life continually presents opportunities for learning and growth.

IMPORTANT ALCHEMICAL FORMULAS

- Either blocking Qi/energy or not having efficient utilization of Qi/energy is the cause of disease.
- We live and die at the cell level.
- We get sick not from what we take in but from what we do not eliminate.
- Fasting is staying away from something, be it food, a thought, or an activity.
- Everything below the soul grows by taking, so we breath, eat, and experience. The soul grows by learning.
- Everyone is responsible for their total beingness.
- Is there anything you fear or block about knowing your True Self? If so, what place in the body reflects this? Place your hands there and give it a voice. Ask for an image of the earliest time you forgot you were divine. What do you feel, sense, see?
- If there are any judgments, do the Forgiveness Process listed previously. Set your intention to let this go for good.
- Look at the Five Phase chart and decide which Thief or Thieves, if any, are recurrent patterns. Transform Thieves into Virtues by making different choices. Get your intention clear, keep the mind calm, and endure to the end.

* * *

Notes

1. HEALTH PALACE

HEALTH AFFECTS ALL THE PALACES. Interestingly, we get sick not from what we take in but from what we do not eliminate.

The Health Palace is under the domain of the gall bladder, which stores and releases bile that separates pure from impure fatty acids, providing building blocks for hormones. Bile also eliminates used hormones. The gall bladder energetically represents the decision-making process, choosing what is and is not beneficial. It is important to make wise choices regarding what is beneficial for us, not only in health, but in all aspects of life.

Cycles of 7 and 8 denote the years from gestation to age seven for women and until age eight for males. These are our formational years that hopefully ensure that we establish strong physical and emotional foundations. Many problems that show up later in life are influenced by bonding or lack thereof and by parental rearing choices; our temperament personality is formed during these early years.

- What is your default decision-making temperament? Aggressive, acquiescing, or balanced?
- What was your family dynamic with siblings and parents?
- Where you breast fed or, if put on a grain or milk formula that was a precursor to food allergies?
- Did your parents smoke when you were a toddler? Were you exposed to smoggy city life? Were you exposed to molds, paints and dyes, insecticides, or pesticides?
- What life-enhancing patterns or destructive habits were established in the home?
- In kindergarten, first, and second grade, did you learn to play well with others, or fight with peers?

Emotional or physical traumas, depending upon severity and duration, can be the causative factor in illness. Modern medicine has ascertained that seventy-five percent of illness comes from our lifestyle, while genetics only contribute twenty-five percent.

Key: Opening the chest allows us to collect Grace/spiritual assistance rather than feel oppressed. Grace can be defined as working with Spirit to find more elegant ways to learn. If we have symptoms or a diagnosis, we look at what lessons are to be learned.

Tian Chi /PC-1/Heavenly Pond-Celestial Pool sees opportunities to love more fully. This acu-point, located on the chest, reaches into the depth of our physical, emotional, mental, and soul.

THERE ARE NO INCURABLE DISEASES, ONLY INCURABLE PEOPLE

There are no incurable diseases, only incurable people. All diagnosis is rooted in Spirit and can effectively be reduced to either too much or too little.

One reason we do not resolve disease is an unwillingness to change or a seeming inability to transform traumas and dramas into learning. It is possible, however difficult the situation, to learn about ourselves. There are many inspirational people showing us, in spite of physical or genetic handicaps, how to thrive.

The *Huang Di Nei Jing, The Yellow Emperor's Inner Canon* was first mentioned in the *Han Shu* or *Book of Han* in 111 CE. It is generally dated by scholars between the late Warring States Period (475-221 BC) to the early Han (206-220 CE). It contains two parts. The *Ling Shu* and the *Shu Wen* each consist of eighty-one chapters.

The *Su Wen/Basic Questions* main teaching asserts that the root of disease is an inability to change; life's situations are likened to the action of the wind, which changes force and direction quickly and often.

The second part is the *Ling Shu/Spiritual Pivot*; it teaches how to practice medicine. The spiritual aspects of *Nei Jing* are most likely not writings from clinicians but rather from enlightened beings, true persons who were in harmony with themselves, with nature, and with Spirit. The *Nei Jing* tells us the greatest acupuncturist is concerned with the spirits because…

> *The heart holds the office of sovereign and master and the radiance of the spirits/Shen Ming stems from it. (Ling Shu, Ch. 8)*

> *The main things concerning the practice with fine needles are not difficult to explain. What is difficult is a deep understanding. The good practitioner guards the body, the great acupuncturist guards the spirits. But if we are unable to examine and know all*

the aspects of the disease, how can we understand and know the origin of the disease. (Ling Shu, Ch. 3)

Excess and deficiency of spirits is seen as deficiency of the Qi of the heart. (Su Wen, Ch. 62)

For the practitioner:

The one who is about to needle must have the spirits/Shen, pulling his heart on the alert, mobilizing all the defense. The spirits maintain their thoughtfulness without any failure and thus control if the illness remains or disappears. (Ling Shu, Ch. 1)

We find this conversation between the Yellow Emperor and his chief physician, Qi Bo:

Qi Bo: *Blood and Qi are determined by the Shen.*

Yellow Emperor: *What is the Shen?*

Qi Bo: *When blood and Qi compose harmoniously, nutrition and defense circulate and penetrate everywhere, the five Zang organs (heart, spleen/pancreas, lungs, kidney and liver) are perfectly achieved, and the spiritual Qi/Shen dwells in the heart-mind. The Hun/Basic Self and Po/Conscious Self possess all their capacities—this perfect achievement is a human being.* (Author note: I added the Basic and Conscious Self to identify Hun and Po for the reader. I have detailed explanations of the Basic, Conscious and High Selves in the Relationship Palace).

Note: *to penetrate everywhere* means there are no blocks of energy or deficiencies of energy, and therefore the cells are healthy and longevity is achieved. Remember the definition used in this Workbook: disease is caused either by a blockage of Qi/energy or an inefficient use of Qi/energy. Extrapolating further, we can say there is only one energy with many manifestations.

Addressing self-responsibility:

Qi Bo: *Through what is called heart/mind, which is my True Self, I make what I receive bright or dull. And if I make it bright, I am bright. If I do not, I am dull. It is through the concentration of the Qi, the way I regulate my life and calm the mind, that I can act in such a way the spirit becomes efficacious. And this is also the means by which I can connect with others. That is the meaning of reaching the spirits (with others).*

There are those who think the reference to the Shen/spirit/heart is only an ancient rambling of unsophisticated/backward people, and they state that spirit as a physical or metaphysical quality does not exist.

During a continuing education course I took decades ago, in a class titled, Systemic/Social Misconceptions, the well-regarded instructor's interpretation of the classics was there is no role for the spirit in diagnosis or treatment. He said Heart Qi was constructed and nourished solely by blood and essence/hormones, and that disorders of the spirit are nothing other than dis-ordered Qi of solely physical origins and components.

My bias is opposite to this instructor's.

Going further back into discovering where we came from, and who we are, the Ling Shu says: *When one speaks of hua/transformation, it is communing with the natural order, with the principles of Li/life through communication with the light of the spirits/Shen Ming.* (*Ling Shu*, Ch. 6)

Shen Ming means deities/gods. The heart is residence of the spirit, and the character for heart is the bottom radical for both intention and will. When internal or external causes/evil Qi block the free flow of Qi, there is a withdrawal of spirit. We are much more than the physical definitions of Qi and blood.

SPIRIT DOES THE HEALING

Quantum physics says we are 99.9999999% empty space. My experience is that Spirit—we could say Qi if we have an eastern orientation or divine loving if western—occupies the 99%.

When I seek to obtain a result through diagnosis and acupuncture, my results are much improved when I needle into the emptiness with the intention to contact the invisible Spirit/Qi/divine loving in the 99% instead of thinking/approaching the patient on a material level: i.e., How does this point affect this meridian channel function of this organ or system. To interpret the classics, acupuncture is *not* about sticking a stainless steel, gold, or silver needle into a point to affect a condition/diagnosis/disease/blood test. We treat the patient and not a disease that is arbitrarily named and arbitrarily diagnosed.

Five acupuncturists treating the same patient with the same acu-points will get five different results. We have to earn the right to get results. On one hand, we cannot take the patient any further spiritually than we have gone ourselves, if we think we are responsible for the healing. If we open to spirit doing the healing, and it does, then the healing can go way beyond the level of consciousness we have individually achieved.

In a class I was teaching, I demonstrated needling **Jianyu/LI-15/Shoulder Bone** to demonstrate this approach. The volunteer, who had never experienced acupuncture before, said he felt the sensation but not much effect.

I chose this point because of its convenient location for demonstration purposes, even though he did not have shoulder symptoms. I took the needle out and then accessed my spirits to prepare myself, as directed by *Ling Shu*, Ch. 1. Then I needled the same point, looking for the Spirit in the 99% space within the point.

I was stunned when the volunteer patient revealed the presence of his soul to me in that instant. A soul revelation had only happened for me two other times in decades of practice. I started to cry in front of the class in response to the sacredness of the revelation.

For me, this type of awareness falls into the category of *true knowing*, which is the domain of the soul and gives veracity to the wisdom in the classics. After such experiences, the human mind wants to doubt, but the profundity of these interactions far outstripped my mind's interpretation, and so it doesn't matter to me whether you, the reader, believe or disbelieve, because, inside of me, there is a *knowing*. Such is one of the benefits of alchemical transformation.

The wisdom from centuries of human struggle and success is that if we try to change our conditioning without using the spirit(s), then the *fire of desires will still rage,* and the Five Thieves have their way with us. Because we cannot force transformation through willpower, there is a relax and letting go, a trusting Spirit component to the process.

* * *

The first health key is to open the heart, to breath and release blockages in the chest. Then we listen for knowledge and direction.

Health is not an absence of disease; rather, it can be defined as being content with ourselves. By this definition, we could be diagnosed of a disease and consider ourselves to be healthy since our focus is correctly on the soul first and the body second.

The ancients believed the most important virtue is being true to ourselves. We use deep introspection to know when to act and when to rest, when to speak and when to be silent, in accord with our nature and the situation in which we find ourselves. Even if we are a science-first atheist with only one life, we still want to have happy, fulfilling days. Opening the chest and breathing fully allows for relaxation and contentment.

- ★ Stretch and open the chest/pectoralis muscles or massage the area for relaxed respiration. Practice a breathing regime of your choice. Rather than behaving repetitively, embrace endless possibilities.

The liver-gall bladder controls the sinews/tendons/ligaments, so postural habituation is an accompaniment to long-term emotional patterns. Releasing the posture does not necessarily mean we release the emotion, just as releasing an emotion it does not necessarily release a posture, although both scenarios can and do take place. We respond in our own ways emotionally (trepidation/fear) and psychically (tighten neck muscles) to a loud noise but we get over it in our own timing. Emotions and body accompany each other, though not in necessarily in direct relationship, but intimately enough so it is beneficial to pay attention to both aspects.

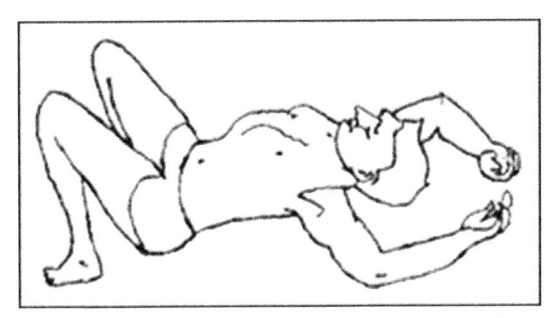

Basic posture to open the pericardium channel to get rid of fatigue, strain, etc.

Advanced posture.

Notice how, when the glute max is engaged in the advanced posture, the axis of backward rotation happens at the hip joint to prevent straining the back. Follow opening the chest with breathing. This can be the opening approach to ALL disease/imbalance.

Notice: the points listed below are all in the heart/chest/diaphragm area and focus on opening blocked Qi. The wisdom of the heart is the purveyor of prevention or rectification of disease. The Health Palace impacts all Palaces. Beside getting acupuncture, massage, or exercising the musculature where these points are located, you can take the qualities/attributes of the acu-points and intend and/or envision the particular function taking place within.

- **You Men/Ki-21/Hidden Gate** calms anxiety.
- **Yin Du/Ki-19/Yin Metropolis** is where blood Qi/oxygen interact, controlling our resources of breathing and digesting.
- **Bu Rong/St-19/Not Contained** indicates where thoughts are not transformed into actionable ideas and Qi rebels in response to the blockage.
- **Shen Feng/Ki-23/Spirit Seal** prevents the spirit from escaping.
- **JU Que/CV-14/Great Tower Gate** affects the diaphragm to relax the breathing.

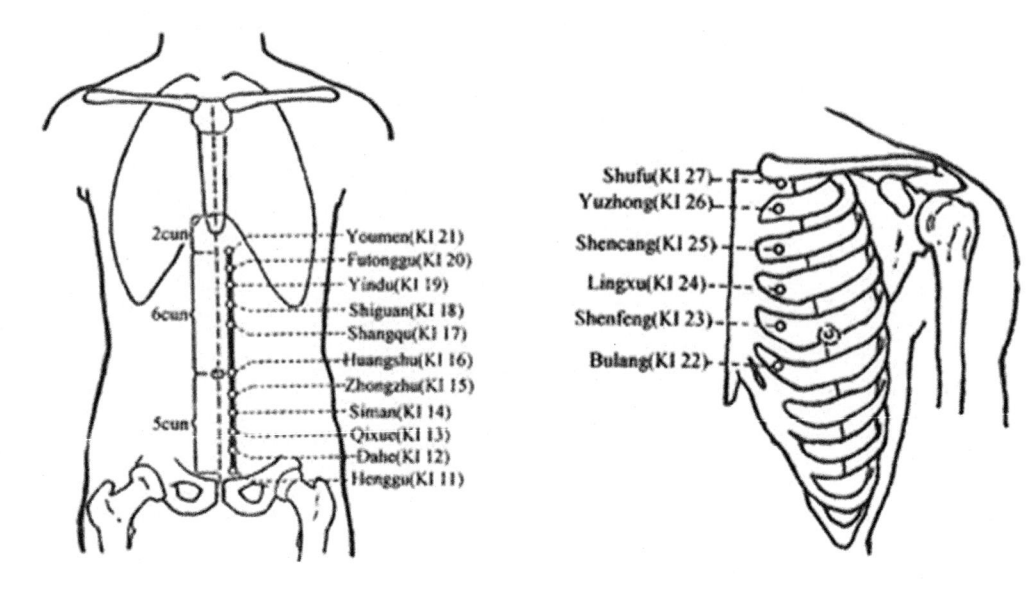

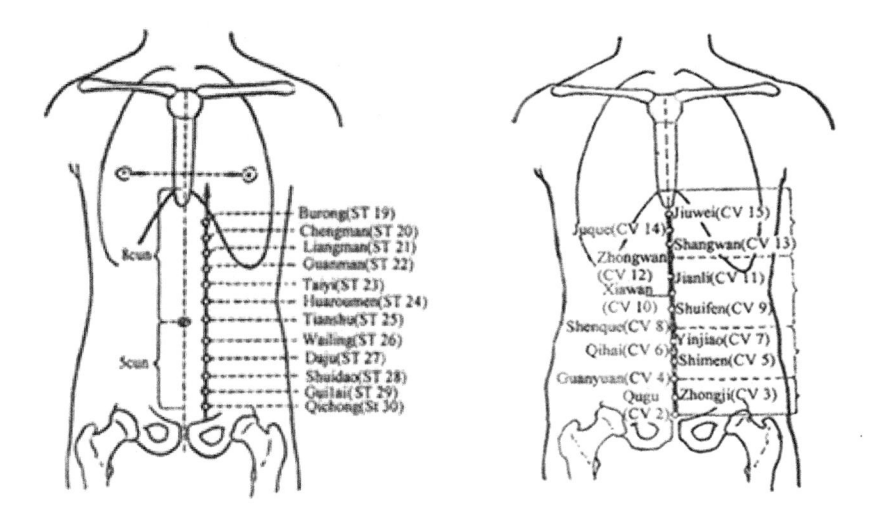

* In the evening, after activities and responsibilities are handled, note what you learned during the day and release any issues that are disturbing you. Since what we do not eliminate makes us sick, we do not need to drag imbalances or unfinished business into a new day. Die to the day at sleep and wake in the morning as would a child, excited about what adventure may be ahead, refreshed, anew, without much prior conditioning.

Using Herbs as Teachers

To effect change, we can use herbs, which can be viewed as concentrated foods. Herbs have a chemical composition, an electrical frequency, and a consciousness, like all things living. Innate objects such as rocks and stones have consciousness as well but understanding this takes digging deeper and can be addressed in another book. Since herbs originate outside of our bodies, they can be viewed as possible teachers, when we ingest or relate to them.

We can take herbal qualities/attributes into our consciousness during contemplation or meditation. One method is to go into nature and see to which tree/plant/flower you are attracted. Call in the light for yourself for the highest good, and ask the tree/plant/flower, *What would you like to share with me*? It may or may not answer. It is here to serve us but treating it with respect is better than demanding. If you buy the herbs listed for the Palace within which you are working, tuning into their frequency while taking them as a tea in either raw or powder form can yield powerful results.

* * *

- **Shi Chang Pu/Acorus Root** opens the heart portal and promotes emotional balance for those who do not trust themselves, so they can make good choices. It is good for people who are unhappy with their lives. Eat it raw to open the senses, clear the mind, overcome illusion, develop intuition, and elevate the Spirit. If it is boiled for tea, it will break down accumulations and gatherings in the abdomen but will not open the senses.
- **Yuan Zhi/Polygala/Everlasting Will** returns willpower to its pristine state as extra strength is needed in a crisis to overcome dampness/resistance and to break through blocks.
- **Fu Ling/Hoelen/Guiding my Soul Destiny** releases what is no longer working, so we are not stuck in the past.
- **Rou Gui/Cinnamon Cortex** is a spiritual plant with much Shen/spirit. Besides circulating Qi/blood in the chest area it protects against pernicious external energies of a toxic environment or psychic atmosphere.
- **Ye Ju Hua/Chrysanthemum** helps guard against overthinking.

THEORY AND TREATMENT OF AGING AND SENILITY

The first chapter of the *Huang Di Nei Jing/Su Wen* states that people have lost the ability to live one hundred years, which is lamentable. Some modern gerontologists suggest a normal human life span should be over one hundred. Present-day Japan has approximately sixty-five thousand centenarians, a majority of whom are women, so we know it is possible to attain healthy longevity.

Both ancient and modern anti-aging experts state that having a quiet mind is the number-one key to longevity. Oriental medicine posits that some level of senility begins around fifty if our life span is one hundred years, and at forty if we live to eighty, unless we take care of ourselves. The average life span in the US is below eighty for both men and women, which, as of 2018, was decreasing, most likely due to increased environmental toxicity, increased stress, and prescription and illegal drug dosing/overdosing. As Qi Po said five thousand years ago, we have forgotten who we are.

As we gain intellectual knowledge and experience, we commonly are less open to living from the spontaneity of the true self and subsequent mental rigidity and repetition stagnate Qi/oxygen, leading to blood stasis and impaired cellular metabolism. Typically, only twenty percent of the micro-circulation of all the blood vessels are open and only twenty percent of our brain cells are developed by the end of our lives. What does this indicate about our untapped potential?

Chinese doctors estimate the prime causative factors of modern disease are excess inflammation (stress, taxations, and toxicity, etc.), oxygen stagnation and blood stasis (lack of breathing, lack of exercise, blocked energy, poor air quality), and excessive/deficient emotions. More emphasis in modern times, even in China, is given to physical causes than one's spirit and emotions, which is, to me and the ancient seers, lamentable.

Western medicine has 68,000-87,000 diagnostic codes, depending upon the system one uses, domestic or international. Of course, Oriental medicine has its myriad diagnoses, but when one dives deep into causative factors of dis-ease, there are only two: too much/excess or too little/deficiency. In relation to aging, the two contributing factors are Qi stagnation and blood stasis. Since we live and die at the cellular level, the delivery of oxygen and adequate nutrition to the cells and the elimination of by-products/toxins is the bottom line.

As I am editing, we are experiencing a *shelter in place* edict, in which most people are likely getting substantially less exercise/deep breathing than normal. The amount of blood circulating is deficient relative to the amount of vasodilation to which the blood vessels are accustomed. This sets up a disharmony of blood flow and cellular health, which will have repercussions that we will notice during the 2020-21 flu season. Italy reported that approximately 97% or more of deaths from coronavirus have one, two, three, or more pre-existing diagnosed illnesses. Whatever the coronavirus mechanism, diminished oxygen and nutrition to the cells and elimination of cellular waste has serious consequences. Additionally, the WHO administered flu vaccines to Italians in the autumn of 2019, so their immune systems were already expressing a cytokine storm when Covid arrived. The healthier and more vital we are, the easier time we have responding to bacteria, viruses, fungi, environmental toxins, injury, surgery and the not-knowing how life will be regarding sheltering in place, travel, access to foods, socializing, etc.

The following section on contributing Western factors and common diseases resulting from Qi stagnation and blood stasis is taken directly from Gunter R. Neeb's *Blood Stasis, China's Classical Concept in Modern Medicine.*

Yan De-xin, one of China's foremost present-day geriatric specialists, identified the physical root of aging as Qi/oxygen stagnation and blood stasis, coming primarily from kidney vacuity/low hormonal levels and brain cell deterioration resulting from deficient/impaired digestion, stress, and aging.

Western factors contributing to Qi stagnation and blood stasis:
- Excessive stress of any nature (see the Five Taxation patterns)
- Poor diet
- Unsupportive habits (lack of sleep, inadequate exercise, stressful lifestyle)
- Lack of oxygen and circulation
- Suppressed emotions
- Psychiatric diseases
- Neurotransmitter deficiencies
- Hormonal deficiencies, imbalances
- Chronic immunological stress
- Chronic diseases
- Surgery/Traumatic injury
- Irregular menstruation
- Reproductive abnormality
- Addiction or substance abuse

Common diseases resulting from Qi stagnation and blood stasis:
- Diabetes mellitus
- Hypertension
- Hyperlipidemia
- Coronary artery disease
- Congestive heart failure
- Cerebral vascular disease
- Peripheral vascular disease
- Chronic obstructive pulmonary disease
- Nephrosis and kidney failure
- Prostatic hypertrophy
- Macular degeneration
- Dementia
- Alzheimer's disease
- Tumor formation
- Cancer
- Low immunity
- Rheumatic and arthritic conditions

- ✓ Hemorrhagic and menstrual diseases
- ✓ Functional impairment in heart, brain, blood vessels, liver, kidney, etc.
- ✓ Numerous skin diseases

Signs and symptoms of Qi stagnation and blood stasis are as follows: Noting which symptoms you have and in what category they fall will give you direction of the needed therapy which you can address this with your doctor.

Pelvic cavity:
- ✓ Qi Stagnation: Stiffness, heaviness, tightness in the lower abdomen and extremities
- ✓ Blood Stasis: Palpable lumps in the lower abdomen, menstrual irregularities, and varicosities
- ✓ Fluid Stagnation: Edema, pitting, dampness
- ✓ Cold Stagnation: Cold abdomen, back, legs and feet
- ✓ Food Stagnation: Constipation

Abdominal cavity:
- ✓ Qi Stagnation: Burping, gas, bloating, tight abdomen
- ✓ Blood Stasis: Blood stagnation felt as a lump in the abdomen
- ✓ Fluid Stagnation: Gurgling abdominal sounds
- ✓ Cold Stagnation: Poor digestion, anorexia, diarrhea
- ✓ Food Stagnation: Greasy tongue coat, epigastric spasms

Thoracic cavity and head:
- ✓ Qi Stagnation: Emotional and mental symptoms, depression, hysteria, headaches, dizziness
- ✓ Blood Stasis: Discoloration, varicosities, blueness, heaviness of the head and arms
- ✓ Fluid Stagnation: Edema, dampness of the head and chest, damp, swollen and scalloped tongue, slippery pulse
- ✓ Cold Stagnation: Cold extremities

Additionally, German Electrical Acupuncture (GEA) discovered obstructing factors that impede therapeutic results. These factors have borne out to be accurate in my forty plus years of GEA practice. If one or more of these sites are affected, therapeutic results will be limited no matter what therapy we utilize. Therefore, these obstructing factors must be addressed first:

- Brain
- Bones/marrow
- Teeth/gum/bone/jaw/sinus/tonsil
- 1st and 2nd Cervical vertebrae
- Gall Bladder
- Appendix
- Testes/ovary/uterus
- Auto-immune diseases

Our body is a laboratory, and similar diagnosis and therapeutic results may not resemble that of the person next to you or a synopsis written in books, including this book. We have individualized biology and individual lessons to learn. Ge Hong, the main chronicler of the Nine Transformation format, wrote about more than eighty individuals who lived to be one hundred twenty-five to two hundred years old by practicing alchemy similar to what is presented here, noting they adapted their individuality to their times, environment, and availability of herbs.

Keep track of the results you get with each technique, herb, and awareness. Herbs and foods have a different effect when you are ill than when you are healthy and in different seasons of the year and different seasons/times of your life. Similarly, recommended exercises change with the seasons, and their effect for us/on us differ under different circumstances. The adage, the only permanence is change, is well taken here. New research and new books and new products tout the latest magic drug/magic food/magic supplement. Individually, we have to ascertain if its workable for us. It is better to understand how to do something than to have a strict regimen of what to do.

Eating and exercising according to the seasons supports the five Zang organs (heart, pancreas, lung, kidney, liver) to detox, balance, and tonify in the correct season. Multinationals importing foods from different locals/continents so that we get to eat our favorite fad foods in all seasons is not necessarily health promoting.

* **Spring:** Emphasize sour and spicy foods. Since vegetables have not fully matured, they are slightly sour and therefore perfect for spring detoxing from the torpor of winter, assisting in burning off fats. The Oriental diet discourages high-sugar vegetables such as carrots, beets, and sweet potatoes in the spring. It emphasizes some protein, small amounts of healthy fat, seasonal vegetables, and medicinal mushrooms.

Do Isometric exercises, stretching tendons, ligaments, joints, and muscles.

* **Summer:** Emphasize sweet and bitter foods, watching not to eat excessive amounts of sweet fruits.

    Do Cardio exercises.

* **Autumn:** emphasize acrid/pungent-tasting foods to assist detoxing the mucous membrane and to enhance immune enhancement for cold/flu prevention; also, eat some salty foods to begin consolidating for winter. Breathing exercises of your choice are to be emphasized in the autumn, since the associated organ is the lungs.

    Stance training in martial arts and qi gong regimens are the recommended exercises to move Qi back to the external Wei protective level for immune defense. One way to relax during stance training is to give more space to go deeper, where more power is found in relaxation. Create muscular tension and observe if you go into more tension or you relax. A martial art teaching is to lift up whatever is pushing you down, as thoughts change the dynamics of exercise. Meditate while the body is in uncomfortable stances to encourage relaxation.

    Passages and Cavities are terms used in Daoist medicine referring to the joints and cavities through which the vital inner breath circulates. In Chapter 57 of the *Seven Slips of a Cloudy Satchel*, Yunji Giqian says the flourishing vital breath can circulate body fluid and blood, strengthen bones and muscles, and sharpen passages and cavities. It is a given in Chinese medicine that Qi/energy/breath moves blood. Breathe faster or deeper and the heart responds with stronger and more rapid heartbeats.

    Forest bathing describes going into the woods and breathing deeply to reduce stress, anxiety, and depression and to improve one's mood. In Japan, where many nature-loving city dwellers can be seen on the trains trekking up into the mountains on the weekends, a small study showed after only six hours of forest bathing over the course of two days the natural T-cell immune activity increased by fifty percent.

* **Winter:** emphasize salty foods for strengthening kidneys or sour foods to assist liver function in preparation for spring detox. Overcome stress by staying relaxed to replenish adrenals/kidneys.

We exercise less vigorously during the colder winter months than during warmer summer months. Rest and relaxation can be a strategy. During the spring and summer, we stay up late and get up early. During the autumn and winter, we go to bed earlier and get up later. This follows the natural cycles of life. As a clinician, in taking pulses at the radial artery, I have to be aware of the season. The pulses are quicker and more superficial in spring and summer, and slower and deeper in the fall and winter. This points out the natural rhythm of the heartbeat in different seasons.

Li Ching-Yuen was a Chinese herbalist and martial artist who was reported to be over two hundred years old when he died in 1933. As a boy, he followed Taoist herbalists up into the mountains and learned their longevity techniques. Beside his martial art exercising, he consumed **Reishi/Ganoderma, Ginseng, Lycium/Goji Berries, Ho Shou Wu/Polygonum** and **Gotu Kola.** When asked his secret for longevity, he answered, *Keep a quiet heart, breathe like a tortoise, walk sprightly like a pigeon, and sleep like a dog.*

There is no such thing as the perfect diet—macrobiotic, blood type, Paleo, vegan—or even a perfect way of eating—salad first, salad last, food combining, juicing, etc. The proof is in the workability: does what and how you eat nourish you? Maybe the foods you liked most as a child are still the ones that give you the most energy, even if not considered the most wholesome or in alignment with the latest fad.

A Taoist recommendation of foods to support energy during intense periods of introspection/meditation at first glance does not seem appropriate. It includes sprouted grains (oats, rice, quinoa), sprouted nuts (walnut), spouted sunflower and chia seeds, vegetables (sweet potato, watercress, winter squash), and small amounts of protein (beef, chicken, lamb, milk). Before dismissing this list as non-vegan, mucous producing, and poor combinations, does it work?

Remember to use your intuition, your taste buds, and a pleasant presentation to enjoy what is appealing. Moving spirit through your hands into the food will make it more compatible for you to extract nutrients.

A balanced alkaline diet is a good place to start when not sure what to eat. Excessive acid from stress or poor eating can corrode the magnetic poles of the cells, making them less efficient. A common food stasis formula in Chinese medicine to break up accumulations from poor combination or excessive intake contains sour tasting herbs such as dandelion, chicory root, asparagus, and bitter vegetables.

Zhuyou/The Power of Words

Zhuyou is treating disease by chanting sacred tones or names, prayer, or visualization. The mythical Yellow Emperor Huang Di (2698–2598 BC) asked his head physician, Qi Po:

> *In ancient times people treated disease by shifting the energy with Zhuyou to change the flow of Qi in the body. Why people now treat internal disease with herbal medicine and external disease with stone needles, and some are cured, and some are not?*

Qi Po answered:

> *It was a calm and peaceful world, and evil did not get deep inside, and people cured disease by shifting the energy by saying the Zhuyou. Today, the world is different: worries stay inside, while hardships and suffering hurt the outside. People are living out of harmony with the four seasons, and Zhuyou cannot cure them.*

To clear worries and hardships:

> When old memories and pains come up, place it all in the Light, send the Light to yourself, and ask for balancing and healing, and then let it go. You will find that for a while it will keep coming up. Just keep repeating the process of letting go and placing it in the Light. Heal the memories. Forgive the past. Then forget it. Let it go. It is not worth remembering. None of it is worth remembering. What's worth experiencing and giving is the joy of this moment. (Ref: J-R)

> Once we lift above the cause-and-effect plane and into the soul, we are allowed, with perfect spiritual protection, to go into the Kal power field and dissolve our karma from a higher place, so nothing is recorded against us. That's why I tell people don't mess around in these lower worlds, trying to correct anything. You can't do it. You're just going to make it worse. If you want to correct what you've done, get in and get high enough where you are above that negative power, so it has to bow down to you and you can correct it with impunity. You just say, "Take that off," and it's removed as soon as you say it. (Ref: Paraphrased J-R quote.)

I modified a Chinese technique using words that convey actions in order to remove blockages and change cellular degeneration with myself and others. While working with others, I repeat the words in the list below, sequentially 1-9, while focusing my attention on certain areas by placing my hands over that area working in the auric field and/or doing acupuncture. I have whomever I am working with simultaneously chant/say the words with me. When working with myself, I repeat the wording and may or may not place my hands over an area, such as the stomach or heart. With myself, the hand placement is more reflexive/spontaneous than thought out.

One result of this technique was with a client whose ninety-five-percent invasive uterine cancer diminished to five percent in seven weeks with no other therapies except acupuncture, moxa, and herbs to support this technique. The reduction of the cancer is not supposed to happen. She came out of surgery strong and focused on what she needed to change going forward, knowing which beliefs and earlier traumas had caused her condition.

This or a similar technique is invaluable since *what we do not eliminate makes us sick*. I might take four or five minutes to complete the process. For a couple of situations that were life-altering, I took more than an hour to involve my whole being in the action.

Start with number 1 and go through to number 9. Move to the next step when you are intuitively complete with each stage.

1. Dissolve
2. Disperse/scatter/dispel/come loose
3. Completely break up/disassociate
4. Clear/Cleanse/Gone/disappear
5. Healed
6. Recover original intent
7. Done/finished/complete
8. Spiritualize
9. Seal

After completing this process, I suggest doing the forgiveness exercise written about earlier, to release any residue. Then reframe how you think/feel about whatever situation you addressed. Out loud, tell yourself or someone else who is willing to listen what is good about the situation and how it ultimately benefits you and others, turning it into a steppingstone rather than a stumbling block.

If you talk to someone who is at least five years past a major trauma, they will tell you the benefits they received from accessing their strengths and resources and by asking others for assistance in overcoming their crisis.

IMPORTANT ALCHEMICAL FORMULAS AND HOMEWORK

Continue with what was presented in the preparing the cauldron section, while taking a deeper look at yourself.

- ➢ We live and die at the cell level. We get sick not from what we take in but from what we do not eliminate. Fasting is staying away from something, be it food, a thought, or an activity. Stop doing and let go of what is no longer working/supportive. Embrace what is supportive.
- ➢ Keep the mind calm, be loving with yourself and others, and finish what needs to be finished.
- ➢ Grace is the key for health on any level, on all levels. Observe your celestial essence/divinity. Is there anything you fear or block about knowing your True Self?
- ➢ If so, what place in the body reflects this? Place your hands there and give it a voice.
- ➢ Ask for an image of the earliest time you forgot you are divine. What do you feel/sense/see? If there is any judgment, do the Forgiveness Process listed previously.
- ➢ Set your intention to let this fear/ block go for good. Embrace the Source/Spirit and allow Grace to assist you in your journey. We often think, *I am doing this*, as we attempt to master life. Everything is already in place and accomplished, so instead of interfering, we are better served by relaxing and letting go. The subject of free will versus fate is deep and complicated. I will be focusing on it in another book.
- ➢ Look at the Five Phase chart and decide which Thief, if any, is a recurrent pattern. You may have more than one. Forgive yourself for any judgments in relation to generalities or specifics. Ask your soul to convey to you what would be the highest choice for you the next time you are faced with decisions in which this pattern is an option. Get your intention clear.

***

NOTES

2. WEALTH-AMBITION PALACE

WEALTH-AMBITION PERTAINS to having an adequacy of resources: enough food and water to feed the family, enough clothes, and sufficient protection to get through winter, and enough loving to feel like surviving. Material resources can be an outer reflection of inner wealth, although being attached to accumulating possessions or wealth could be detrimental, depending on one's attitude.

The Wealth-Ambition Palace is under the domain of the liver, which alters blood volume depending on physical activity. The liver is the location of the Basic Self energetic; the ability to plan, be resolute, have creative drive, and be assertive, all of which determine a smooth or interrupted flow of Qi is located here. It is interesting that the key for Wealth-Ambition is gratefulness. As we are still working in the first three Palaces, the Basic Self and its survival reaction are very much in play. Being grateful moves a survival reaction up to the thoughtfulness of the heart level.

The Cycles of 7 and 8 in this Palace correspond to ages 7-14 years for women and ages 8-16 for men. With our relative abundance in the Western world, often we don't worry about resources the way many people on the planet are forced to, but even in affluent households, the dynamic of abundance or lack is formulated within the family. At the end of this cycle we can procreate and therefore have the capacity to understand life, loss, and death

- ★ How was your early relationship with money? Did a parent or guardian teach you about this medium of exchange?
- ★ Did you have too much with little of your own effort and now feel entitled?
- ★ Do you understand the bartering process?
- ★ Are you a taker?
- ★ Are you a giver but do not feel worthy to receive?
- ★ Were you instructed about spiritual resources by people you respect?

Key: Gratefulness for our blessings, abilities, opportunities, and resources.

Tian Quan/PC-2/Heavenly Spring—Celestial Spring of Kidney supports a balanced accumulation of wealth and assists us in understanding that challenges are opportunities designed for learning and growth. It took me many years to learn this. Humans mostly will put more effort into avoiding pain than going after pleasure. With neutrality, it is easier to see what opportunities present without labeling situations with emotionally provocative words.

At this stage in our alchemical journey, we encounter the first three upper-grade herbs of Shen Nong's *Ban Cao Jing, The Divine Farmer's Materia Medica Classic,* which originated in approximately 2700 BC. Shen Nong is credited with developing Chinese agriculture and herbal medicine and assisting a transition to a cultivated grain and vegetable diet.

The *Divine Farmer's Almanac* is most likely the first recorded medical theory and is very much in practical use today. It systemizes how each herb represents an observable progression of pathology and describes how their use can counter degeneration and confer long-life. I have gotten remarkable results with my alchemy patients using the first three herbs in the series. I recommend buying these herbs and taking them together before meditation/introspection on a daily basis. If bought in powder form, two grams each together once a day can be a good alchemical dosage. When we use upper-grade herbs for alchemy, we use smaller doses than when curing an illness with lower-grade herbs or restoring Qi with middle-grade herbs.

* * *

- **Ling Zhi/Reishi/Ganoderma/Guide the Soul** is the herb to which all other herbs and plants and vegetation evolve. It assists us to cultivate virtue while exploring the mysteries of life as we transcend the palace in which we are working. It is said that those having desires in this world see only the manifestation, while those with the desireless desire to know their True Self see into the mysteries behind the manifestation.

    Reishi opens the portals/sense organs to enhance perception of our self-assigned meaning of life. It promotes calmness, balance, and strength by building essential kidney Qi, and so is used for dementia, forgetfulness, and degenerate diseases. Reishi lightens the body and consciousness so one feels like flying over the dross of life.

- **Tian Men Dong/Asparagus/Door to Heaven** flushes out stagnation and procrastination by purging turbid sticky phlegm that blocks cellular respiration. By extension, asparagus can break curses, psychic insults and lingering or outmoded thoughts/beliefs by increasing oxygen utilization.

- **Bai Zhu/Atractylodes/The Granary/The Great Harmonizer** conducts other herbs throughout the body. It also diffuses food stagnation and removes mucous that slows decision making.

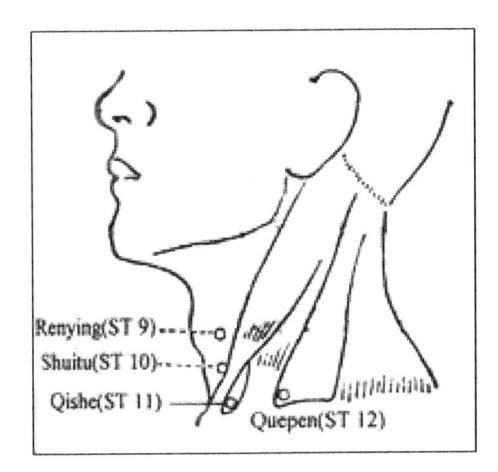

★ Massage above the clavicle to free up **Quepen/St-12/Empty Basin.** We need blood sugar and oxygen getting to the brain to process thoughts and eyes and ears to implement survival strategies. This area can be opened by rotating the neck 360 degree in both directions. Be careful not to rotate too fast or far. Do not cause pain. Use a rolled-up towel around the back of your neck to limit the extent to which you roll the neck if there is pain. Repeat daily, if stiff.

★ Tonify the stomach and digestion by ridding phlegm in the gut with **Chen Pi/Mandarin Orange Peel** to discourage procrastination.

★ Use an enema or colonic, if needed, to eliminate that which is better eliminated.

★ Enhance life with a workable lifestyle.

A more complex formula is the common Taoist Jade Purity School longevity herbal formula called **Tian Ling Xian**. It can be infused in rice wine. Soak nine grams of each raw herb in rice wine for at least two months. If using powdered herbs, soak four grams each for at least two weeks. Take one ounce of liquid each evening to nourish the spleen/pancreas, which controls thoughts and memory and therefore is good for focused meditation.

- **Ling Zhi/Ganoderma** is a Lung Qi talisman.
- **Tian Men Dong/Asparagus** holds the lung Qi.
- **Mu Xiang/Saussarea** is a stomach and spleen Qi tonifier.
- **Sheng Ma/Cimicifuga** rids evils and parasites while tonifying the spleen-pancreas.
- **He Shou Wu/Polygonatum** tonifies liver/kidney yin.
- **Gou Qi Zi /Lycium berries** are good for the eyes and nervous system.

Exercise and Movement

The human body is composed of four basic tissues:
- ✓ Nervous
- ✓ Muscular
- ✓ Epithelial
- ✓ Connective

Connective tissue/collagen holds our organs in place, but because of its relative impenetrability, the connective tissue also creates knots and nodes that impede and block circulation of Qi and blood, and thus ultimately are partially responsible for our death, since obstruction creates illness. On the positive side, connective tissue is included in the acupuncture channel matrix and is part of the body-body and body-mind communication.

Dao-yin/stretching the body, developed during the Early Han dynasty (206 BC-8 CE), is referred to as nourishing life when combined with breath work, as together they increase circulation and cellular metabolism and keep the connective tissue supple, allowing easy and relaxed movements and preventing pain. Stretching is necessary as we tend to become less elastic and more plastic-like with aging. Dao-yin exercises copy animals in their natural habitat:

- ❖ **Tigers** are bold and pounce, suddenly dash to strengthen heart and legs. Modern high-intensity HITT training and sports such as cycling, tennis and basketball fit this phase.

- **Deer** are meek and arch their head to stretch muscles. Yoga, Pilates, and Gyrotonics.
- **Monkeys** are agile and jump, climb, and stretch. Climbing trees, free running in the woods, and parkour.
- **Bears** are vigorous and crouch and stretch. Weights and CrossFit.
- **Cranes** are carefree, flying and flapping and expanding the chest to strengthen heart and lungs. Rock climbing and dance.

Many exercises and/or outdoor activities fit these patterns. If you are stiff or experience a lack of flexibility with certain movements, concentrate on creating suppleness in that area, without creating pain or injuring yourself.

Sexual Practice

It is taught that for a man's longevity and spiritual focus, it is better to use Jing-Essence/hormones in an inward, upper meditation than releasing Qi into the world through ejaculation. This attitude varies according to one's choices of intention and lifestyle. Strictly for health benefits, the Chinese medical recommendation is for men to reduce orgasms as they age: a fifty-year-old man can ejaculate once every five days if robust, and once every ten days, if not. A sixty-year-old man in good health may emit once every ten days if robust, and every twenty days, if not. At seventy, once a month if robust, but not at all if in ill health.

There are ways of enjoying sexual expressions without ejaculation and forms of sex can be part of one's spiritual expression. Women differ physiologically, and these recommendations do not apply to them.

Circulating Qi/The Microcosmic Spirit

The nine stages of transformation focus on minimizing the negative aspects of the physical, emotional, and mental knots and nodes, and on emphasizing one's positive aspects. The Conception Vessel and Governing Vessel together make up the Chinese version of the chakra system. A meditation and breathing technique called the Microscopic Spirit moves Qi up the spine into the head and down the front to be stored in the lower Dantien energy field.

One way to look at injuries or body-born structural abnormalities is that they give us information on what to balance/clear/heal. An acupuncturist, chiropractor, osteopath, doctor, yoga teacher, etc., who knows the esoteric aspects of the points can assist clients to open blocks. For example, opening **Ming Men/GV-4/Door of Life** in the lower back helps to get past materialism or **Zhi Yang/GV-9/Yang Extremity** in the mid-back assists to transcend emotional blocks. Alchemy is a gradual practice. Some yogis have premature white hair from forcing their practice.

It is easy to get hung up between **Zhi Yang/GV-9/Yang Extremity** and **Feng Fu/GV-16/Wind Mansion,** because of the entanglements of human emotion. We energize and relax the physical body to allow us to focus more easily on our spirit at **Shen Ting/GV-24/Spirit Court-Third Eye** and at **Bai Hui/GV-20/100 Convergences-Crown Chakra** to become clairaudient and clairvoyant to ourselves.

- ✱ To activate the Governing Vessel, arch and curl the spine, adding lateral circular movements. Stiff, sore, or injured spinal segments can point out how we are blocked or misuse energy. Movement becomes both diagnostic and therapeutic.

Unwillingness or Inability to Change Is a Major Cause of Disease

We complain about the unfairness of life when what is so does not match what we think should be so. When we approach life in this way, we know ourselves only through reflection and not through direct experience.

An alchemist wants liberation and freedom. We do not like lingering situations or conditions of illness and endeavor not to allow illness to take up residency. If illness does take up residency, it is possible we lost our will/kidney Qi to change; if so, refer to breathing exercises and foods that tonify kidney yang/adrenals.

If our emotions are out of balance, check points on the chest for knots and nodes, and exercise and/or massage the muscles, tendons, and ligaments to unblock Qi/energy both on the front and back of the body. Do the Forgiveness exercise to release emotions and judgments.

What is Natural?

Having lights in our houses that brightly illuminate the late of night stimulates the pituitary gland to interpret it is daytime and that the mind and body should be active. If the mind/body cannot fully relax to recover from activity, how can we expect to greatly influence our longevity with pills and herbs and exercise?

Many years ago, I read about a cure for nervous breakdowns. The doctor put his patients in a darkened room for two weeks without stimulation from other people, TV, radio, phone, books, newspapers, etc., and he let them relax and sleep as long as they wanted and eat whenever they were hungry. Modern researchers measuring telomere length know the importance of a quiet mind.

Our body is a laboratory, and results may not resemble a synopsis written in a book or the person next to us. We have individualized biology and individual lessons to learn. Herbs and foods have a different effect on us, depending on whether we are healthy or ill, in different seasons, and in different seasons of life—youth, maturity, retirement, or old age. Fads or scientifically documented drugs, nutraceuticals, herbs, or foods do not take into consideration age, sex, body weight, hygiene, stress, season, karma, beliefs, etcetera, so when you read a study or report know the results may or may not be forthcoming for you in particular. To add to our stress, the chief editors of the *Lancet* and *New England Journal of Medicine* have indicated that some of the articles they printed were submitted with *inaccuracies*, so just because someone makes a statement or we read *a fact* does not make it so. We must discern what does and what does not work for us individually.

When we feel stress and tighten our diaphragm/breathing, it is difficult to feel blessed. To relieve oxygen stagnation and blood stasis, acceptance and cooperation with what is so are key. This does not mean we placidly accept. It means that a starting point is first to survive and secondly to learn and grow. As I edit this in May 2020, there are political, economic, and health situations that some of us will not survive. Relaxed breathing and a calm mind and emotions allow a clearer picture of what our next best action can be. Alchemy teaches that learning and growing is a full-time job, and thinking we know what others should think or do is best left to each person to decide for themselves. The herbs listed, the spinal exercises, the neck rotation, and Basic Self survival strategies (details in Relationship Palace) are very appropriate for the stresses it appears we will deal with during the 2020s.

Wealth and Longevity

Having experiences equates to aging. To counter normal aging, we can regenerate and extend our life span by moving Qi and blood, minimizing the Five Taxations, letting go of attachments and limiting beliefs, cultivating mental quietude, and accessing our True Self. To return to the True Self, it is said we should practice cultivation for ten months. This timeframe is mathematically symbolic, referencing the lunar cycle from gestation to birth, and is extended out by multiples depending on one's karma and curriculum.

***

- Continue modalities that are working for you.
- The key to Wealth is gratefulness. What are you grateful for? Where in your life are you operating from lack and ungratefulness? Forgive your judgments regarding this.
- Make sure your sense organs are open. Do a daily breathing technique, combined with mindful physical exercise of your choice to open the chest and diaphragm. A complete breathing regimen is found in Palace 6.
- Get rid of an overly busy life and maintain some degree of quietude. Nourish hormones with foods, herbs, or Western prescriptions, as peak hormones diminish yearly after approximately age twenty-eight for men and in the thirties for women.
- Keep in your mind images that you want more of, so your conscious and subconscious mind can assist you. We have many examples of successful athletes who use mental repetitions; e.g., imaging a successful free throw over and over while sitting on the sideline.
- Get home at night and review what you learned. Let go of any lingering feelings and thoughts and move into peace. Affirm issues in a positive manner.
- Locate and amplify your ability to use the inner eye and inner ear. Meditate on and release blocks in the Governing and Conception Vessels. (See page 152 for diagram)

***

NOTES

3. PROSPERITY-HONOR PALACE

WE BEGIN THE TRUE MOVEMENT of the alchemical Three Treasures/Three Selves in this third Palace, as we open to and decide how much of the overflow of our manifestations we share with others. The analogy here is the Dead Sea in Israel, which has no outlet. The circulation of Qi flow is blocked, so the mineral salt concentration is too high to support life. There has to be an outflow as well as an inflow.

In this Palace, we include whether others are betraying our sense of honor by being jealous of our successes and/or stealing from us or lying about us. If this is the case, we explore how we respond.

The small intestine channel receives, transforms, and assimilates food, absorbing the pure, and passing the impure to the large intestine for excretion, so we examine our ability to assimilate not only food but interactions with people, places, and things. Observing our interactions, we then decide going forward what/who we are and what/who we are not; i.e. absorbing the pure and passing the impure for excretion.

School exams and competitions give us snapshots of our strengths and weaknesses, how we compare, and what natural talents and abilities we possess which can be utilized.

Everyone is sovereign unto themselves, and each of us decide how we live our lives. The Nine Transformation model does not support one person imposing beliefs or lifestyle upon another.

Loving another can be defined as respecting, caring, and supporting them. It is not appropriate to tell others how they should think/act/be unless they ask for our opinion. In answering someone, we keep in mind that treating them with respect and care means asking inwardly the best way to share. If nothing comes forward, we can offer what worked for us in a similar situation. Giving two or more possibilities allows them free choice and keeps us from being over-responsible. Teaching by example, not words, is the most effective method.

The Cycles of 7 and 8 include the years 14-21 for women and 16-24 for men. In the first two Palaces of Health and Wealth, hopefully we were able to rely on our parents and guardians. In this Palace, we grow up, mature, and become self-responsible. Since we are able to procreate, we understand life and death and recognize that conflicts exist. We learn morality serendipitously from parents, peers, schools, and society, so hopefully we realize we are a work in progress, there are no absolutes, and we do not take ourselves too seriously. As we mature, we overcome indecisiveness, drop a know it all attitude, and see illusion in endlessly outward seeking or being mesmerized by the world.

In ancient times, boys and girls grew into men and women at an earlier stage than today, commonly working in the fields by age seven or eight and marrying by age fourteen to sixteen.

In this Palace, we learn how to respond in stressful situations. If we collapse, hide, or get angry, hopefully we have role models or guardians who can reflect back to us what works and what doesn't. Personally, I did not fully mature until about age twenty-three, the tail end of this cycle, so I understand how youth wants to enjoy life and have money and opportunities given freely to them. From a humanistic standpoint, an interesting discussion can be had about how much teenagers should be served and protected versus left to rise and fall by their own merits. Within us, we have an inner family of father (kidney), mother (pancreas), grandparent (lung), and child (liver), and supreme guidance (heart) so we have the attributes to counsel ourselves, if we do not have guardians or mature teachers.

Our physical constitution stabilizes in this Palace, so it is important to continue to open the heart/chest and connect the upper and lower parts of the body to accommodate a spiritual/physical connection though breathing and stretching the chest, intercostals, and ribs, and by strengthening the abdominal muscles.

Key: We recognize that conflicts are learning opportunities, so we develop strategies to harmoniously deal with circumstances. We begin to realize the difference between the true and false selves and develop a sense of purpose.

Qu Ze/PC-3/Crooked Marsh is a reservoir of vital Qi/energy and brings stability to both spiritual and physical manifestations as it connects the upper and lower parts of the body. Happiness is inherent in the consciousness of the True Self and is realized by traveling an inner path.

THE BIG PICTURE

This is a good time to step back and look at the big picture: How did we get to 2020 and its myriad apparent inconsistencies?

We can divide Oriental medicine's long history into four parts, namely:
1. **Early Shamanist**
2. **Classical medical theory** of the Song Dynasty (960-1279 AD)
3. **Innovative** during the Middle Ages (1279-1799 AD)
4. And finally, the more recent **Crisis,** with the advent of the opium addictions and war, modernization, toxins, congested city living and viral pandemics.

I place this information here, in the Prosperity-Honor Palace, because taking a key from the small intestine's function of separating the pure from the impure, Chinese medicine has been able to grow and thrive by assimilating what is needed/demanded by new situations in new times.

China's long chronology has been impacted by external forces (pandemics, epidemics, extreme climate, war, famine, peace), internal choices of social thought (Daoist, Buddhist, Confucian, Legalist, 100 Schools), and governments (tribal, unified, warring, peaceful, Mongolian, Han Chinese, institutional, dictatorship, Japanese invasion, communist, controlled capitalist). Their history reminds us that the only permanence here on Earth is change.

The Early Shamanistic period: Herbal extracts preserved in alcohol dating from about 7000 BC were found in Jiahu. Bone and shell needles fashioned during the Stone Age were replaced by metal needles around 5000 BC. A high-ranking government post was assigned to an herbalist around 1500 BC. Shamanic medicine of the Wu, Yue, Min, and Chu tribes of southeast Yang Tze River area during the Shou Dynasty (1046-256 BC) employed herbs, acupuncture, chanting, musical instruments, incense, and altered states of consciousness.

Some of us today would say these early shamanic medicine practitioners exceeded the rational when they pierced the air near a patient with arrows to ward off evil Qi. These early Shaman were the priests, doctors, and spiritual leaders to their communities, so in this context, I don't find this much different from modern churches and practitioners using prayer, faith healing, and laying on of hands to focus attention on a desired outcome of health to a patient and ultimately to the benefit of the community.

The early Chinese believed disease was caused by invasion of Gui/evil spirits and or Gu/parasites. The character for Yi/medicine used before the Warring States Period (475-221

BC) was made up of the radicals for shu/ancient weapons made of bamboo, a yi/quiver of arrows, and a wu/shaman. They wanted to liberate evil that was thought to reside in xue/caves, which is the same character as acupuncture point. Today we say, I caught a cold, still using the same thought process that the evil came into us from the outside.

Waving needles or wooden arrows over the body was practical, as the bone and stone needles were large compared to our modern needles and were painful upon insertion. Most people likely opted for prayer, if it was effective. I would have. Modern acupuncture needles do not hurt as they are machine-made with a rounded tip that pushes skin cells aside, unlike injectable hypodermic needles, which are cut on the bias and slice the skin. Additionally, modern needles are referred to as hair needles, because the width is thinner than a hypodermic.

Jeffrey Yuen points out how the early connection between shamanism and acupuncture is mirrored in many *Nei Jing* passages describing how the skill, intuition, and sensitivity of the acupuncturist depends on his or her Shen/spirit and, as such, acupuncture is a very subjective art. An acupuncture doctor may get excellent results with a certain treatment, but when he or she repeats the treatment at the next visit, the results differ because subjective factors in both doctor and patient have altered over time.

Modern science estimates that placebo treatments can be fifteen to seventy percent effective over time and, under the right circumstances, can be just as effective as traditional Western or Eastern treatment, or, in the very least, can increase the efficacy of a drug or treatment. As such, medicine is very subjective. Dr. William Osler defined the practice of medicine as an art, based on science.

How the shaman's Shen/spirit interacted with the patient's Shen/spirit and the patient's beliefs hold answers to successful therapeutic outcomes. Sometime during the Warring States Period (475-221 BC), the radical for shaman was replaced by the radical for herbal decoction in the character representing medicine, replacing the shaman with the herbalist, as the use of herbal treatments became more popular than the painful acupuncture. Chinese comprise one-fifth of the world's population, so their sample sizes are extremely large. That we still use similar techniques after thousands of years speaks to efficacy.

Classical medical theory of the Song Dynasty (960-1279 AD): The Chinese invented the printing press around 400 AD which allowed the dissemination of Chinese medicine books to be widely studied. The Northern Song Dynasty (960-1127 AD) established medical schools and edited the Classics (the *Nei Jing* was edited three times by Imperial committees), constituting the second of the four components in this long history. The **Classics** depicted the inability or resistance to change as being the main cause of disease. It is interesting in 2020 to observe doctors and patients of all persuasions/ beliefs and see how many of us are rigid, unyielding, and resistant to change.

Humans often look down upon ideas and techniques outside of their tradition. The Northern Song in the Chinese classical approach labeled the southern shamans barbarians, called their gods demons, and their healing methods useless. This attitude toward *the other* is evident today too, as Western medicine typically looks down upon holistic medicine/Oriental medicine/nutraceuticals or any methodology that is not theirs, while touting their own. Usually this comes down to ego and financial concerns. We must always go back to workability, regardless of who *owns* the technique. Combining East with West is superior to utilizing only one or the other. A wonderful example is the combination of Chinese medicine to alleviate the side effects of western cancer therapies or to enhance the effect of chemo or radiation or surgery. Chinese medicine has been successful in cancer cases without any western-style intervention. Rigidity blocks the free flow of Qi, of life, of ideas, of creativity, of healing.

Innovative during the Middle Ages (1279- 1799 AD): During the mid-1000s, inquiring minds went past prevailing thought and became innovative. This was a necessity to survive pandemics/epidemics, and society enjoyed a philosophically and artistically rich life. Four main herbal schools were developed, which broke the causes of disease into finite categories that we still use to prescribe today.

Crisis: Finally, during the more recent fourth stage of modernizing the culture, a myriad of crises forced Chinese medicine to develop new herbal formulas and new treatment strategies for pandemics such as SARS. As I write, we are under siege from the COVID-19 coronavirus and bird flu, along with cancer, auto-immune diseases, and the stress of modern life. Evidence shows that when Chinese medicine is used in conjunction with Western during acute pandemics, patients respond better to lower doses of steroids or antiviral drugs, have fewer complications, and recover faster.

Today, Oriental medicine and Western holistic practices use similar techniques from all four periods:
- ✓ Herbs
- ✓ Acupuncture
- ✓ Clinical studies of blood and cellular pathology
- ✓ Autopsies

- ✓ Modern formulas for new pandemics
- ✓ Combining modern Western diagnostics, drugs, and surgery with traditional Chinese medicine
- ✓ Diagnostic laboratory results
- ✓ Research
- ✓ Psychology
- ✓ Fasting
- ✓ Breathing
- ✓ Prayer
- ✓ Accessing altered states to bring back information useful in healing methodology
- ✓ Intuition
- ✓ Intentionality and changing beliefs
- ✓ Improving feelings toward situations/health/disease
- ✓ And more

Personal experience and belief are enormous deciders of what and how we individually decide to proceed, as it ought to be, meaning I am free to seek the health methods with which I am congruent and not have medical intervention forced upon me.

LIFE CAN DEPEND ON HOW WE PROCESS INFORMATION

The mind leaves the body when we are drawn to an outside object. Since the mind is a great servant and a poor master, it is better to keep the mind empty of opinions, judgments, and attachments. We perceive more clearly when we neutrally observe, freeing us from having to balance/clear/forgive misconceptions at a later time.

An inferior doctor treats a disease that is already manifest. A superior doctor addresses the patient's spirit and physical condition, works to keep one's vital force at optimal levels, and anticipates where an illness will manifest and treats the disease at that point. Often, people, businesses, and governments address issues only in crisis mode. Taoist thought puts forward the idea that, if we deal with issues when they are small, they never evolve into a crisis. An ounce of prevention is worth a ton of cure.

China's Hundred Schools of Thought thrived from the 6th century BC, Spring and Autumn period and into the Warring States period (221 BC). The following four are the most prominent schools from that time period that exist today. As you read through them, see which approach you use most. Commonly, we have a predominant approach, but we utilize all four at different times.

Sometimes, we manufacture a reason to support a fixed belief or emotion to our detriment; other times, we use the decision-making process to our benefit. Sincerity and intention, informed by the heart without pre-conceptions, allow us to use these processes to our benefit. Examine whether you have a go-to reactive style or whether you mostly access heartfelt values.

Legalism: Legalism is symbolized by the element wind, which often changes direction. If we are unable or are resistant to change, we leave ourselves open to disease, as emotional and/or mental rigidity stagnate liver metabolism, leading to blood stasis, irritability, anxiety, depression, poor digestion, poor decisions, and premature aging. A positive Legalistic approach would be *Steady as the North Star and flexible as the wind.*

Confucianism: The Nine Palaces provide a lesson plan for a Confucian to achieve individual peace, health, and transcendence through harmonious activity: eating when hungry, sleeping when tired, and honoring one's spirit. Self-responsibility is important. By utilizing the Five Virtues and being a contributing member of the community, we attain social harmony and become more of ourselves.

Buddhism: We transcend desire, attachment, and suffering through neutrality and subsequently do not suffer from wanting the world or our life to be different than it is. Our quiet mind allows for longevity.

Taoism: We become a real human being by embracing Wu Wei/effortless action through Ziran/naturalness, which can be defined as listening to our higher mind/spirit to determine what action to take. We complete our curriculum by focusing on self-cultivation rather than living the dualistic nature of defining health/disease, good/bad, desirable/detestable.

CHANGING THE MIND TO CHANGE THE CONDITION

Taoist Chuang Tzu (370-287 BC) suggested that intellectual honesty requires we explore the exact opposite of what we believe to be true. For example, if I eat organic foods and avoid GMOs, can I entertain that the Source/Creator foresaw GMOs and insecticides and built into my body the ability to detox deleterious genetics and poisonous chemicals? Maybe it takes great effort, time, and money to procure and prepare GMO-free organic foods, which takes time and energy from focusing on self-cultivation. Does the extensive effort ultimately serve me in the bigger picture of my life's curriculum?

We can use the process of being healthy as part of our self-discovery, but we can also create problems when we read something or listen to someone who says we should eat or avoid X or do Y, or we will get sick. Using fear to scare a consumer into buying a certain product/technique is an oft-used method. Consensus data does not take into consideration emotions, feelings, beliefs, lifestyle, stresses, hygiene, or genetics, all of which inform our individual metabolism.

A high-fat/high-protein/low-carb diet is not good for everyone. Nor is veganism. Oriental medicine takes into consideration the seasons of the year, the seasons of our lives, and matches foods and activities that are appropriate at various times of the day or year and life. The sour taste of spring fruits and vegies is recognized by the tongue and will assist liver and gall bladder detoxing of blood, hormones, and fats from winter's relative torpor. These same fruits and vegies sweeten in summer and provide cooling to the external heat. From this model, eating the same foods with the same flavors and same carbon-nitrogen-phosphorus composition the year round is not what nature intended, and ultimately does not serve us.

Since the only permanence is change, openness to change needs to be part of life's equation. The *Shang Hun Lun, Treatise on Febrile Diseases,* which has been China's description of the progression of pathology and the main arbiter of herbal formulary for two thousand years, emphasizes that the inability or resistance to change is the main cause of disease. We change herbal formulas with seasonal changes. We change formulas for the same disease as a person either moves in the direction of health or worsens.

Oriental medicine highly values our sense organs' ability to provide us with valuable information to stay alive. It points out that we do not stay healed unless we remain open to what feedback our sense organs are giving us to alter thoughts and behavior based on this feedback as a continuum. A patient can see many doctors without getting results and might blame the doctor. Possibly, what needs to change is the patient's belief and behavior, based on self-observation.

People with either a too-rigid viewpoint or a lack of awareness as to what they see/hear/taste/touch and smell will likely lack awareness of necessary behavioral changes. We all know people who keep doing the same detrimental action over and over and who wonder why the situation does not change. It is much harder to observe our own rigidities/blocks/lack since we often protect our weaknesses.

To assist us with prosperity and honor, the following points and intentions address making changes:

- **Qimen/Lv-14/Gateway of Time** addresses the Qi of chest and shoulders, opens the breath, and regulates time-related issues such as finishing projects or cycles and/or Palaces, getting over an illness, irregular menstruation, menopause/andropause, jet lag, etc. Open the intercostals with lateral stretching exercises and let go/release issues that bind or inhibit moving forward. How many of us are flexible when stretching laterally? The correlation to those of us who hold onto past issues/projects past their usage is high.

- **Sp-15/Daheng/Great Horizontal** at the level of umbilicus helps release issues that haunt us or take us away from enjoying life. Moxa Sp-15 or exercise the abdominal muscles.

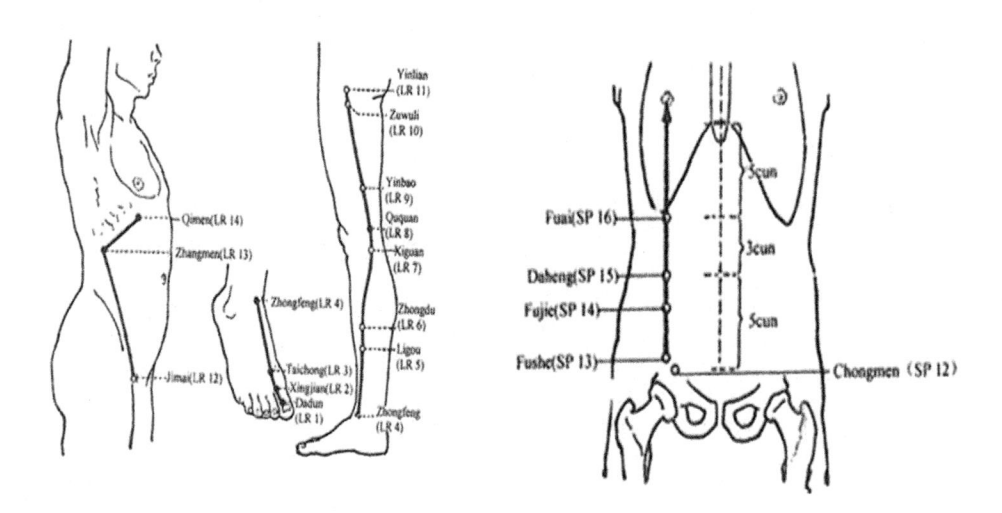

THE FIVE TAXATIONS

One of my patients sent me what they thought was a great quote: Life is not a journey to the grave with the intention of arriving safely in a pretty, preserved body but rather to slide in sideways, completely worn out shouting, Wow, what a ride!

The idea of wearing oneself out is an inferior coping mechanism according to the Nine Transformation model. Too much activity, whether mental or physical, wears out mind and body in specific ways before its time. Too little activity can also be detrimental.

Let's examine the Five Taxations.

1. **Sitting too much injures the pancreas/spleen**. When we decide what is in front of us is not worthy of our engagement, we sit too much and injure the musculature by non-utilization. This encourages obesity and blood sugar discrepancies.

2. **Lying down too much injures the lungs**. This translates as swallowing one's pride, good works, breath, and life; being too patient, too tolerant; feeling one cannot rebel, having to toe the company line, allowing others to dictate our expression. This manifests as lung disorders.

3. **Standing too much consumes kidney-adrenal energy** by putting pressure on the articulations of the spine/Governing Vessel, which curves at GV-4 lower back area of original energy/adrenals and GV-14 upper back/immunity. Standing means there is something that stimulates and motivates us to accomplish. In contemporary society, low-back pain and stiff necks are common because society encourages people to be busy, interactive, to accomplish. Chronic fatigue and early aging are a result of this taxation.

4. **Walking too much** is akin to preparing to reach an objective but never reaching it because we change our mind about what the objective actually is. Having much to do and too many plans **damages the liver** because with excessive strategizing and movement one cannot maintain a smooth flow of energy for a harmonious life.

5. **Looking too much** at the same event, idea, or having the same emotional response over and over **insults the heart** because the heart wants to be present and spontaneous. Most people have rituals or routines that they follow (e.g., waking up, getting ready for work, driving the same roads, doing the same activities at a job, etc.). Repetition without spontaneity makes the heart/mind go numb. As we gain experience and knowledge, we often are less open to living from the beginner's mind, the spontaneous state of the true self, and our essence dims. Rigidity stagnates Qi and causes blood stasis, which impairs cellular metabolism. Aging can be defined as becoming rigid, doing the same things over and over.

An example of liver taxation is Napoleon's military defeat in 1812, when he decided to attack the Russian army with his Grand Army, the largest army assembled up to that time. The Russian general utilized a scorched-earth tactic of burning food and supplies as he retreated, knowing the Russian winter would be formidable. The Little Ice Age was also a factor, making winter particularly harsh.

At the beginning of the campaign, when planning on supplying his troops, Napoleon did not consider he would march from Paris to Moscow. He never was able to engage the Russians in battle, never reached his objective, and had to constantly change plans. Only thirty-thousands of his six hundred thousand-plus troops survived the Russian winter's snow, cold, and lack of food to return to Paris.

That campaign was the beginning of the end for Napoleon's career and life.

Personality Temperament

Which Five Taxations we end up expressing is the result of a combination of our karma, our constitution, and our personality temperament that is imprinted and learned during the first Cycle of 7 and 8.

These early years are the domain of the Basic Self, and its job first is survival. As an infant, toddler, and child, our learning curve is steep, and we do not have a mature rational mind to calmly analyze what is stressful or feels like stress. Our personality temperament traits are played out through feelings, decisions, and actions, mostly decided unconsciously. Bruce Lipton, PhD at Stanford University estimates, as adults, we react/respond unconsciously ninety-five percent of the time. It takes a great deal of education, introspection, and reprogramming to track down and change why we believe what we believe and do what we do. This opportunity is one of beneficial results of the Nine Transformation process.

Below is a categorization of constitutional temperaments I excerpted from an excellent document by Eeka King B.H.Sc (Acup) of Bayside Acupuncture and Herbal Medicine, located near Byron Bay, Australia. These are typical associations common in Oriental medicine, as observed over more than two thousand years.

- ✶ First, go through the Five Phases constitutional typing and decide which one or which two fits you most. Most people will have one primary and possibly a secondary, less prevalent one.

I will go through my example, to give an indication of how to proceed:

➢ I am a Water Phase type. If I have any energy (adrenals), I will use it to be productive. I follow the beat of my own drummer and am not afraid to embark on little known/not common paths. Each of the attributes listed below is accurate for me:

- ✓ Articulate, clever, and introspective: Lots of meditation and study. Likes to get to the bottom of a subject. I have long contemplated the meaning of life, starting in my youth.
- ✓ Self-contained and self-sufficient: Likes to work alone rather than in group.
- ✓ Penetrating, critical, and scrutinizing: Likes to get to bottom-line understanding.
- ✓ Seeks knowledge and understanding: I study everything I can about a topic.
- ✓ Likes to remain hidden, enigmatic, and anonymous: I live in a rural community outside of the U.S. I'm not involved in social media, do my own thing, travel alone, don't carry business cards, and don't look to expand my social or business circle.
- ✓ Prefer to read about a subject rather than listen to lecture about same subject or discourse with someone: Writing and studying books is a very singular occupation. On the challenge side, some people have said I am emotionally inaccessible. I do isolate myself, so I fit neatly into the Water phase.

➢ I am born in the year of the Fire Pig, and pig is a water animal, further enhancing my temperament in this category.

➢ From a physical standpoint, kidney Water Phase rules the bones. My left femur bone is eight millimeters longer than my right, so when I step forward with the left leg, my sacrum and lumbar spine excessively thrust to the right. From this pattern and sports injuries, I have degenerated lumbar discs. Further up my spine, at Thoracic-5 vertebra there is a compensatory stiffness that reflects into the first and second cervical vertebrae.

There is a Taoist saying: You cannot pick a flower without troubling a star. This points out the interconnectedness of everything in the universe. In our own universe, similarly, if we keep looking deeply enough, we find many interconnections. One can look at a blood test, an orthopedic test, or an Oriental medical exam, and make a fairly accurate assessment of personality temperament.

> I also exhibit qualities from the Earth type in my caring for others:
> - Likes to be in charge but not in the limelight
> - Seeks harmony and togetherness.
> - On the problem side, I go over things too much instead of deciding and acting. I could use more self-worth, and I can become overprotective to those close to me.
> - In Western astrology, I am born under the sign of Taurus, which is fixed earth, as is my moon location, so this further supports the personality temperament traits.

I have added the Thieves and Virtues that I listed earlier in the description of the Five Phases into Ms. King's document. Thieves and Virtues will be important to consider when answering questions later in this chapter. The Thieves steal our Qi/energy, and the Virtues enhance. We are our own most interesting topic, so enjoy exploring your correspondences.

* * *

WOOD TYPES: Liver-Gall Bladder people either excel or have trouble in planning, making decisions, and acting. Their ability to see the future can be their strength. When out of balance, they may procrastinate, become indecisive or have a no sense of hope.

Virtue: Receptivity and flexibility
- Seeks challenges and pushes to the limit
- Enjoys and does well under pressure
- Admires speed, novelty, and skill
- Loves action, movement, and adventure
- Likes to be first, best, and only

Typical problems:
- Thief: Irritability, impatient temperament
- Intolerance and impatience
- Volatile emotions, anger, irritation, frustration
- Extremism, impulsive or over-disciplined, self-indulgent, or self-punishing

FIRE TYPES: Heart/Small Intestine/Pericardium/Triple Heater people love to reach out and be in relationship with all people. They enjoy having a laugh, and sometimes they carry a sadness or lack of joy deep within.

Virtue: Open consciousness, integration of the Three Selves
- ✓ Relishes excitement and change
- ✓ Delights in intimacy
- ✓ Intuitive and passionately empathetic
- ✓ Believes in the power of charisma and desire
- ✓ Loves sensation, drama, and sentiment
- ✓ Likes to be hot, bright, and vibrant

Typical problems
- ✓ Thief: Closed off, righteous
- ✓ Anxiety, agitation, and frenzy
- ✓ Bizarre perceptions and sensations
- ✓ Nervous exhaustion and insomnia
- ✓ Abuse of mind-altering substances; addictive personalities

EARTH TYPES: Pancreas/Spleen/Stomach people have the ability to nourish like a mother nourishes a child. Food and understanding are important. Sometimes, an Earth person can feel a sense of emptiness or neediness in their own life.

Virtue: True intention, coming from the heart, Thy will be done
- ✓ Wants to be involved and needed
- ✓ Likes to be in charge but not in the limelight
- ✓ Agreeable and accommodating; wants to be all things to all people
- ✓ Seeks harmony and togetherness
- ✓ Insists upon loyalty, security, and predictability

Typical problems
- ✓ Thief: Arbitrary willfulness, my will be done
- ✓ Worry, obsession, and self-doubt
- ✓ Meddling and overprotective
- ✓ Over-extended and inert
- ✓ Unrealistic expectations and disappointments

METAL TYPES: Lung/Large Intestine/Immune/Skin people search for what is pure and spiritual. They set the highest standards for themselves and others; respect is important. Sometimes, they live in a sense of what could have been.

Virtue: Doing the right thing because it is the right thing to do
- ✓ Likes definition, structure, and discipline
- ✓ Organized and methodical
- ✓ Seeks to live according to reason and principle
- ✓ Holds self and others to the highest standards
- ✓ Reveres ceremony, beauty, and refinement

Typical Problems
- ✓ Thief: Misdirected feelings
- ✓ Indifference and inhibition
- ✓ Autocratic, strict, and difficult to please
- ✓ Formal, distant, and unnatural
- ✓ Self-righteousness, and prone to disillusionment

WATER TYPES: Kidney/Bladder/Adrenal people have a persistence and determination; they will often excel in situations that others find too scary. Sometimes, they may hide a deep sense of being frozen by their fear.

Virtue: Pure wisdom
- ✓ Articulate, clever and introspective
- ✓ Self-contained and self-sufficient
- ✓ Penetrating, critical and scrutinizing
- ✓ Seeks knowledge and understanding
- ✓ Likes to remain hidden, enigmatic, and anonymous

Typical problems:
- ✓ Thief: Desires and wants
- ✓ Emotionally inaccessible and undemonstrative
- ✓ Isolation and loneliness
- ✓ Tactless, unforgiving, and suspicious

* * *

- Examine your life in detail. Decide which constitutional phase you are, and if you have one that is secondary.
- Next, when you have time, utilizing each of the Nine Palaces, mark down the ages associated with each Palace, and add which calendar years match these palace years.
- Add, in broad-strokes, major life elements during those years. Include additional details when they come to mind. Put in the accomplishments you are proud of, any situations that were challenging, and those you considered a failure.

This will give insight into which Palace(s) have had more importance up to this point. You are totally responsible, as you either created, promoted, or allowed all of it. If you are less than seventy-two years old, you can be aware of the portals through which you will pass in the future, as part of your alchemical journey informed by chronological age.

* * *

Here is a sample exploration, using myself as an example:

Transitioning into the 5th Palace of **Creativity-Children-Friendship,** while aged 32-40, I was busy with my career and had no interest in being a parent. I was the valedictorian of the first-ever OMD class in California. We moved our Baraka Holistic Center to a large, 7000-square-foot facility when the only other holistic clinic in the country was the Berkeley Holistic Clinic—and we didn't know to spell holistic *or* wholistic. We learned how to creatively triage a patient between various forms of holistic and Western medical care. I started the Sacred Tone Workshops at the clinic, focusing on meditation, and also Health Care classes at night for our patients, to teach self-responsibility.

I studied with Emanuel Rivici, MD in NYC, an oncologist who used his own radical delivery system of non-lethal chemotherapeutics for his cancer patients, and who had a unique blood-testing panel and interpretation. I fully immersed myself in the Electrical Acupuncture according to the Voll system of blending German diagnostic machines to match homeopathic remedies with acupuncture meridians and points. I studied in both the U.S. and Germany. I was creatively seeking knowledge and understanding and was on purpose, critically scrutinizing the medical field from ancient to modern.

In the 6th Palace of **Global Adventure-Joy-Happiness,** from ages 40-48, I opened my own Center for Regeneration in Beverly Hills. During this phase, I had more German diagnostic and therapeutic machines than anyone on the West Coast. I was sent to Dharmsala, India to be with his Holiness, the Dalai Lama and his doctors to see what part of Tibetan medicine could be brought back to the U.S. I got married and divorced during this Palace and took vacations to Europe, Tahiti, Jamaica, St. Maarten, St. Kitts, and Fiji.

As I look at my chronological timeline in each of the Palaces and what I was attracted to, engaged with, and accomplished during each Palace, I see how uncannily precise it is.

So lay this out for yourself. As you go through the Palaces, see which Palaces are most active and which give you the most fulfillment. For me, obviously, the Health Palace is a primary one since I deal with my own and others' health on a daily basis. Additionally, I have always been interested and deeply involved in Palace 8-Wisdom Palace and the 9th, Going Home, as evidenced by my daily meditation, wide reading/study, and writing this Workbook.

The ultimate purpose of the Nine Transformations is to assist one to graduate from all the Palaces, to redeem one's spirit from the materiality of the lower levels, and to express the truth of who we are.

* Decide which Palace(s) contain your heartfelt decisions. What is the overriding purpose of your life? How can you fulfill your spiritual promise if you have not already?

Personality Temperament and Choices

Next, examine if your beliefs and methodology for processing information and if your subsequent choices support or necessitate altering what you do.

* Look at the lists you created detailing the Palaces, chronological years, calendar years, and activities. Contemplate the times you chose certain behaviors that led to successful outcomes.
* Which choices led to consequences you wish you did not have to experience? What beliefs and choices do you want to embrace, and which do you want to leave behind?
* What opportunities did you have and how did you act/re-act?
* What were your feelings/thoughts about levels of success or failure? If you were successful, did you enhance that quality? If failure was the outcome, did you change your beliefs or behavior?

* Did you mimic Napoleon, fixed and rigid, rather than being adaptable and flexible?
* Have you had an open consciousness or been righteous?
* Are you able to give up arbitrary willfulness and embrace the greater good?
* Do you do the right things because it is the right thing to do, or do you tell yourself a story defending your actions?
* Do you value truth over desires and wants?
* As you examine the Palaces, ask yourself if your choices have been *on purpose* or a nice detour on your road to self-discovery. Write an evaluation for each Palace.
* Look at your choices and determine if you stayed with a certain temperament or whether there was a successful event or a haunting trauma that contributed to you altering your temperament. If you stayed the course and your original temperament served you well, congratulate yourself. Job well done. If you changed temperament, congratulations! Job well done. You gave yourself more choices to explore and learn about yourself.
* If you experienced a trauma (large or small) that made you choose actions that were incongruent with who you are, examine your payoff listed in E-motions. Do the free form writing exercise to remove excess thoughts and feelings and then the Forgiveness exercise to allow you to move forward in ways that are more harmonious.

***

As I write this in December 2019, I am 72 (or 73, if counting by the Asian method, wherein we are one year of age when born), so the #10's sharing and touching to others with all that I learned fits this model as I complete the Workbook. (For a woman, the age is 63+.) Most likely, I needed to learn how to negotiate and graduate all the Palaces and understand their import before being able to complete this Workbook so as to write from experience, and not conjecture.

The Nine Palaces and their corresponding Pericardium channel points are:

1. **Health Palace:** Affecting all Palaces, good health means our attention is not drawn to health issues; poor health impacts our ability to plan, initiate, and complete in any palace. Under domain of the gall bladder/making decisions.

Tian Chi/PC-1/Heavenly Pool opens the chest to allow us to more easily collect the Grace that comes from heaven reaching into our physical, mental and spiritual depths.

2. **Wealth Palace:** Do we have enough resources to survive, feed our families and have protection from heat, cold, danger and death? Under domain of the liver/choices.

   Tian Quan/PC-2 Heavenly Spring of the Kidney/Fountain of Life assists us to be grateful by understanding that challenges are not against us but designed to teach us about loving, caring and sharing.

3. **Prosperity-Honor Palace**: Do we have enough resources to share with others? Are people jealous, betraying, or stealing from us, and if they are, how does that affect us? Under domain of the small intestine/assimilation.

   Qu Ze/PC-3/Crooked Marsh is a reservoir of clear non-salty water/vital Qi that brings stability to what we manifest.

4. **Relationship Palace**: Relationships with spouses, family, and intimates as a heartfelt response. Under domain of the heart/loving.

   Xi Men/PC-4/Gate of Accumulation/Path of the Spirit heals emotional pain and suffering. It is interesting that this point is tonified with moxibustion to keep someone alive until they are transported to a hospital during a heart attack.

5. **Creativity-Children-Friendship Palace**: It is a basic belief that creativity comes from relationships and interacting with our children, acquaintances, and colleagues. We do not have as many children as the ancients did, but we have many avenues of creativity. What do we want our testimony of life to be? Under domain of the large intestine/letting go of what is no longer needed, a natural process of creativity.

   Jian Shi/PC-5/The Intermediary/The Passenger is the pericardial minister point that protects the heart under duress.

6. **Global Adventure-Joy-Happiness Palace**: In ancient days this was a small Palace as one could not travel quickly or far. Today we have planes, trains, and autos and we spend/waste time on the Internet/social media so this Palace has become more important in our time. Under domain of the lung/breath of life.

Nei Guan/PC-6/Inner Gate/Perfect Love Point/Gate to Success opens the chest, regulates Heart Qi to calm the Shen/spirit, and is the best point for restoring balance between the body and the mind.

7. **Career-Knowledge Palace**: What is our chosen work? What do we do with the knowledge we gain in our endeavors? Under domain of the bladder, which has the most acupuncture points of any meridian channel, affecting every system, relationship, and interaction.

   Da Ling/PC-7/Big Mound/Spirit Gate is used when we do not know which way to go, or what to do in our career.

8. **Wisdom Palace:** Turning relationships, experiences, and knowledge into wisdom. Under domain of the kidney, which rules DNA, bones, spinal fluid, and brain, relating to our deepest physical aspects.

   Lao Gong/PC-8/Palace of Toil and Weariness is used for mental fatigue/Taxation Syndrome.

9. **Home Palace:** We follow the inner path to bring ourselves to the true self, whereby we achieve spiritual fulfillment. Under domain of the spleen-pancreas/stomach/our physical center.

   Zhong Chong/PC-9/Balanced Friendliness opens the eyes, ears, nose and mouth allowing us to perceive ourselves, others, and the world for what it is.

10. **The Hero's Journey**: Classically, there is this tenth aspect, the sharing with others what we have learned. We tune into Spirit to dictate how and what we share, not allowing the ego to dictate we *must* share with the less enlightened. We share what emanates from the heart. Since there are only nine points on the pericardium channel, there is no point associated with this aspect.

It takes time and energy, an entire lifetime really, to go through the Nine Transformations. If you have read only up to this point and have learned more about yourself, this Workbook has been successful for you. The percentage of books that get read from start to finish is frighteningly low.

However, if you are committed to doing the work to transcend the lower planes of consciousness and become aware that you are one with God and the glorified states that accompany knowledge thereof, continue on. There are many of us lifting and being lifted.

The Three Worms/Karma

We have three types of karma, known as the Three Worms. Karma means action that we are to take to complete our stated curriculum, i.e., what we are to learn about loving and what do we need to do to balance past deeds.

A common interpretation of karma is that we reap what we sow, i.e., do something good and good comes to us; do something bad and bad comes to us. However, what is commonly left out of this explanation is that there can be long periods of time between events, either in this life or going back to past-life existences. What is said is we are held accountable down to the last farthing. Also, that explanation leaves out the Grace plan, which is a more elegant way to navigate life.

Earth is a classroom, and our ultimate curriculum is to learn unconditional loving. We can look at our abilities and opportunities positively, as in, I was born to do this, or negatively, as in, I am a victim.

> Karma can be created in several ways and through seemingly infinite situations. Basically, karma is accrued by transgressing your own consciousness or the divine consciousness in another person.
>
> Any action, emotion, thought, or word that is put forth in an out-of-balance way may cause karma. For example, if you become angry and strike your child, that may very well create a karmic situation. Later, you may apologize, which clears the karmic action. But if the child has done something he or she should not do, and with love you do discipline the child… you create no karma, nor will you feel it necessary to apologize. You are merely helping the child to learn. As this example shows, attitude can make a big difference in whether or not you create karma.
>
> You can bring many karmic situations to yourself through misuse of your emotional nature. If you feel anger, if you feel hate, if you desire revenge, if you feel guilt or any of the other negative emotions, you bring karma to yourself. If you bring it in and hold on to it, you will be held accountable for it.
>
> The Soul is perfect; the personality is imperfect. But since the Soul has contracted to experience the physical realm with a particular personality and consciousness, it will re-embody to fulfill the karmic situations accrued by the personality.

When you get so angry that you are out of control, when you continually get so emotionally upset that you cannot control your tears and your sobs, when you get so drunk that you cannot remember or control what you do, when you get so "spaced out" on drugs that you are not in control—these situations bring karma to you.

And, probably more than any other single thing, the guilt you feel after these overindulgences will bring karma to you. Most of them are not inherently "good" or "bad," but the attitude with which they are carried out may very well create a value judgment, which, if the judgment is "bad," may create guilt, and that, in turn, will create karma. In fact, the biggest thing that builds karma is guilt. If we do something and then have a second thought—"I wonder if I should have done that…"—we have karma. It is important to watch the attitude and keep it as neutral as possible. (Ref: J-R/MSIA.org)

If you want to know what your karma is, see to what you are attached or attracted. Herein lies the Nine Transformation encouragement to move toward neutrality first, and then clear karma/attachment/curriculum from above, which is much easier than from trying to balance it directly, as was discussed previously.

The Three Worms are:

1. The collection of unfinished business from past lifetimes, in which we did not fully learn what was intended for us. These can be completed by changing behavior/action, through a spiritual practice and awareness, prayer, being of service to others, working with a master, in the dream state or purged through forgiveness and Grace to find redemption and contentment.
2. Accrued karma from actions this lifetime. Similarly, these karmas can be completed by changing behavior/action, through a spiritual practice and awareness, prayer, being of service to others, working with a master, in the dream state or purged through forgiveness and Grace to find redemption and contentment.
3. Inherited with the family lineage. As this involves other souls, we purge our part/participation to release indebtedness from parents'/relatives' actions so that it does not have to affect us or future generations. Other family members are still responsible for their actions, though some assistance can be done for them through prayer and forgiveness and asking for Grace to support their journey.

***

There are several ways to balance karma. The most common is the eye-for-an-eye and tooth-for-a-tooth approach. People used to say to me, how wonderful you are a healer. My response has always been, No, Spirit heals. I might be a facilitator, but this is something I have to balance from a past action.

In the earlier years of my practice, when giving acupuncture treatments, more than a few patients joked, Wow, this is like torture. To me their response was not a joke as I knew I had to balance my karma by working in the healing profession.

> It takes quite a while to clean up karmic debris. But if that influence is not utilized, some way or another it starts to go to the next level of behavior and locks in there. So, if you don't clear up a sprained ankle and you don't do anything about it, it might get into your lower back. If you don't do anything there, it might get into your head. Or it might reverse.

> So, we need to look at our life and say, "I am today an accretion of everything that has happened to me up to this moment. Good or bad, right or wrong, blaming and not blaming, helping not helping, whatever—this is it." And for you to not like what you've got is then to declare yourself inept at the way you went through your life.

> You have the right to do that, by the way. It's called: finding your mistakes, finding your errors, changing and correcting them, reaching in, and pulling them out. (Ref: J-R)

> Chant Ani-Hu or an initiatory tone or a sacred chant into specific areas of your body to quicken the vibration of the cells and bring in a healing vibration.

> Chanting and listening are a method of focusing. Chant the sacred tones, then stop chanting and listen. Start searching inwardly. Look for the golden thread, and, when you find it, ride on it into awareness of your Soul.

> As you chant the ancient names of God, you clear enough karma to evolve to each succeeding level. It is not by your mental, physical, or creative ability that you do this. It is specifically by your putting in the time, loving, and disciplined focus. (Ref: J-R)

I reference two counselors to assist in identifying and clearing karma and working with situations one finds difficult to master. They work in both Workshop and individual format. Alisha Das (ALISHADAS.COM) and Michael Hayes (www.Awaketolove.com).

* * *

Palaces Four to Six relate to the decision-making Conscious Self, the intermediary between the High Self direction and the Basic Self preferences and actions. Here, the Taoist alchemical firing process refers to conquering our inner demons of the false-self proclivities and selfishness by aligning the human mind with the higher spiritual mind. Sometimes spirit will assist the High Self to give information directly to the Conscious Self, bypassing the Basic, where we get a gestalt type *aha*, but this is not the common pathway.

Moxibustion

A healthy body, a strong mind, and a focused will are three essentials that make it easier to make self-supporting choices to successfully move through the Nine Transformations. Moxibustion is a superior physical method to energize these three aspects.

A Japanese folk tale from the Edo era (1603-1867 AD) relates that Farmer Manpei's secret to maintaining his long life was daily direct burning of moxa on **Zusanli/St-36/Leg Three Mile,** as his ancestors had done. It is recorded that Manpei lived 243 years, his wife Taku lived 242 years, and their son Mankichi 196 years.

Detailing the functions of moxibustion, the authors of an oft-used text in modern Chinese schools, *Chinese Acupuncture and Moxibustion, Vol. 2,* states that: since cold obstructs and stagnates Qi, the use of moxa warms meridians, expels cold, and increases Qi flow. Since Qi is the foundation of life, if Qi is sufficient, a man lives a long life. But when lost, death occurs.

Yoshito Mukanino, M.D., at the Sports Science Laboratory at Fukuoka University in Japan found that moxibustion on **Zusanli/St-36/Leg Three Mile** increased maximum oxygen uptake improving recovery time from hypertension and diabetes, and decreased cancer rates.

Bian Que's *Book of Heart Teachings* from China states: Moxibustion has a warming action and supports yang, frees the flow of the channels and network vessels, moves the Qi, quickens the blood, dispels dampness and cold, disperses swelling, scatters nodulation, secures yang, and stems counterflow Qi.

Both texts instruct that moxibustion is the way to achieve longevity of more than one hundred years.

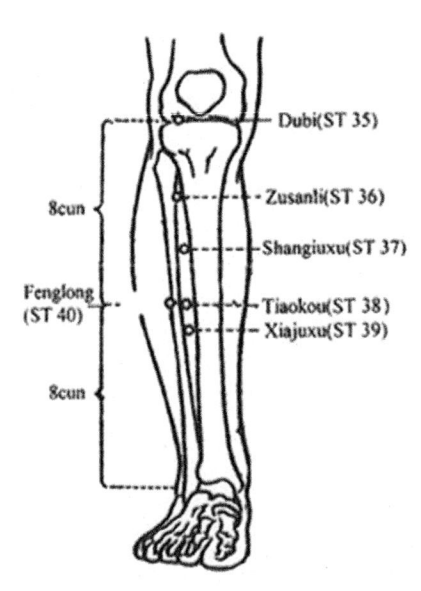

Zusanli/St-36/Leg Three Mile is named to indicate moxibustion at this point facilitates it being easier to walk three miles, regardless of age.

Additional moxa points for longevity synthesized from moxibustion's long history are:

- **Shenque/CV-8/Qi Abode- Spirit Gate** replenishes Qi and strengthens the body, especially if a lack of determination in the middle-aged and elderly.
- **Guanyuan/CV-4/Source Pass** is the source of Original Qi.
- **Qihai/CV-6/Sea of Qi** is where Qi emanates from and returns to.
- **Zhongwan/CV-12/Middle Cavity** is one of nine points for returning yang energy.
- **Da Heng/SP-15/Great Horizontal** is a main Kidney Qi point.
- **Huangshu/KI-16/Vital Shu point** is the crossing point of the kidney channel and the Chong Vessel genetics.
- **Tianshu/ST-25/Celestial Pivot** regulates Qi and blood.
- **Mingmen/GV-4/Gate of Life** tonifies Kidney Qi and Yang, Original Qi/constitution and strengthens the lower back and knees.
- **Zhi Shi/BL/-52Will Power Chamber** tonifies the kidneys, benefits urination and strengthens the low back.
- **Shen Shu/BL-23/Kidney Shu point** strengthens Kidney Yin and Essence, benefits the ears, bones and lower back.

THE NINE TRANSFORMATIONS

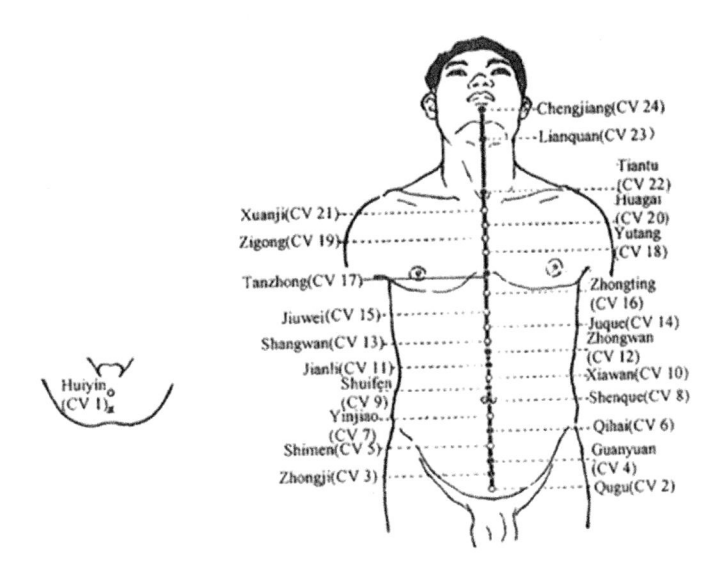

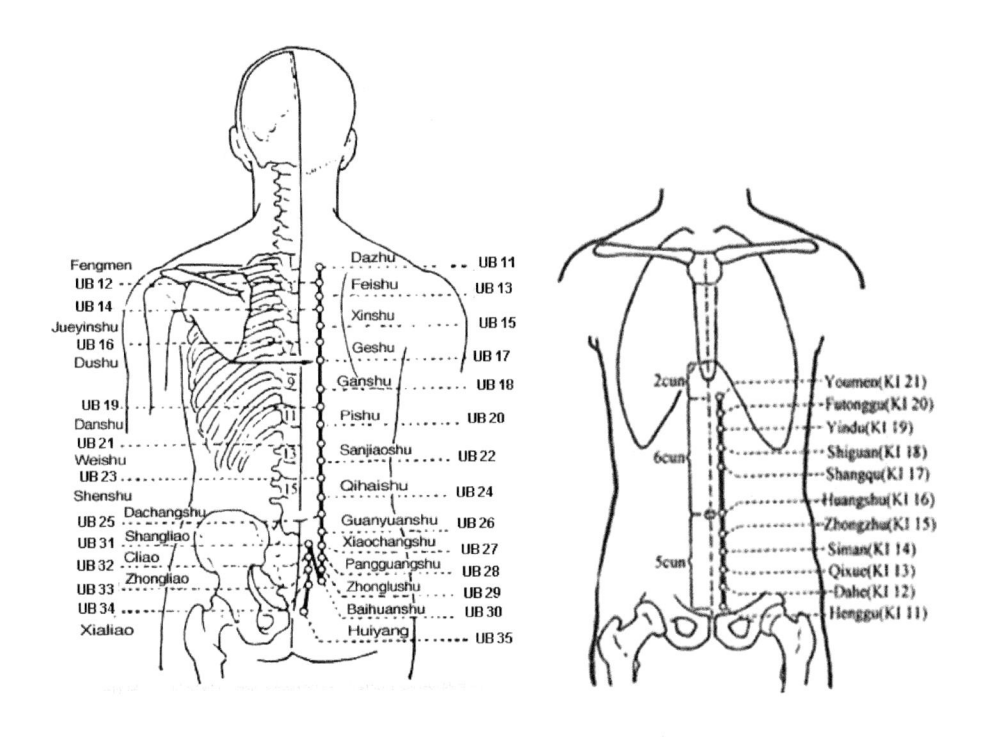

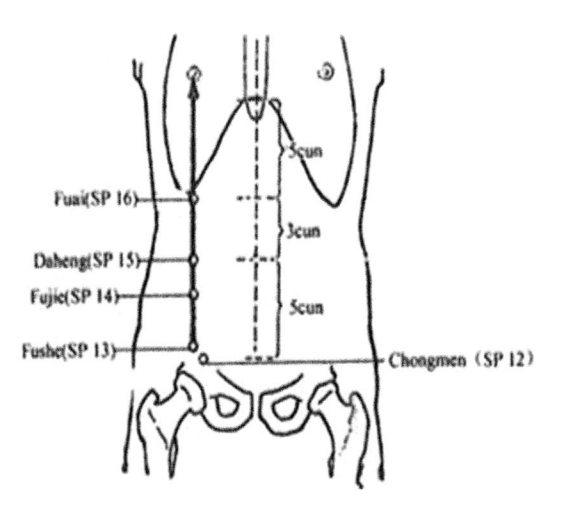

Strengthening the body and achieving longevity requires perseverance over time. During convalescence, it is suggested to moxa three to four times per week. If healthy and wanting to strengthen the body or promote longevity, moxa twice a week to start, and when some effect is noted, reduce to once a week.

One can use a moxa stick to hold near a point, put moxa on the end of an acupuncture needle, or place directly on the skin. The skin can be burned, and scarring can occur with all three modes, especially with direct moxa. It is important to get instruction from a qualified professional before embarking on your indirect moxa stick protocol and leave direct moxa to licensed practitioners.

* * *

Notes

4. RELATIONSHIP PALACE

THE RELATIONSHIP PALACE is an important time of self-examination, reflecting on life and destiny. Besides the enjoyment of sharing and relating with spouses and family, we learn about our strengths and weaknesses, and if our communication skills are effective. This Palace also explores the High, Conscious, and Basic Selves of our inner family, a little-known, to our detriment, aspect of consciousness.

Cycles of 7 and 8 target the years 21-28 for women and ages 24-32 for men, when relationship successes and issues provide feedback as to how we are handling our Ming/fate—the cards we have been dealt—and the opportunities that spirit presents. What we do with our Ming/fate/opportunities is our destiny and depends on our choices and subsequent actions. This Palace is the major player of our destiny, as it acknowledges both the totality of one's action and the unification of consciousness under the domain of the heart.

It is said the great medicine is extremely close at hand, equal to the Western perspective that the kingdom of heaven is within and the blessings already are. The alchemical process requires accessing the human mind less and less and accessing the Spiritual mind more, until figuratively there is no human mind left.

The processing of choices by the Conscious Self is the focus of Palaces Four through Six: Relationships, Creativity and Children, and Adventure-Joy and Happiness. We realize the value of merging the Three Selves into one cohesive unit to complete our curriculum more easily.

Depression may be a result of not being in alignment within ourselves. One idea here is, instead of excessive physical activity to produce a runner's high or getting a prescription for a psychological drug, or drinking alcohol or taking recreational drugs, (the National Center for Health Statistics in 2017 indicated that 12.7 percent of the population over age twelve had taken antidepressants in the month prior to their evaluation), drop whatever is causing depression and embrace that which is uplifting and gives you joy.

By examining the intention behind how and why we interact, we can decide if that intention supports or detracts from who we are and where we are going. Taoism suggests we develop virtue if we follow our destiny. Healers can bring out benevolence, and monied people can share prosperity, while community organizers can spread compassion. It depends upon intention, however, as healers can be less than altruistic, monied people can be greedy, and community organizers can sow diversion, separation, and violence.

Key: Make wise choices with relationships to facilitate your soul's life path. Detours can be interesting but possibly not worth the suffering.

Ximen/PC-4/Gate of Accumulation-Path of the Spirit is a point for emotional suffering and pain. Suffering teaches us to look for alternate actions that are more beneficial and on-purpose. Using the higher spiritual mind, we realize loving and inclusiveness conquers all, turning obstacles into stepping-stones. Since moxibustion is used to tonify this point during a myocardial infarct/heart attack, to keep a patient alive until they are transported to a hospital, and because we are in the Relationship Palace, inquiry could be made into relationship imbalances as one source of heart disease and strokes.

THREE TREASURES, THREE SELVES

Chinese culture observes Nature to understand the movement of Qi through forever-interchanging polar opposites yin-yang, and to categorize all things into Five Phases to comprehend the universe. The Five Phase model is subsequently used in governing, strategizing war, economics, health and longevity, medicine, martial arts, flower arranging, art, diet, agriculture, architecture, feng-shui, fate and destiny, philosophy, education—everything! Obviously, many people do not avail themselves of this knowledge, but it is readily available.

To illustrate:
- ❖ Alchemy's Three Treasures of Jing, Qi, and Shen is comparable to Chinese medicine's hormones, oxygen, and spirit and Taoism's humility, frugality and compassion.
- ❖ Qi Gong, martial arts and Taoist meditation use the same orientation of Jing-Qi-Shen.
- ❖ Medicine uses these three levels in diagnosis and treatment: the lower Jing/constitution, the middle Ying/blood level, and the upper Wei/superficial-immunity level.

- ❖ The level of needle insertion is referenced by superficial/Qi—heaven, man/middle, and earth/deep insertion.
- ❖ Herbs are classified as earthly lower-grade curative, humanity's middle-grade restorative, and heavenly upper-grade for prevention and alchemy.

About ten years ago, I was putting myself through a mini version of the Nine Transformations I had designed and given in a monthly seminar format. Much of the presentation had to do with meditation, mental focus, inner awareness, what foods to eat, breathing techniques, etc. It was well received. However, I knew something was missing.

I went back through Three Treasure translations of the classics, which spoke about the energy in the lower Dantien, below the umbilicus, that has no definite location, somewhere between the spine and body front… And it struck me. OMG! They were talking about the Basic Self.

This realization came after forty years of familiarity with the subject! Medical descriptions reference physical attributes of Jing/Qi/Shen and only peripherally the psychological attributes of the Three Treasures, but do not allude to the western identification of the Three Selves, first noted by Plato in the third century BC. The Basic Self is located in the pelvic cavity, the Conscious Self accessed in the chest and head, and the High Self in the higher spiritual centers, corresponding to Jing-Qi-Shen.

When studying a mystical format, there is an outer teaching that is available to all and an inner teaching, revealed only to initiates of that teaching. To fully understand the *Tao Te Ching*, it is necessity to be taught the myriad symbolic references. The Forbidden City's inner sanctum was only open to the Emperor, his families, retinue, and support personal. On our bodies, **Weiguan/TW-5/Outer Gate** acu-point on the outside of the lower arm refers to the outer courtyard while **Neiguan/P-6/Inner Gate** located on the inner lower arm references the inner sanctum to our fate and destiny. Solomon's Temple in Jerusalem had outer and inner sanctums. Ezekiel and the Southern Tribe codified the secrets of consciousness in the Old Testament to protect themselves from their Babylonian captors using knowledge against them. One needs to know the symbolism from the old Testament to fully understand the New Testament. Religious orders, governments, and companies are set up similarly, with an inner sanctum reserved for a few and outer, general information available to all.

Some of this bifurcation is practical, some protective, and some secretive. If I had been initiated into a Taoist order, I possibly would have been taught outright that the Three

Selves of consciousness are the Three Treasures. As it was, I was taught within MSIA.org, and thus I am able to extract a deeper understanding from Taoist teaching since universal knowledge is universal.

As I gazed inwardly yesterday (as I was editing this Palace) to see who my patient was at that moment, I found a lack of communication between their three selves. Remember: the doctor works with the patient, and the herbs, acupuncture, drugs, supplements, foods, exercise, etc. treat the disease. This is a situation I commonly find. The Taoists reference *Three in One*, which means, as I understand it, to illicit excellent communication between the Basic Self/physical vitality, Conscious Self/emotions and decision-making, and High Self/life plan and spiritually is necessary for vibrant health and alchemical advancement.

The patient in question was rehashing a small situation, attempting to rectify why she acted in a certain way in response to a male neighbor's request that came across as an order. We tracked back in her life to age eighteen, wherein, as a young woman, she was learning how to survive in a patriarchal society. Her instinctual responses that had served her then were now no longer necessary. My advice to her was, in these moments when she is caught off-guard, to pause for a second, place the situation in the light for the highest good, and see the appropriate self to express from. The High Self might provide her altruistic wisdom as to why the neighbor was acting in such a way and/or what the opportunity for learning was for her or the neighbor. The Basic Self might react in an angry or aggressive manner to ensure her survival in the moment, which might or might not be the correct response. The Conscious Self might say to the neighbor, I am busy with these other people right now. Can we talk later?

> The Three Selves are a perfect marriage. The High Self holds our spiritual direction and passes the information to the Basic Self, which has the responsibility of maintaining the body and getting us involved in life. The Conscious Self chooses whether or not to go along with the information that the Basic Self passes up to it. In physical sickness and in health, the High Self always holds the spiritual design. If the Conscious Self gets out of the way, the Basic Self can balance and heal the physical body. When we maintain a positive image in our minds, the Basic Self will accept and work with it. (Paraphrase, J-R)

HIGH SELF-WISDOM AND BEYOND

The High Self holds the keys to being a real human being. The High Self has total knowledge of our life plan and is the intermediary between our soul and our consciousness;

it turns experiences and knowledge into wisdom.

Shen/Spirit—High Self
Wisdom

Neurotransmitters

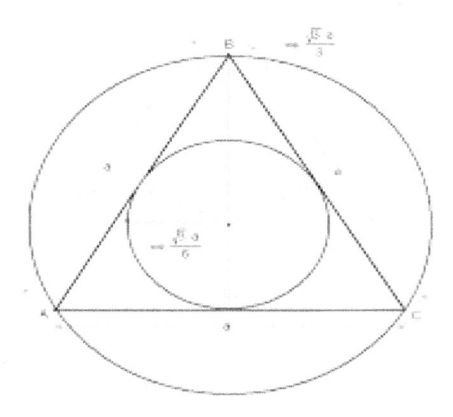

JING/VITALITY-BASIC SELF   **QI ENERGY-CONSCIOUS SELF**
Survival-Hormones   Gaining experience-Oxygen/Immunity

When you understand the nature of your beingness, you have the key to all creation, and the key is this: when we pray fervently from deep within the conscious self, where we are now, we charge our lower self with this prayer, and it will release energy up into the high self. The high self will then send the energy back down into the lower self until the lower self is so charged with energy that it forces the energy back up into the conscious self. With the spiritualized energy, our consciousness rises. That's why we don't have to go anywhere except within. (Ref: J-R)

- **Organs**: Frontal brain, psyche

- **Function**: We deal with that which is greater than us, deciding what is of value and letting go what is not useful. We swallow the gold pill/get initiated into a mystery school to access techniques to transcend the levels below the soul, or, if we are already initiated, we rededicate ourselves to our discipline.

- **Treatment**: We mature parts of consciousness that are fearful, stagnated, or feeling victimized. We look again at endless possibilities, as we probe our self-identity. We rebuild the parts of our constitution that have been injured. We wisely interpret that which we see, hear, smell, sense, and touch. We pray and/

or chant the names of God and avail ourselves of spiritual counsel. We are open to the benefits of contemplation, meditation, and spiritual exercises, of taking upper-grade alchemical herbs and acupuncture, psychological counseling, and group growth-awareness seminars to assist getting deeply embedded issues to come to the surface and be cleared. Often, these embedded issues are mirrors to what we judged as our ugly part(s). Once we are aware, we change our behavior to get results we want.

- We connect with the crown chakra at **Bai Hui/GV-20/100 Convergences**, the meeting point of the Governing Vessel, which represents our curriculum with the Bladder, which rids what is no longer needed, the Gall Bladder, which makes decisions, the Triple Warmer, which integrates the Three Selves, and the Liver, which is in charge of taking action.

THE BASIC SELF—SURVIVAL

Taoism is one of the few philosophies that teaches the Basic Self is a wonderful asset to overcome lower levels of consciousness. (MSIA is another. There are others, but I have not been exposed to them.)

Once the personality temperament of the Basic Self is accepted by the Conscious Self as part of our personal story or identity, by definition we have conflict/disparity with beliefs/ideas that are positioned outside our story. When we are exposed to situations/beliefs outside our personal story, we have the opportunity to be neutral toward them, to incorporate them, or leave them alone. It is difficult to be neutral and not judge what we do not want to incorporate. In Palaces 8 and 9 we identify with unification and how not to have conflict.

The High Self communicates the karmic plan to the Basic Self and the Basic gets us involved in life. The Basic Self grows our bodies when in the womb and is responsible for keeping the body healthy throughout life. Survival and defense are its primary physical focuses. It corresponds to hindbrain's function and the instinctual responses of lung breathing and pancreas and stomach digesting and in the way we use muscles to move about and engage with the world. The Basic Self is highly referenced in the first three Palaces of Health, Wealth and Prosperity.

Medically, we look for acute problems/disease under the Basic Self's domain first, as the lower mind and emotions attempt to work things out when feeling hurt/misunderstood/victimized, or we have an opening to an external pathogen.

If not in effective and harmonic communication with the Conscious Self, the Basic will eat foods, engage in sex, be judgmental or violent, or act out as a way of feeling productive/creative. If we attempt to use willpower to overcome the Basic Self's interpretation of how to support completing our curriculum, the Basic Self will win ninety-plus percent of the time, and our willpower will be defeated. This is why it is vital to have flowing communication between the Three Treasures/Three Selves. The Basic Self responds well to images, so the advice is to keep uplifting images in our conscious mind that we want more of. Professional athletes get profound results doing mental reps in their specialty while sitting on the sideline.

The Basic Self will lie, cheat, steal, or murder, and then make up stories why we are justified in these actions. It might fight to the death to defend made-up beliefs and positions.

The Basic Self is referred to in Chinese medical classics as the Hun, one of the spirits that must be addressed during the therapeutic encounter. The Basic Self likes harmony and balance, and the Thief/Virtue model works very well in this context.

- **Main organs associated with basic self:** Lung, Large Intestine, Stomach and Spleen influencing breathing, digestion, muscles, and acute and chronic pain.
- **Function**: Self survival, defense, adaptation, and response to stimulus.

Below are parts of an article from the May 2015 issue of *Current Psychiatry* titled "Psychoneurogastroenterology: The abdominal brain, the microbiome, and psychiatry," by Henry A. Nasrallah, MD, detailing some of the physiological actions of the Basic Self/gut.

Existence of a gastrointestinal (GI) nervous system, distinct from the CNS that comprises the brain and spinal cord, has been recognized for more than a century—yet it has been ignored by psychiatry and rarely is included in residency training. This nervous system is located inside the wall of the GI tract, extending from the esophagus to the rectum. Technically, it is known as the enteric nervous system but it has been given other labels: second brain and abdominal brain.

The ENS includes 100 million neurons (same as the spinal cord) with glia-like support cells. It contains >30 neurotransmitters, including several closely linked to psychopathology (serotonin, dopamine, γ-aminobutyric acid, and acetylcholine). It communicates with the brain via the vagus nerve. It is of great relevance to psychiatry that 90% of the body's serotonin and 50% of dopamine are found in the gut.

Association of GI disorders and psychiatric symptoms:

Irritable bowel syndrome is associated with panic disorder, generalized anxiety disorder, social phobia, dysthymia, and major depression.

Inflammatory bowel disease (IBD), such as Crohn's disease and ulcerative colitis, is commonly associated with mood and anxiety disorders and personality changes.

Celiac disease has been repeatedly associated with several neuropsychiatric disorders, including ataxia, epilepsy, peripheral neuropathy, headache, anxiety, attention-deficit/hyperactivity disorder, autism spectrum disorder, and schizophrenia.

(Ref: Henry A. Nasrallah, MD)

* **Treatments**: Access and lovingly communicate with the Basic Self. Make sure your gut health/microbiome is optimal. Avail yourself of counseling/psychiatry/psychology, acupuncture, moxibustion, chiropractic, etc. Practice Qi Gong, breathing exercises, physical exercise, yoga, adjust the diet, eat foods in season, take herbal formulas and nutraceuticals.

* An effective way to eliminate fearful stress that is felt in the stomach is to stick the tongue out when inhaling and breath into the lower belly.

* Observe the subtleties when you realize you are judging. There may be unconscious suffering or judgments from earlier in life or from a previous life that either your soul or the Basic Self experienced and needs acceptance and loving. Both the Basic Self and High Self come from repositories and most of the time the Basic Self and High Self have had prior lifetimes in bodies serving other souls.

* Connect with the Basic Self which traditionally occupies the space between **Qihi/CV-6/Energy Sea and Ming Men/GV-4/Gate of Life,** but not in a precise location. The Basic can also be behind the umbilicus or slightly above. Thank the Basic Self for doing such an exemplary job of keeping you alive. It may take several weeks of lovingly asking and listening to the Basic to gain its cooperation after years of not knowing its function. After expressing gratitude and gaining some level of communication we can ask, as we would our own physical children: How would you like me to support you? What do you need? What would you like to tell me?

* Once we connect and have a level of communication, we can start to give them images of what we want, not as a demand, but as a loving direction, by keeping

positive images in our mind.

Conscious Self—Having Experiences

Looking spiritually, the Conscious Self comes in blank, as a tool of the soul, with access to both the High Self and Basic Self. If we perfect our consciousness and move our awareness up into our soul, we can break reincarnation patterns by the technique mentioned earlier: moving up into the soul and declaring with impunity to "take that off," so that karma is expunged from our karmic record. (Excerpted from J-R info.)

After learning survival strategies in the first three Palaces, the next phase involves having relationships and interacting with the world. The Conscious Self mediates between the Basic and High Selves, utilizing the mid-brain to choose the actions we take.

We create, promote, or allow everything that happens to us, as we are totally self-responsible. Illness becomes chronic when we suppress or dismiss acute issues that we do not resolve. An arbitrary belief or our personality temperament can be causative factors as to why we do not resolve. Refer back to the notes you took for questions in the last Palace. The Conscious Self portion of life corresponds approximately from about age twenty to fifty or sixty for us in modern society, where we get a job, have a family, and are in the world in our most expansive, involved manner (if we are dividing our lifespan into three portions corresponding to the Three Treasures/ Three Selves).

We use middle-grade restorative practices to repair any decay from poor conscious choices, as the characteristics and frequency of the middle-grade herbs resonate well and are effective for the Conscious Self. We remain open, checking that our choices/actions are not habituated or causing stagnation.

- **Organs**: The circulatory system of the heart channel and the locomotion of the skeletal system of the kidney channel carry us into the world.

- **Function**: If we are tolerant of others, we can thrive and live harmoniously within society. Negative thinking or emotional flooding can poison the body by turning the blood acidic and toxic, so we wisely choose in what we participate and monitor our progress.

- **Treatments**: Acupuncture, massage, chiropractic, moxibustion, dance and movement therapies, diet, and taking middle-grade restorative herbals.

- **Da Zhui/GV-14/Great Hammer is** a famous immune tonification point. One aspect of this point is reflected by whether we embrace the world or stubbornly act like it is separate from us. Acupuncture and moxa are useful.

- Connect with **Tanzhong/CV-17/Center Chest**, the Mu point for pericardium and convergence point for Qi. Stretch the associated small muscles and ligaments in both the chest and upper back/ lower neck and practice your preferred breathing exercises. Moxibustion is beneficial with these two points.

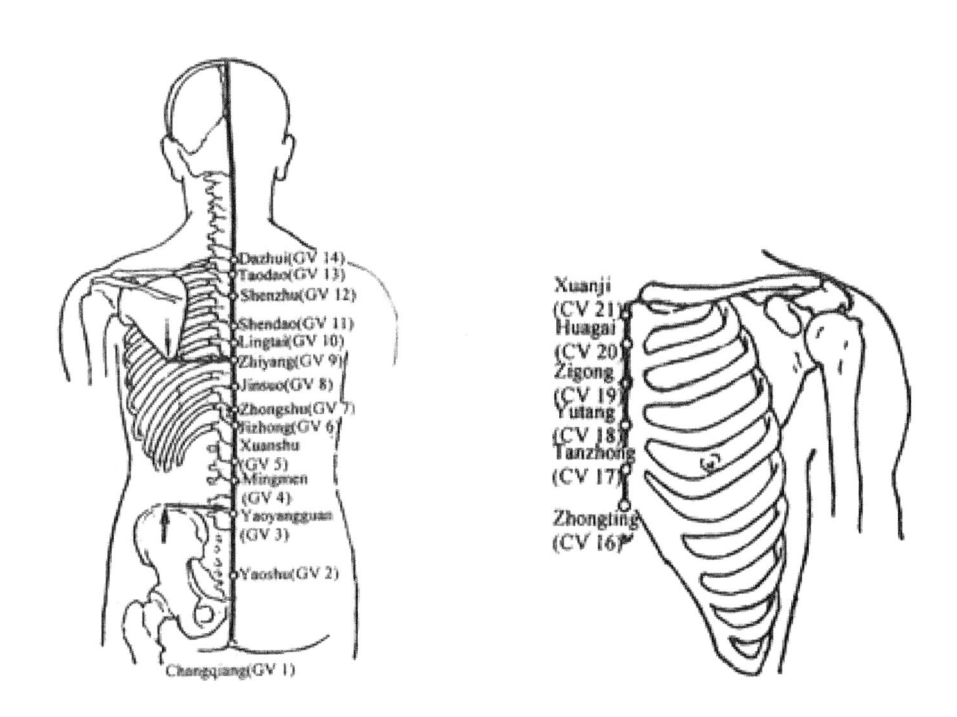

Working with the Three Treasures/Three Selves to Balance the Five Phases

It is interesting to note that infants, children, and animals respond more readily to energetic homeopathic medicines than adults, as they do not have limiting beliefs that block healing. When our intention is clear, life is not a negotiation. Once the Basic, Conscious, and High Self are aligned, we more easily awaken to the sacredness of our being.

What is the main personality temperament that blocks healing and a successful alchemical journey? Authors throughout history have depicted heroes failing in their endeavor because of one fatal flaw. It is the same flaw in the Five Thieves that the Chinese marked as the most egregious: that of arbitrary willfulness.

Christopher Booker in his *The Seven Basic Plots: Why We Tell Stories* says:

> *What is it that brings the hero or heroine of a tragedy so inexorably to catastrophe? The first people consciously to ask this question were the ancient Greeks; and they had no doubt that all the great tragic figures in their mythology had something profoundly in common. They called it hubris, which we usually interpret as a form of over-weaning pride, a reckless arrogance. But the literal derivation of hubris was from the word hyper, meaning "over." It meant a "stepping over the bounds," a defiance of the cosmic order, that state of perfect balance which ultimately holds the universe together (characterized in the motto "nothing in excess," written up over the temple of Apollo at Delphi, the most sacred spot in the Greek world).*

The alchemical cure is sincerity of intent.

One poetic Taoist wrote, *If we try to change our conditioning without using the mind of Tao/spirit, the fires of desires rage inside, allowing the Five Thieves to attack us and tragedy ensues.*

To direct and calm the mind to receive and integrate higher wisdom, massage, or acupuncture the following points/areas:

- **Tong Zi Liao/GB-1/Pupil Bone Hole,** at the side of head lateral to eye, accesses the brain marrow to tap our innocence for new beginnings.
- **Yifeng/TW-17/Wind Screen,** at the bottom back side of the ear, stirs up the wind to elicit change, like a shaman moving Qi with arrow or a modern practitioner laying on of hands.
- **Da Zhu/BL-11/Great Shuttle:** Rotate neck slowly in both directions to get circulation moving in the joints and bones. If it is painful, roll up a small towel, wrap it around neck and let neck relax onto towel support as you rotate. If we change our bones/constitution, we can change our alchemy.
- **Feng Shi/GB-31/Market Wind.** Once upright, we have a willingness to change and take on challenges. Use if afraid to make changes.
- **Bai Huan Shu/BL-30/Dew of Heaven** prevents stagnation in the sacrum, allowing us to let things go on a moment-to-moment basis. A level of salvation can be found in going with the flow. Emotions deplete us because Qi/energy is needed to maintain them. Often, it is not necessary to fix emotions/attachments. If we observe how a reaction was triggered and forgive ourselves for forgetting we are divine, we move back into innocence and experience life without judgment, as the real person

THE NINE TRANSFORMATIONS

we inherently are.

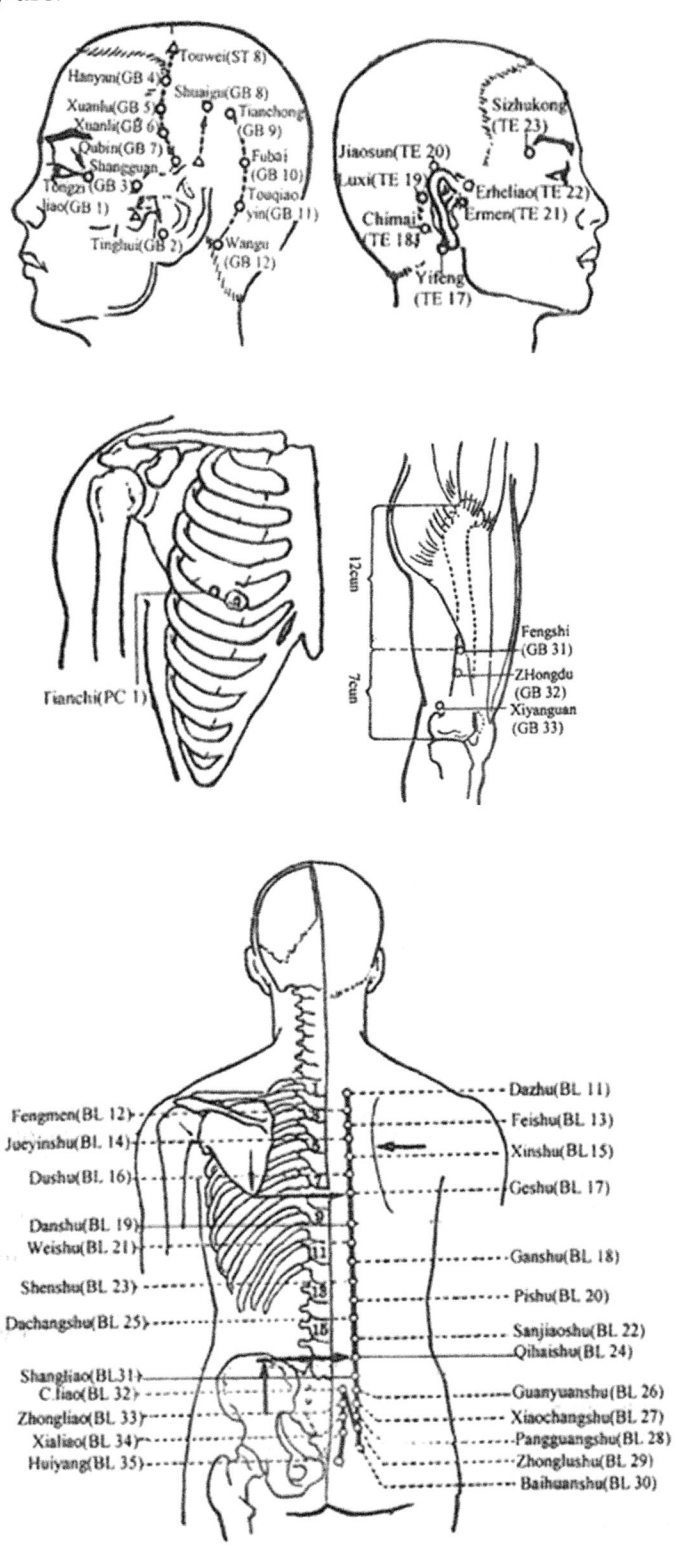

When we prepared the cauldron before entering the first Palace of Health, we asked and answered three basic alchemical questions:

- ➢ What is my ORIGIN? From where did I come?
- ➢ What is my FATE? Who am I?
- ➢ What is my DESTINY? Where am I going?

Tali Sharot, in a TedTalk, revealed that modern researchers have identified three principles that drive the mind and behavior.

1. First are social incentives, our response to the opinion of others.
2. Second, we value immediate rewards rather than some reward that might come in the future.
3. And third, the brain processes positive information better than negative information.

Looking so far at what has been presented in this Workbook, we participate with like-minded individuals. Second, we immediately feel better/good/content when clearing emotions, breathing, stretching, and meditating. Third, the Nine Transformations presents a viable outline/timeline for enlightenment and freedom; by monitoring our progress in our journals, we are motivated by seeing results. If you have not adequately answered the three alchemical questions, do so now.

From the step-by-step Nine Transformation method, we open the sense organs to assist accurate perception. We do this physically by clearing mucous out of the head and sinuses, but really this implies going deeper as we meditate on the area between the eyebrows to open the third eye, and we listen inwardly between the tips of the ears with the third ear, to be clairvoyant and clairaudient to ourselves. We align the Three Treasures/Three Selves for unified communication. With this attunement and alliance, we can clear self-imposed obstructions and change behavior. If these actions resonate with you, take some notes on what actions to take and implement.

**

So that we do not become overwhelmed and abandon our cultivation at this point in our journey, Nine Transformation practitioners know the wisdom of building back that which was broken down. Take the following herbs orally as a tea or infusion.

- **Yu Zhu/Polyganatum odoroti/Jade Bamboo** represents the evolution of one of our objectives: health and longevity through flexibility. This herb used to repair sinews, sprains, and tears.

- **Huang Jing/Polygonum/Solomon's Seal—Will Strengthener.** It has been said that will power/willingness is the fourth treasure in the Three Treasures system, being a necessary ingredient to breaking habits and holding through until *this too will pass*. Polygonum also connects the sexual Kidney energy with the loving heart, linking sexual function with good feelings, bringing new levels of happiness.

- **Di Huang/Rehmannia/The Marrow of Yellow Earth** is used here to build back the flesh, treating broken bones, torn sinews or tendons, and emotional rips or tears.

- **Sheng Ma/Cimicifuga** clears heat in head around **Touwei/St-8/Yin Yang House** at the side of the head and prevents our dying before we are destined. Sheng Ma draws out things hidden in deeper layers of subconscious and unconscious that can cause problems, such as ghosts, demons, toxins, obsessions, unfulfilled desires, and toxins inherited from parents. **Cimicifuga** will also assist our freeform writing exercise.

- **Chai Hu/Bupleurum** clears blocked Qi energy in the chest, abdomen, and throat, ridding obstructions in head that block communication between the Basic Self and spirit. **Bupleurum** impacts the liver, which deals with time, so it is good for acknowledging the past is past and embracing the new.

It is important to point out again that herbs treat the condition, while the doctor treats the patient. We choose herbs for a condition, but simultaneously we look within for awareness regarding what to change and what to continue. Alchemy is about treating the spirit of an individual, not chasing symptoms.

***

Meditation of Three Selves:

* Sit upright, if preferred, and close your eyes
* Call yourself forward into the Light for the Highest Good
* Begin saying or chanting the Ani-Hu chant, inwardly or out loud. Have intention that the tone will move through the subconscious and into the Basic Self. (Full explanation of Calling in the Light and the Ani-Hu chant in Appendix).
* Once you feel attuned and integrated, thrust the tone up into the High Self. The High Self gives back spiritual energy in return. Energy patterns can be re-assembled and new direction brought forward out of our own conscious guidance. (Excepted from J-R/msia.org)

When leading group meditations, I have experienced the Qi/energy from our chanting go up above our heads and then descend, bringing new energy patterns for us to assimilate and utilize, and then rise again, taking us out of the body. Over the years, in leading groups at the clinic and elsewhere, I have been amazed that people who have never meditated will experience the subtleties in guided meditations, such as the Ani-Hu, Flame Meditation, and White Light Healing Meditation.

We all inherently have, as Hermes pointed out, *The fire of Spirit and the vessel of our gross and subtle bodies are One. Nothing needs to be added. Just remove the impurities that surround it.* (See *Inner Worlds of Meditation* booklet at www.msia.org for explanation of the Flame Meditation, the While Light Healing Meditation and more).

***

Once we have built back up what was broken down and the upper portals are open, we can work on vitality and longevity. Qi/energy is necessary to transform traumas and dramas into wisdom, so we tonify **Mingmen/GV-4/Gate of Life** and **Da Zhui/GV-14/Great Hammer** on the spine. If not getting acupuncture, moxa, or chiropractic, move the spine with yoga-type postures, front to back and side to side.

- **Mingmen/GV-4/Gate of Life** tonifies kidney Qi and yang, tonifies original Qi, nourishes essence/hormones, and strengthens the lumbar region and knees. It is one of the most effective points to strengthen the constitution, if moxa is used.
- **Da Zhui/GV-14/Great Hammer** clears heat/inflammation and regulates the defensive Wei Qi/immune system.

- **Baihui/GV-20/One Hundred Convergence of Experiences** is crossing point of the Governing Vessel with the six yang meridians and Sea of Marrow point. It raises yang, treats prolapse, subdues excessive yang, clears the head, calms the Shen, dispels interior wind, and treats manic psychosis. It responds well to acupuncture and moxa.

These three Governing Vessel points relate to the physical and psychological aspects of the Three Treasures/Three Selves. The three corresponding points on the Conception Vessel on our front are **Qi Hai/CV-6/ Sea of Qi, Tanzhong/CV-17/ Chest Center** and the **third eye.**

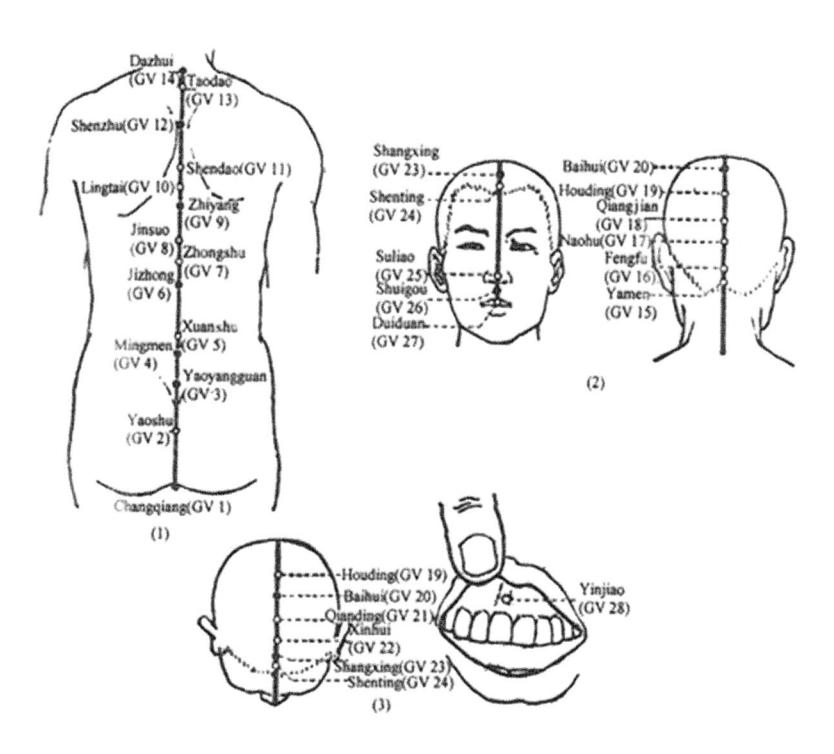

***

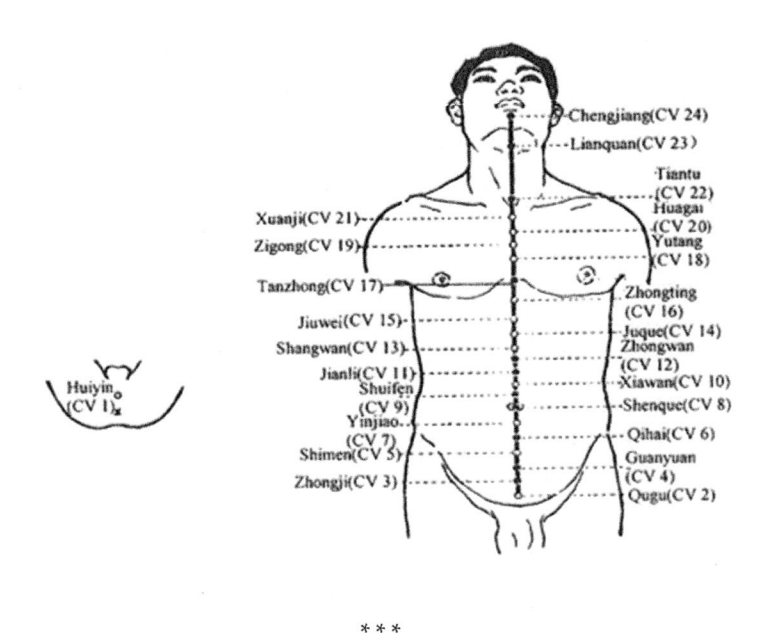

- The key to successful relationships is to make wise choices, keeping in mind your life path. Continue to refine goals and directions for your ideal scene and detail your action steps.
- Communicate daily with Basic Self/selves, giving appreciation for their good work and support, and asking them what support or attention they would like.
- Optional: Continue moxa treatments on St-36 by a licensed practitioner or by yourself if you have been adequately instructed. Have a practitioner moxa the GV points on the back listed above.

Aligning the Three Treasures/Three Selves

Techniques to align the Three Treasures/Three Selves vary with lineages, teachers, and preferences. The steps below offer but one approach. An oft-used method is breathing through a body part that appears tight/ blocked. Here, the area of focus is the approximate locations of the Three Treasures.

1. First, call in the Light for the highest good and intend that the Three Selves come into alignment. If convenient, ground yourself, putting bare feet on soil, grass, or sand.

   Through visualization, extend Qi/energy from the bottom of the foot at **Yongquan/Kidney-1/Gushing Spring** like tree roots pushing into the earth. The earth will reciprocate. Feel Earth Qi come back into the lower Dantien/abdomen, approximately three finger widths below the naval. If not convenient to be outside, extend your Qi down through whatever you are sitting or standing upon and down into the earth for a foundation.

2. We want to locate where the Basic Self is residing at the moment. Place your hand and attention at the umbilicus, **Shenque/CV-8/Spirit Gateway.** If you do not feel a connection, focus three finger widths below the umbilicus at **Qihai/CV-6/Sea of Qi** or two finger widths below that at **Shimen/CV-5/Stone Gate** or at **Guanyuan/CV-4/Gate of Origin.** If not there, place your hand two finger widths above the umbilicus at **Xiawan/CV-10/Lower Epigastrium.** The Basic Self is dynamic and not locked into a specific point.

   Place you hand over the area in which you feel affinity. The body will likely relax, maybe taking a deep breath. Extend loving to your Basic Self for doing such a marvelous job of keeping you alive and to the degree of health that you enjoy. Now is not the time to judge what you might consider to be ill-health. Perform either regular or reverse abdominal breathing. When feeling vitalized, go to step number three.

3. Place the hand on the heart center, at the sternum between the nipples at **Tanzhong/CV-17/Center Chest.** Change the breathing pattern to full lung breathing, breathing air into the bottom third of the lungs.

   If your breath is not full, inquire why you feel stress, or why you are not present in the body or wanting to do something else. Place whatever awareness in the Light. What belief or behavioral change might rectify this?

   If you become aware of a beneficial action step that needs another time frame, write it down. When you feel aligned, move to number four.

4. Place a finger on **Yin Tang/Third Eye/Hall of Impression,** between and slightly above the eyebrows, to access the High Self. Focus breathing in and out of the **Yin Tang/Third Eye** until it vibrates, or you feel an expansion of consciousness.

5. Focus now on the intersection of the Third Eye and the tips of the ears, in the center of head, at the **Purple Palace**. Ideally, you have access to your soul. Begin chanting Hu or Ani-Hu, either inwardly or out loud. Rather than thinking we are meditating, realize we are being meditated.

6. Experienced meditators will expand awareness such that it appears they are moving out of the body. If it does not happen naturally, one way is to focus about twelve inches above the crown chakra/**Bai Wei/GV-20/Place of One Hundred Meetings** and *breathe* from there. Actually, we are expanding awareness to include subtle levels of what is already so. Stay with your experience as long as it lasts.

Spiritual masters recommend that however one can get out of the body is good, but the ideal is to rise up the spine out through the crown chakra/**Bai Wei/GV-20/Place of One Hundred Meetings**. If we are successful in moving from the unconscious and into the soul, past and future do not exist, since we are not bound by time or space in the level of soul and above. We have spiritual sight, and we expand our consciousness to become aware of what is. The longer we stay in the soul body where everything is *here and now*, co-creating with the divine, life takes on an effortless quality. The trick is to hold this consciousness after meditation sessions as we move about our daily lives, interacting in life. The sage will stay in his/her center and act rather than re-acting to outside stimulus. Who we choose to be in any given moment is always up to us.

* * *

It is helpful, almost necessary, to view life in an objective, non-attached manner to keep the mind clear. It is said that the Gold Elixir is finally restored when the alchemist merges the human mind with the mind of Tao/Spirit, giving up doing and accomplishing to enter the state of Wu Wei/non-doing/cooperating with spirit. When we cease efforting to increase or decrease, we experience freedom, as the false self takes a secondary position to the true self. When we allow Spirit to direct us, we do not create more karma for ourselves. We give spirit the credit and spirit gets the karma, and we walk free.

A technique to obtain oneness is to embrace opposites into one viewing point: Day and night become a full unit of time. Man and woman become humanity. Hot and cold become variations in temperature. Winning or losing are representations of keeping score.

Settling the consciousness with this viewing point, coupled with relaxed breathing and chanting sacred words, the mundanity of conditioning of the false self will be burned away, leaving the pure True Self. People notice our transformation when we realize, without fanfare, what has always been so. A Taoist saying is that we leap out of the cage of the ordinary to live as long as heaven and earth. They ask, Would that not be wonderful?

The *I Ching* teaches when we assume our proper position in the family, the community, and the world and we act sage-like, there is no wasted energy, no squabbles, no war. We keep a Light consciousness while walking, standing, eating, sitting, working, sleeping, and dreaming. We put the Light around us that filters all elements coming into us and going out from us. We bless our food and drink, our brothers and sisters, wherever our attention is drawn.

* * *

Notes

5. CREATIVITY-CHILDREN-FRIENDSHIP PALACE

IT IS COMMONLY UNDERSTOOD that interactions with others stimulates creativity. Raising children is the highest human creative activity. Artistic endeavors obviously fulfill this Palace. As such, all forms of creativity can be a testament to our character.

Cycles of 7 and 8 in this Palace for women is between 35-42 years and 40-48 for men.

Key: In the last Palace, we repaired injured or ripped aspects of the body and consciousness. Now, we rebuild consciousness with new understandings. We examine whatever bitterness/suffering we still identify with and use the Light to transcend same, realizing how situations are for learning and not punishment.

Since our bodies have lost some of their natural capacity to purge by this age, and since the Creativity Palace is under the aegis of the large intestine, keeping the bowels open while eliminating beliefs and feelings that are no longer useful is recommended; as a result, we have less heaviness in the body and consciousness.

Jianshi/PC-5/The Intermediary—the Passenger is used when one wonders why God has forsaken them. This acu-point loosens rigidity felt in the Basic Self/abdominal area, making it easier to let go of what we are holding that no longer serves us.

If we accept and understand our Basic Self, the child in our inner family, creativity flows more easily. Bruxing, clenching the jaw, and grinding one's teeth is from unresolved Basic Self issues as the stomach meridian innervates the jaw/ masseter muscle.

Key: Ask for assistance from the Greater Shen/Spirit. It is best not go inward wanting something but rather acting *as if*, affirming that the desired outcome has already taken place. Healing does not have to answer to reason.

We have the Shen/spirit herbs to assist us in this Palace. (Notice: Shen/spirit is used in names of the herbs listed in this Palace.)

- **Ku Shen/Sophora root** awakens us to the lessons inherent in suffering.
- **Xuan Shen/Scrophularia** After getting in touch with the cause of suffering, we reframe how we view the situation and which beliefs caused the suffering.
- **Dan Shen/Salvia** allows us to change who we think we are.
- **Ren Shen/Ginseng** re-orients how the consciousness will flow to the extremes of our lives. Ginseng tonifies yang Qi and gives us endurance.
- **Sang Ye/Morus** increases oxygen utilization.
- We add one more herb to move Qi into the pelvis, in alignment with large intestine's influence in this palace: **Niu Xi (Huai Niu Xi/Achrysanthis Root—100 Slops-Knees of the Ox.** It guides other herbs to the pelvis and consolidates energy for healing after stagnation has been addressed.
- Exercising the **quadriceps** with squats, biking, swimming, yoga, etc. also assists here.

True Self—False Self

Shakespeare famously said in *Hamlet*, *To thine own self be true*. Being true to ourselves necessitates knowing what to be true to. In knowing ourselves, we realize that everyone is part of God, without exception, since out of God comes all things. It is wise to make spiritual awareness a priority, whether in a relating to others, a marriage, a demanding career, running errands, in all situations.

Possible areas of self-judgment/infliction that go very deep and block us from self-knowledge are related to arbitrary willfulness, the Thief in the Earth Phase. They are:

- ✓ Lack of trust in self, others, or God
- ✓ Lack of love for self, or having a hatred of self
- ✓ Viewing the world and situations as being out of our control
- ✓ Wanting the world to be different from what it is
- ✓ Wanting to be someone else than who we are
- ✓ Having desires that cannot be fulfilled
- ✓ Having goals that cannot be reached

Deep introspection might be necessary to find acceptance and self-love. Harmonizing the Three Selves and balancing the Five Phases by adapting new behavior is essential, whether we do this through the Nine Transformations, or another model.

Ears are shaped like upside-down kidneys and referenced as the external orifice of the kidneys. Kidney disease often inhibits auditory function. Palpate points around the ear to see if any areas are binding or blocking you from honestly listening. If you find any sore points, massage them. Check internally to ascertain to which voice you are listening. Are you listening to the one that encourages the Five Virtues/Ten Commandments, or the one encouraging Five Thieves/the Seven Deadly Sins?

Release thoughts that promote excessive attachment or are not supportive to your goals. Resolve issues that need attention. Relax and let God/Tao/Source. Do not ask why things happen but accept divine purpose. Ask for Grace and bless the light that resides in all things. Celebrate each moment. Be a messenger of the divine. Emanate Light. Everything we touch is lighter after we put our attention upon it, if we act for the highest good.

Unfortunately, some people think/feel that real people/sages who act in an uplifting way shine an uncomfortable light on their false self/inadequacies, so to protect their weaknesses, they slander or kill these sages.

One of the *I Ching* hexagrams teaches us there are times to hide our light and there are times to shine. If we shine 100 watts of light on someone who can only handle 20 watts, they will close their eyes and look away, maybe even strike out, if reactive. Be wise and ask Spirit when and how to shine.

When we are loyal to our soul, we no longer have extreme attachment to external gratification or even being respected or appreciated by others. Often, we are content to be quiet and hold the Light for someone, allowing them to find their own way. We respond to and enjoy life but not from a need level, and amusingly, the more we express from the true self, the more we are loved and adored.

Opening the Portals Further

As we untie the knots of attachment, healing takes place in reverse order, from the deeper and more entrenched positions to the more superficial and less severe.

In the clinic, I would watch an illness exit one system such as the emotional response of fear and its associated lymph or kidney and stop at the liver's inability to cleanse the blood, necessitating a new strategy to address the new condition. Within this context, the Nine Transformations points out that healing does not become a cure unless our portals/sense organs remain open, such that we see/sense and perceive clearly and enact new behavior based on new awareness. A behavioral change is key. There are patients who see multiple knowledgeable and talented doctors for the same condition without results, wanting the doctors to fix them without introspection or behavioral change on their part.

Early in my career, I thought it was my fault if the patient did not improve. Then I looked at the mathematics of my being with a patient one hour a month and the herbs and homeopathics I prescribed influencing them two or three times per day. The patient was operating within their beliefs, emotions, and choices approximately seven hundred hours per month. I began to look into patient responsibility for their own health.

> As you change behavior, you change the emotion. As you change the emotion, you change the thinking. As you change the thinking, you're getting wisdom. As you gain wisdom, you go into forgiveness. (ref: J-R)

***

The following points for acupuncture assist the senses to improve perception, so we can balance or change our emotions, beliefs, and behavior. Acupressure will not do too much for clearing these points as they are over bone (the point on the outside of leg is not over bone). A more subtle technique may be more effective over bony areas. If acu-points are sore to the touch, consider acupuncture or osteopathy or cranial adjustments. Meditation or strategic fasting is also viable. How Spirit conveys its wisdom to us is enhanced when we practice meditation/spiritual exercises. The time between the intuitive awareness and the mental recognition becomes shorter when we spend timing listening within, and it will seem that knowledge appears spontaneously.

- **Shuai Gu/GB-8/Valley Lead** clears phlegm in the head and is good for those having difficulty clearly perceiving themselves.
- **Tian Chong/GB-9/Celestial Hub and Fu Bai/GB-10 Floating White** calms the Shen, clears inflammation, and removes obstructions from the jaw and masseter muscle. The stomach meridian/Basic Self enervates the masseter muscle/jaw, and bruxing often is the result of unresolved issues in the Basic Self.
- **Tou Qiao Yin/GB-11/Head Portal Yin** has the same function as **GB-9/10** above and releases the sense organs and holding the breath from unconscious stress through these senses.
- **Wan Gu/GB-12/Completion Bone** benefits the head, calms the Shen, and relieves pain from unfinished karma. Good acupoint for sleepwalking.
- **Feng Shi/GB-31/Wind Market** assists in removing obstructions by strengthening our ability to stand up in who we are.

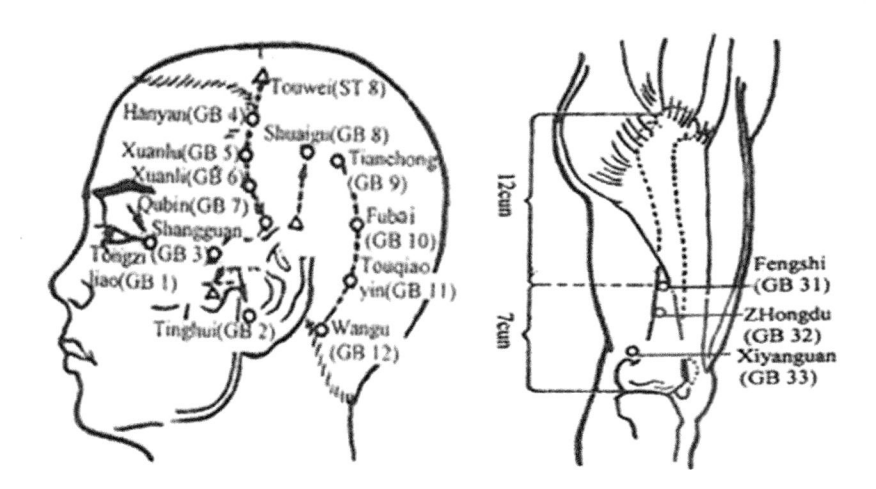

EXERCISES

> Our primary relationship is with our Soul. We do not allow external objects to excessively influence us. We practice discipline, concentration, and insight. If we are clear about this, everything else will follow closely.
> The key in the Creativity Palace is to replace suffering with a new understanding by reframing how situations benefit us. We no longer ask why things happen to us. We accept that we are emissaries of divine purpose, even if we do not know exactly what this is. We celebrate each moment and emanate more Shen.
> We turn 5 Thieves into 5 Virtues.
> We utilize therapies that harmonize and balance the Five Phases and the metabolic function of the heart, pancreas, lung, kidney and liver.

* * *

Notes

6. GLOBAL ADVENTURE-JOY-HAPPINESS PALACE

GETTING A GLOBAL PICTURE through travel and study is beneficial in understanding the similarities of humanity, regardless of race, creed, color, or religion. Under the aegis of the lung meridian, we inhale, expand, and transform our bonds to significant others and to society at large. We are inspired by methods, discoveries, and opportunities utilized by others outside our immediate environment.

Cycles of 7 and 8 for the Sixth Palace align with ages 42-49 for women and 48-56 for men. The Global Adventure-Joy-Happiness Palace was small in ancient times, as you could not travel far or quickly. Today, we have access to long-distance travel, phones, and the Internet, where people productively spend or waste a lot of time, energy, and money.

Key: We continue to use sense organs to extract information about the world. When we see possibilities, we sense life has order, and we can more easily visualize healing and the attainment of our destiny. This envisioning of outcomes calms our mind, relieves psychological issues, and balance is more easily restored between body and mind.

As I edit this, we are experiencing global lock down. We are very connected through the Internet, which is in alignment with this Palace, and viruses engage our immune system, ruled by the lung, which is also in alignment with this Palace. In the Metal element of Five Phases, we have a sense of knowledge and learning. Notice that sense of knowledge is not real knowledge. We are in process. We are certainly learning many things about ourselves and others through Covid. The world is irrefutably changed, and it is yet to be determined how each of us gain wisdom, about ourselves, from these events.

Within this Phase, the Thief of misdirected feelings opposes the virtue of doing the right thing. Many people say and allege many things, mostly claiming they are right and someone else is wrong. Since there are opposing views, all statements cannot be true. Maybe the statements are true for the person speaking, but not for the person they are speaking to or about. Maybe the statements spoken are not true because the speaker has an agenda, hidden or in plain sight.

Personally, I delete the abundant images of the virus that seemingly accompany every article about Covid and do not check daily about how many cases/deaths, etc., since my job does not necessitate me tracking that information and I do not want to be over-responsive to external information. I would rather spend my energy/Qi, of which there is only a finite amount, on assisting myself and my patients and friends. To note, loving is infinite. From an alchemical standpoint, how we respond to a situation is what is important, not deciding which situation is better/worse than another. Life is about learning and growth.

Remember back to the discussion about survival and personality temperament? When we are confronted with life/death situations, whether purported or real, we often revert to our learned responses from birth to ages seven or eight, unless we have done much internal processing. Besides having to monitor our own response, government representatives, doctors, experts, bloggers, friends etc. are, for the most part, reacting and communicating from a Basic Self/human-minded survival consciousness.

The sages who are holding a loving respect, caring, and support for individuals and humanity are few in number. They are acting, not reacting. The bottom line here is to go within, access the Spirit, and ask, *Where do you want me? What am I to do?* This approach is the recommendation for literally every situation in life, if we live alchemically. Obviously, this present situation is intense, which gets our attention. Palaces seven, eight, and nine focus on the subtleties of being sage-like.

Nei Guan/PC-6/Inner Gate—Perfect Love Point—Gate to Success opens the chest, regulates Heart Qi, and calms the Shen/spirit. It is the best point for restoring balance between the body and the mind. With perceived order, we visualize healing and recover from illness. Referencing the Covid situation, we have control of our internal environment and where we place our focus. **PC-6** is used in chronic diseases, revitalizing the Qi/energy and opening the diaphragm for relaxed breathing.

The herbs below utilized in this Palace can be viewed as alchemical harmonizers.

- **Ren Shen/Ginseng** is known as the root of humanity. It works with the Three Treasures/Three Selves, opening the heart and quieting the Shen, and settling the Basic and Conscious Selves. Ginseng moves spiritual attributes along the bladder channel on the back to be distributed to the main organs.
- **Shi Hu/Dendrobium** nourishes and preserves the integrity of the five Zang organs (heart, pancreas, lung, kidney, liver) and treats taxation syndrome.

- **Gan Cao/Liquorice** goes to all the organs, making sure we remain physically strong, protects against adverse Qi, and addresses the uncertainty of whether to move quickly or hesitate.

***

By now we acknowledge that we are spiritual beings learning and growing, and our meditation/initiation practice has jelled into a daily format. On Earth, we have many avenues of expression compared to being between incarnations, so it is advantageous to pay attention, as one hundred years goes by in an instant. We dwell less on the past or future and more on the present moment. As a result, life becomes more effortless. We limit distractions, move into a less hectic schedule, and return to innocence.

> Happiness comes out of the mind, emotions, and body, which are always changing, but joy comes from Spirit. When you rise to the spirit of the occasion and truly partake of the Spirit, you have joy—even during physical, emotional, or mental despair. (Ref: J-R)

The following points enumerate what to focus upon in the Global Adventure-Joy-Happiness Palace:

- **Tian Shu/St-25/Celestial Pivot** is an entryway to access heaven and see our destiny more clearly.

- **Taiyi /St-23/Supreme Unity- Tai Qi realm** transforms phlegm, so we can move forward. It calms the Shen and treats psychological issues.

- **Fu Tong Gu/Ki-20/Open Valley** harmonizes the abdominal cavity organs and opens the chest as Qi moves up.

- **Jiu Wei/CV-15/Turtle Dove Tail** relieves psychological issues.

- **Ling Xu/Ki-24/Soul Ruins** is like a tombstone marking what is left over of one's existence, after embracing Wu Wei. After mixing our essential energies in the internal cauldron of purification, we redeem our primordial Qi/spirit from materiality. This point therefore is regarded as a place of celebration. Its location on the chest corresponds to the physical location of the pericardium and heart.

- **Yu Tang/CV-18/Jade Hall** is the termination point for the liver, and is used to treat situations that have to do with time, as in concluding an event or beginning anew. Here we are terminating our focus on the material world, so we can focus on spiritual awareness.

- **Zi Gong/CV-19/Purple Palace.** There are five shades of red, including the color of a red flower, cinnamon, vermillion, red peony, and purple. Purple symbolizes the color of the highest peaks of Taoist mountains. We go to the highest mountains where the air is clear. We do not see anything as toxic, and we affirm, I am the celebration of life. Purple is the color of transformation, being closest to pure white, which cannot be seen and is formed from red/heart spirit and black/kidney essence, spirit and matter.

- **Tianxi/Sp-18/Celestial Stream-Supporting the Ravine of Heaven.** Water that is stirred up from the kidney and contained by earth symbolizes the importance of Earth Phase's clear intention controlling Water Phase's willingness and willpower.

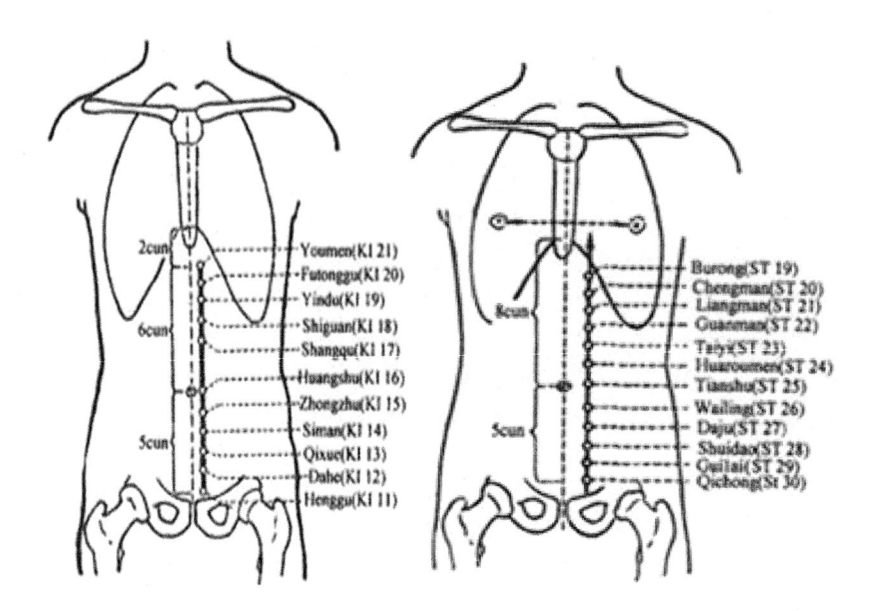

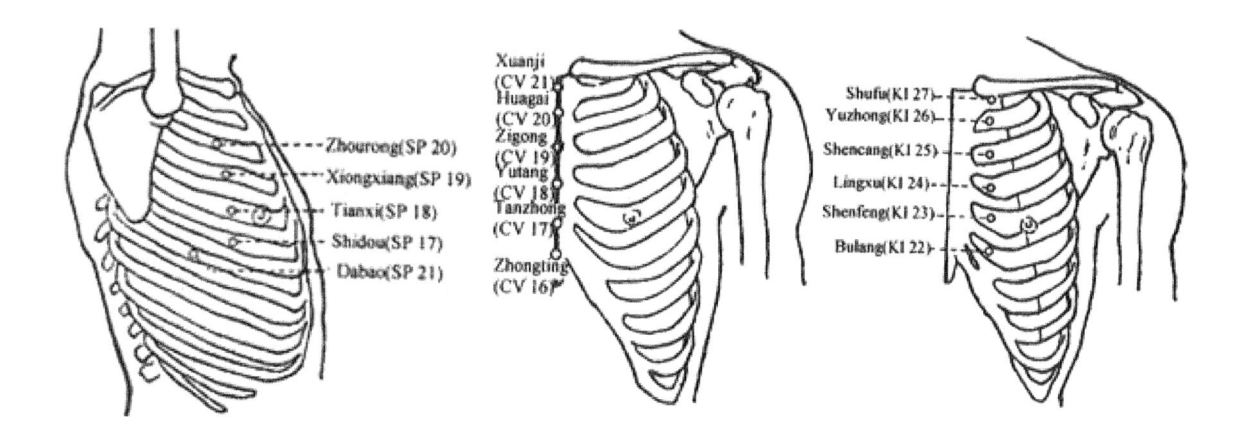

BOUNDLESS BREATHING

Ancestral Teacher Qiu said, *If the breathing is at all unsettled, life is not your own.*

After focused breathing exercises, thoughts and feelings are left behind as attention naturally goes to the spiritual body. After breathing exercises and meditation, which follows easily, it is beneficial to avoid entanglements that are not in accord with one's nature, and to refrain from being overly responsive to the outside world for a period of time. This allows us to release blockages and balance/harmonize metabolism.

Any discussion on breathing leads to the importance of releasing the diaphragm and being relaxed. The Sinew Channels, which conduct Wei Qi/defensive immune system energy that is necessary for survival, terminates at the diaphragm at **Yuan Ye/GB-22/Armpit Abyss.** Relaxed breathing enhances immunity.

The diaphragm muscle moves without our awareness, but we are also able to consciously control it. We will hold our breath during a shock or under duress. How soon thereafter we are able to adjust back to normal depends upon many factors. It is beneficial to have a breathing method/regime to assist us to come back into balance during stressful times. When utilizing the breathing techniques, the five Zhang organs of heart, liver, spleen, lung, and kidney are stimulated.

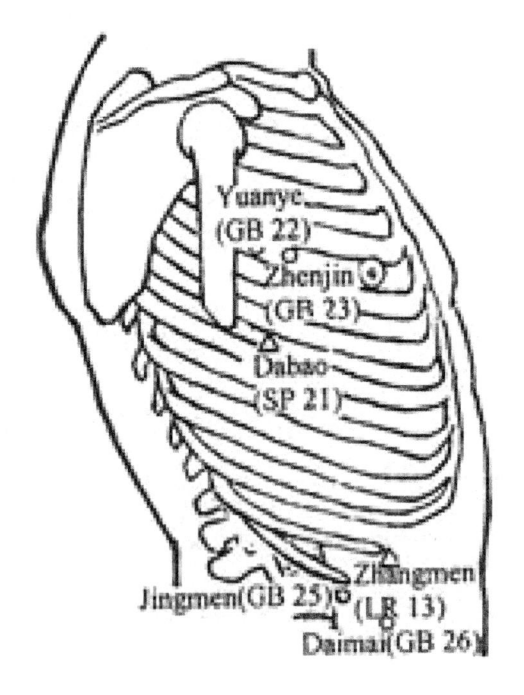

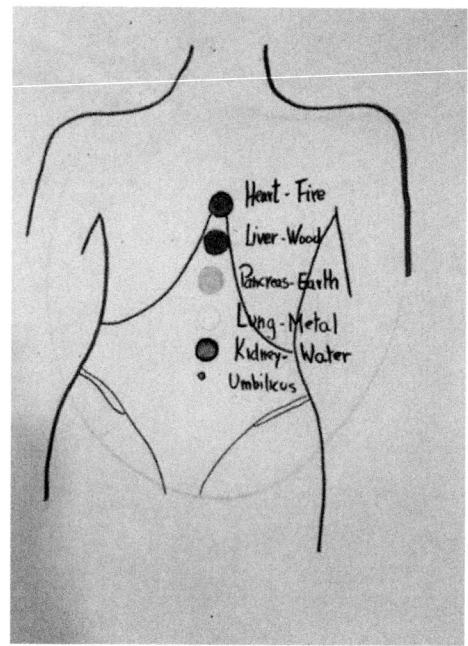

In the Chinese medical vernacular, reducing the consumption of hormones, blood, and thick and thin fluids is the key to longevity because activity consumes these resources. By extension, ancient life cultivators nourished their essence by emulating the long-living, slow-breathing tortoise, which lived longer than the quick-breathing leopard or tiger.

Some breathing exercises are called Wu Ji Shi. Wu means boundless, and Ji means beginning, as in infinite. Since spirit comes into the body first through the breath, breathing protocols are highly regarded. Mucous-forming foods are minimized to keep the lungs and sinuses open and infection-free.

Energizing breathing exercises are ideally done between midnight and midday, as energetic yang Qi is growing, in accord with the Earth's position relative to sunlight. Relaxing breaths are more in accord with nature when done from midday to midnight, though breathing exercises done anytime are beneficial.

The breath comes into the body in the following order:

1. Breath
2. Nerves/meridian channels
3. Blood/blood vessels
4. Muscles
5. Bone marrow

6. Tendons and ligaments
7. Bones
8. Whole body

Observation of the in-breath becoming an out-breath becoming an in-breath to become one continuous breath is the basis of returning to naturalness when discussing the breath. The following is extracted directly from *Qigong, the Secret of Youth,* in which Dr. Yang Jwing-Ming outlines simple to advanced breathing techniques necessary for a robust constitution and calming the Shen to facilitate making wise life choices.

Natural breathing: The rate and depth of breathing determines blood circulation and subsequent cellular health. If we are depressed, we breath more shallowly. If we hold our breath it is easier to be depressed. If exercising, we breath more deeply. When we inhale deeply, we become energized. Breathing is necessary for survival.

Chest breathing: It takes some conscious effort to fill up the bottom third of the lungs while sitting. Vigorous exercise will demand filling the lungs to capacity. An energizing breath.

Normal abdominal breathing: Breathing past the lungs and into the abdomen, expanding the belly with inhalation and relaxing with exhalation. A relaxing breath.

Reverse abdominal breathing: Breathing past the lungs and into abdomen, pulling belly up and in to stimulate kidneys with inhalation and relaxing with exhalation. I was shown this technique by the head monk at a famous Buddhist temple in Kyoto and is one of my favorites. An energizing breath.

Holding the breath breathing: With our mind, we lead Qi to specific areas. Akin to acupuncture stimulation at various points. It is well accepted that Qi/energy moves blood. Breathing into an area, holding the breath, and then moving Qi through that area, especially if location of a blockage will allow for cellular metabolism to normalize. A healing breath.

Body breathing/skin breathing: When we inhale, we draw in Qi from outside, and pores close. When we exhale, Qi moves to the skin and the pores naturally open, like exposing the skin to sun on a winter day. A meditative, restorative breath.

Hands and feet breathing: Communicating with universal elements. If we are cold, we place our feet and hands in warm water. We can absorb Qi from the Earth when standing barefoot. By opening our palms to trees, the sun, moon, or a star, we can absorb elemental Qi. A balancing and energizing breathe.

Ingesting the Five Sprouts Breath: The Chinese place great emphasis on the energetics of nature. The compass directions have Five Phases associations. The alchemist faces the five directions and inhales directional Qi.

- Ideally, put your bare feet on soil, grass, or sand.
- Call in the Light for the highest good.
- Close your eyes and ground yourself like tree roots growing into the earth, extending Qi/energy through visualization from the bottom of the foot at **Yongquan/Kidney-1/Gushing Spring**. (The usual depth to which I visualize extending is about twenty yards. Use your intuition to find the depth for yourself.) Extend deep enough to access the earth's Qi, not just the superficial topsoil. The earth will reciprocate and give back Qi that can be felt in the lower Dantien, approximately three finger widths below the naval.
- Now, facing the rising sun in the east, inhale universal Qi of growth and renewal into your hands at **Laogong/PC-8/Labor Palace** and into the liver/gall bladder to energize metabolism, make decisions, tonify tendons and taking action.
- Face south. Inhale universal Qi of the right use of the Three Treasures/Three Selves into your heart and circulation and affirm what quality of day/life you want.
- Face west. Inhale universal Qi of energy and vitality into lungs, skin, and immune system and for the highest good, envision yourself doing correct actions.
- Face north. Inhale universal Qi of regeneration into the kidneys, brain, genitals, and bones.

Practicing for thirty-two consecutive days will assist in balancing and calming Shen. Refer back to Bruce Lipton's discovery that we can change our temperament with new programming, if done repeatedly. We have found that initiating a new behavior, technique, or thought process will change the Basic Self program if done for thirty-two consecutive days.

Thread breathing: Freely move the breath throughout body and organs and the Eight Extraordinary Vessels (see explanation in next Palace). A healing breath.

Hibernation breathing: Slow the breathing down and be still. Draw out the inhalations and exhalations as long as possible, while attempting to be as still as conceivable, as if you held a feather in front of your nose and the breaths are so soft the feather will not register air passing through it. A restorative breath.

Tai His/Embryonic breathing: Similar to when you were in mother's womb. Making sure the sinuses and lungs are open, lie down, cut thoughts to pacify the mind, hold the thumbs inside the fingers like a newborn, and *ingest the breath* by inaudibly inhaling through the nose and exhaling without sound through the mouth. After creating a rhythm, exhale with the sound of *He* (sound for pericardium and endocrine system) out loud, if you are hot, and *Chew* (kidney sound), if cold. Repeat until soles of feet perspire. As you do this, the physical breathing process becomes increasingly subtler for periods of time and may cease altogether. 3-5 a.m. is the best time to practice breathing and meditation, as this two-hour segment corresponds to the lungs on the horary two-hour timeclock, and the psychic energy of the area in which you live is at minimum, since most people are asleep. A return-to-origin breath.

Microcosmic Breath: Qi/energy revolves around the creation of ATP within the mitochondria, the power-plant of the cells. If our bodies are functioning according to post-natal principles, this cellular process is fueled primarily through the workings of our digestive system, in conjunction with respiration.

Using the Microcosmic Orbit, inhale as you envision Qi moving up the spine/Governing Vessel. When you arrive at the crown chakra, place the tongue to the palate, and exhale as you move the Qi down the front of the body/Conception Vessel. Store the breath/oxygen Qi in the lower Dan Tian, located below the umbilicus at Qi Hai/CV-6/Sea of Qi and Shi Men/CV-5/Stone Gate area, the approximate location of the Basic Self. An alchemical breath. (A further explanation can be found below under Microcosmic Orbit and balancing the Eight Extraordinary Vessels.)

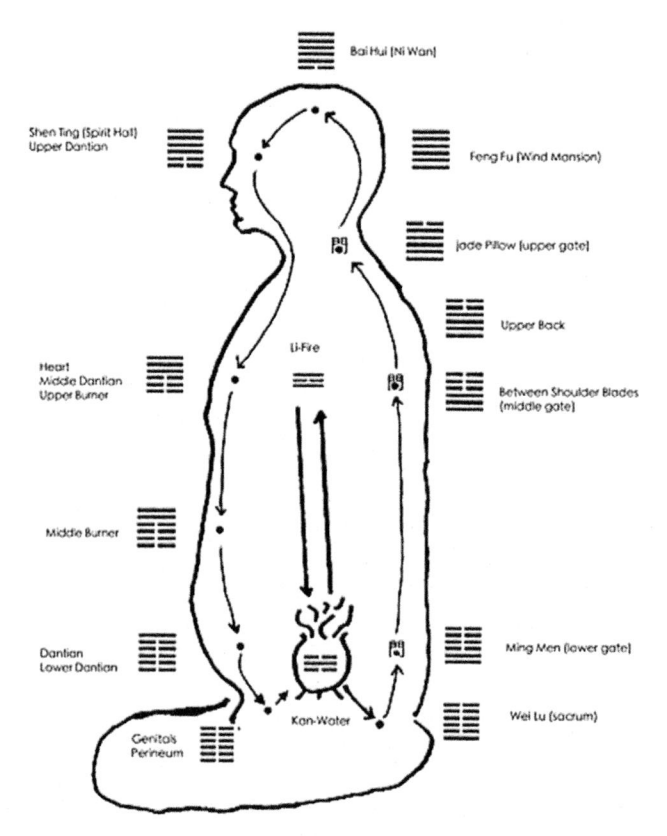

The Waxing and Waning of Qian and Kun (Yin and Yang)
Qian - The Opening of the Gates - Inhalation
Kun - The Closing of the Gates - Exhalation

Taoist "Waterwheel" depicting important chakra points when performing the Microcosmic Spirit meditation.
The Complete System of Self-Healing: Internal Exercise, Dr. Stephen T. Chang
Tao Publishing, 1986.

11. Shen Breathing: This is unconscious breathing, since practitioner has exteriorized the body, initially traveling in the astral body, but with certain initiations and diligent practice will access the Soul body. Intention and breath are in sync, at one. There may be extended time periods during which the practitioner does not appear to be breathing. A spiritual breath.

***

To assist in releasing the mind and getting back to the mystery, having a practitioner moxa the following points assists us to give up our personal stories/identification, contractions, and limitations. In the clinic, I have been well-pleased with patients' resulting self-awareness and subsequent changes in behavior.

- **Po Hu/Bl-42/Door of the Corporeal Soul** treats the lungs and deficiency taxation, giving us a foundation upon which to stand.

- **Shen Tang/Bl-44/Spirit Hall** unblocks the heart and chest and calms the Shen.

- **Hun Men/Bl-47/Hun Gate** treats the liver, frustration, mental confusion, excessive dreaming, and lack of direction.

- **Yi Shi/Bl-49/Reflection Abode** assists the pancreas and its ability to concentrate and contemplate.

- **Zhi Shi/Bl-52/Will Chamber** strengthens the kidney and will power.

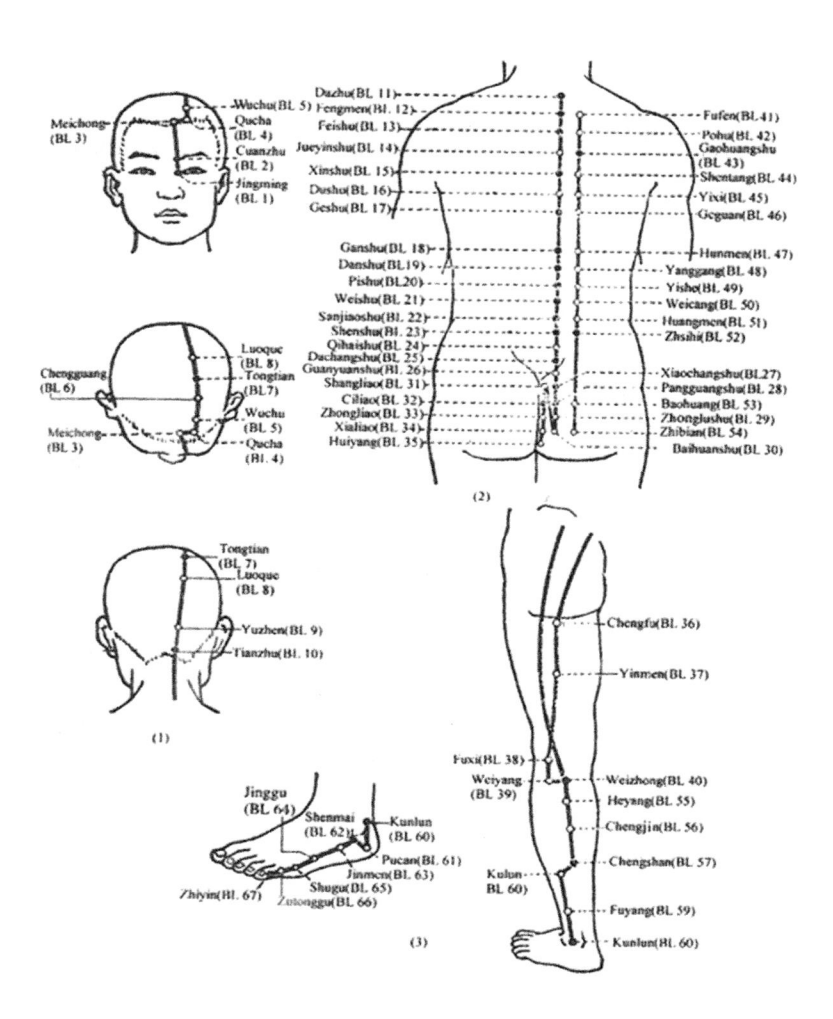

★ Another way to enhance harmony and balance is having a feeling to match every thought and then being able to physically move the thought to completion. Examine what thought, feeling, or action needs completing. www.msia.org has a meditation booklet called *Inner Worlds or Meditation,* in which the So Hawng meditation describes how to balance thoughts and emotions.

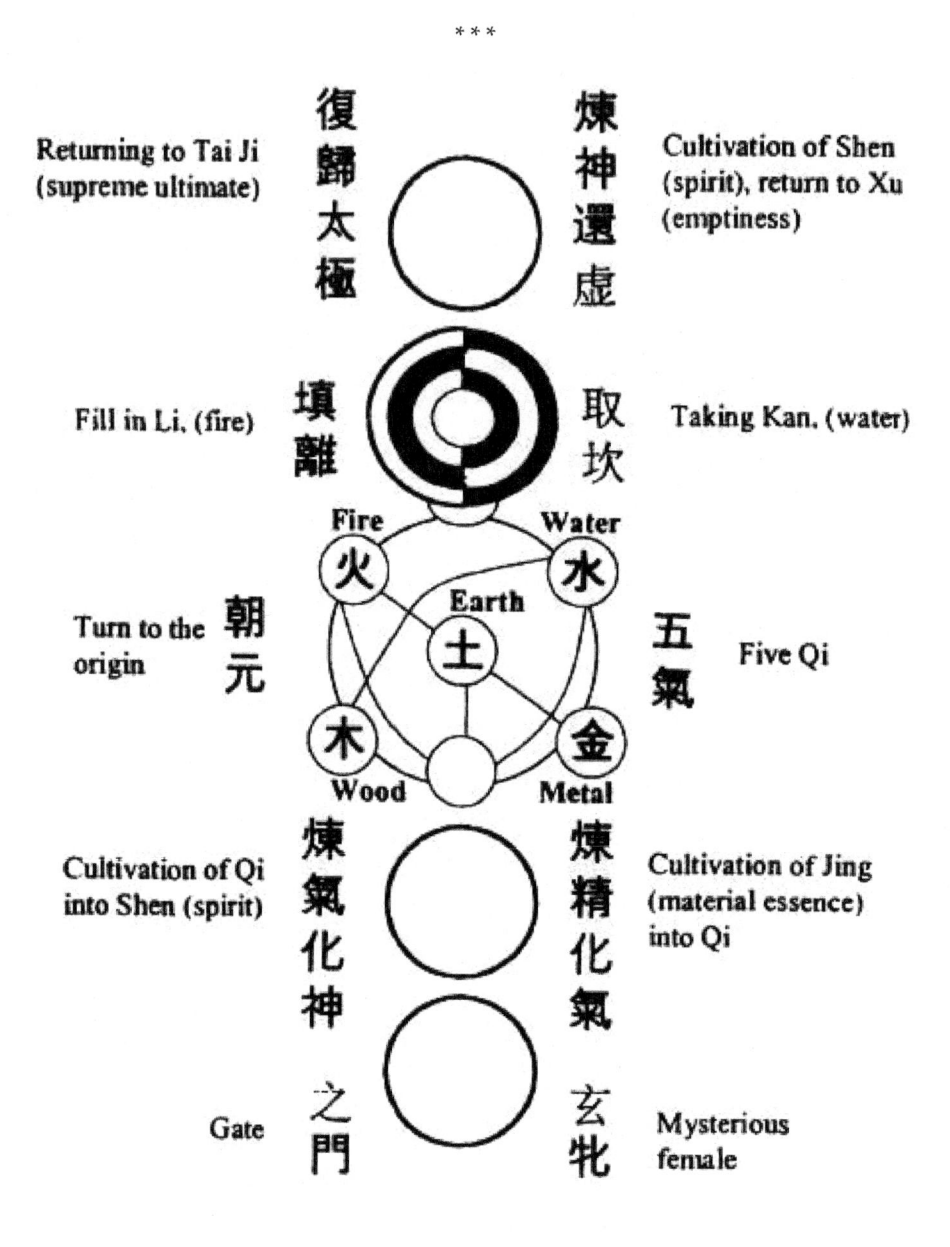

* * *

Returning to Tai Ji (supreme ultimate) 復歸太極

Cultivation of Shen (spirit), return to Xu (emptiness) 煉神還虛

Fill in Li, (fire) 填離

Taking Kan, (water) 取坎

Turn to the origin 朝元

Five Qi 五氣

Cultivation of Qi into Shen (spirit) 煉氣化神

Cultivation of Jing (material essence) into Qi 煉精化氣

Gate 之門

Mysterious female 玄牝

Chen Tuan's Wujitu (906-989), *A Construction of Confucian Metaphysics*

As we graduate to the Palaces Seven, Eight, and Nine, we do not attract as much poverty, illnesses, or have as many relationship problems because we ask for and intend to be in Grace. We make better choices by attuning more to Spirit and less to the human mind, and we are lifted above some of the chaos of life.

* * *

Notes

7. CAREER-KNOWLEDGE PALACE

AFTER MANY EXPERIENCES, we realize we are not what we think or feel, and joy appears when we choose loving, which can be defined as respecting, caring for, and supporting ourselves and others. Like fresh, clear water, loving cleanses and purifies.

The Career-Knowledge Palace is under the domain of the bladder, which stores and excretes non-essential metabolic by-products. Hence, the reference is applied to eliminating what is not of value. The bladder's ability to transform depends on the strength of its paired organ, the kidney, and adrenal glands, the location of our will. The bladder, having more points than any other channel, starts at the head and runs to the feet while innervating all organs and influencing all aspects of life.

Cycles of 7 and 8 correspond to ages 49-56 for women and ages 56-64 for men. We realize at this stage that we do not need to continue striving and efforting, and we take a more philosophical or spiritual attitude toward our chosen profession. Letting go of personal stories and the false-self driven expressions allow us to understand we are truly taken care of by Spirit for our highest good, though often we prefer other outcomes. We relax into regeneration, longevity and immortality. Spiritually, we cannot break down the doors to heaven as they open outwardly, and so relaxing and letting God is appropriate. In Spirit's timing, in accord with our karma, the doors will open.

Key: We match feeling and thoughts as we focus on transforming base personality traits into the gold of our True Self.

Da Ling/PC-7/Big Mound-Spirit Gate is used when we do not have career stability, do not know which way to turn or what to do or are haunted by past events. We may dislike our lessons, but **Da Ling/PC-7/Spirit Gate** opens a gate so our little Shen can travel to Source Shen so we can understand the perfection of what we have been presented.

A great time to examine what thought, feeling, or action needs completing is when you are stretching, especially matching what body parts we stretch to the acupuncture points delineated in particular Palaces. In this Palace, stretching the wrists, working the abdomen, and stretching the back are highly recommended. Releasing the body supports releasing the mind. One does not need a mind to have knowledge. In the upper Palaces of Seven, Eight, and Nine, we ask divine Source for direction and answers, realizing that Spirit knows more than our limited minds and emotions are designed to know.

The Taoist *I Ching* tells us, when we succeed in emptying the mind and reach a state of *non-doing*, the heart is clear and calm, and the inner work is done. Worldly people who are excessively attached to careers, possessions, and families often exhaust themselves and the lamp goes out. If we are congruent with our destiny, unattached to wealth, poverty, position, fame, or power for its own sake, and if we follow the Light, it is said the outer work is done. Utilize moxibustion on the following points to assist your career:

- **Moxa Dahe/Ki-12/Great Luminance-Manifestation** until it vibrates. It reflects the blueprint of life. Accumulations that create blockages will be broken up as we transform our baser characteristic personality traits into the gold of our true self. We do not need to have a mind to have true knowledge.

- **Moxa Qixue/Ki-13/Qi Cave** is the meeting point of the kidney's willpower with Chong Mai/the keeper of life's blueprint, to ascertain if you are on the correct career path.

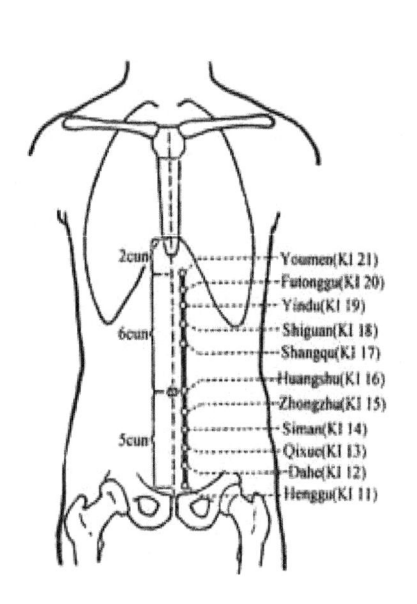

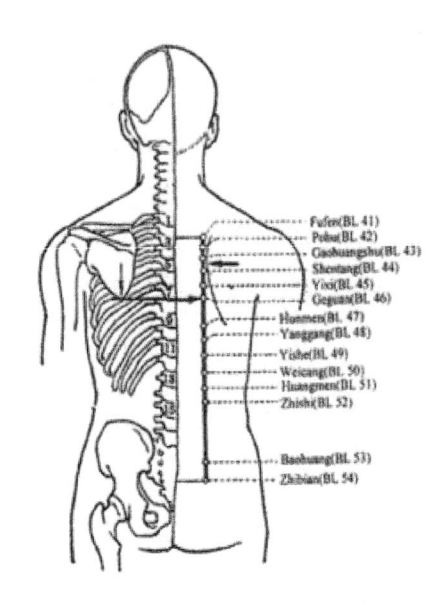

After generating warmth on the front, turn over and have a practitioner moxa the following back points for you. These are the same points as suggested in the last Palace:

- **Po Hu/Bl-42 Door of the Corporeal Soul** gives a foundation on which to stand and is good for deficiency taxations of the lung/swallowing one's pride.

- **Shen Tang/Bl-44 Spirit Hall** unblocks the chest and calms the heart Shen.

- **Hun Men/Bl-47 Hun Gate** treats frustration, nightly fear, mental confusion, excessive dreaming, and lack of direction.

- **Yi Shi/Bl-49/Reflection Abode** assists concentration and the quality of contemplation.

- **Zhi Shi/Bl-52 Will Chamber** strengthens the kidney and willpower.

THE EIGHT EXTRAORDINARY VESSELS

Although the Extraordinary Vessels are not within the Nine Transformation model, I include them as they are applicable alchemically as they can alter the personality temperament and constitution.

The Eight Extraordinary Vessels begin forming in-utero and mostly complete around ages seven to eight. They are considered able to alter both our fate and our Ming/destiny, our choices of how and what we do with our opportunities by altering perception of self and the world. Because of this, they are approached and used with reverence. Traditionally, they are used when treating constitutional issues, with developing youth, and with aging.

After birth, a child is usually dependent on the mother or caretaker, spontaneously in sync as they gaze into each other's eyes while the baby's Conception Vessel and yin organ channels are pressing against mother's Conception Vessel and heart during nursing or carrying.

As the months go by, the foundational Ancestral Chong Vessel, the holder of life's blueprint, extends itself through the Governing Vessel on the lower back to source points of the primary meridians adjacent the spine and then innervates the organs to complete forming of the constitution and basic temperament. The personality temperament further develops during the toddler and young-child stages of cognitive development.

In each section below, under cure, notice ways to balance the personality temperament. During patient sessions, I like to address chronological ages during which a characteristic was either established or, later in life, when situations or choices instituted trauma. This can be done through inner gazing, if we are attuned, or through intuition, muscle testing, or questioning.

I will ask the patient to focus on the time, place, and situation that we identify and invite them to forgive any judgments of self or others pertaining to that situation. I instruct them to reframe the story narrative in a way that they take total responsibility for choices and outcomes. Next, I have them re-frame the situation as they would have desired it to have been. The consciousness can then grasp the new story, and the old story will not have as much power to *run* the mature adult. Studies have shown that how we remember a situation is not necessarily in actuality; rather, it is how we interpret what happened. There is nothing wrong with changing the story to one that is more pleasurable and beneficial.

Within the listing of the Eight Extras, I included herbs to enhance particular vessels. Besides taking the herbs in tea form, with enough intention we can take on the quality listed to assist in altering attitude or behavior. Additionally, we can utilize the Thread breathing technique detailed in the previous Palace by freely moving breath through the Eight Extraordinary Vessels. (I give a Thread Breathing technique explanation at the end of the Eight Extra discussion.)

Ann Cecil-Sterman, a fellow student of Jeffrey Yuen, published an exhaustive study of the Eight Extras, entitled *Advanced Acupuncture, A Clinical Manual, Protocols for the Complement Channels.* I added some information from her book to my Yuen seminar lecture notes, in addition to noting my clinical experience. The Eight Extra Channels are given in order of how Yuen suggested they be treated. We approach the Eight Extraordinary Vessels with reverence, treating one Extra, or one plus its pair, during one clinical session.

Also please note, that rarely will a person reveal a lot, much less the entirely of their soul nature, to another, such as a doctor, so we approach another with sensitivity, without forcing them to work on an issue, as it is *their* choice. We inquire first asking if they are open to proceeding. If you are cultivating yourself with the Eight Extras, you can go as deep as you allow yourself to be open to change.

Bruce Lipton, Ph.D. posits that ninety-five percent of life's decisions come from what was programed during the first seven years of life. These programs of how to be a *functioning member of a family and of a community* are stored subconsciously, and as adults, he says we only make conscious decisions five percent of the time, unless we introspect and *do the work*.

This modern explanation is in accord with China's ancient hypothesis found with the Eight Extra model and further emphasizes how we should be conscious and not mentally/emotionally habituate. In lieu of getting treatments from an acupuncturist trained in this approach, one can take the herbs and meditate on the herbal qualities in areas that are congruent.

Lipton says, as an adult, the way to change the program is to initiate a new program and repeat it over time. My colleagues and I have found that continuous daily programming of a new behavior for thirty-two days is effective in altering choices, direction, and involvement.

***

1. **Chong Mai/Thrusting or Penetrating Vessel** holds life's blueprint. Our karmic curriculum combines with our parents' Jing/essence and Cosmic Qi/Spirit to become engraved in the Chong Mai; what needs to be accomplished in this life. Respecting the individual, this is viewed as an expression of a combination of their spiritual heart and their constitution associated with the kidney meridian, with Spirit's assistance. The *Su Wen* describes the Chong Mai Vessel, together with the Conception Vessel, as supporting the blood, which controls the life Cycles of 7 and 8.

   Gong Sun/Sp-4/Yellow Emperor-Grandfather Grandchild is the opening point and deals with digestion and immunity, necessary for survival and imprinted by our inherited genetics. Our gender, ethnicity, and disposition give us a sense of self that is reflected in the blood and the twelve channels. In-utero and childhood emotional and physiological experiences are reflected in this vessel, as is our genetic constitution and acquired constitution, such as exposure to man-made toxins, mental stresses, traumas, etc. One branch reaches the marrow of the spinal cord Qi and moves up the Chong Vessel into the brain center, nourishing the brain and calming inflammation that may lead to accelerated aging.

   I use a diagnostic method called Electrical Acupuncture According to Voll, or German Electrical Acupuncture, in which low-voltage electricity is introduced into the body through a hand-held probe. How a meridian or specific point reacts to the electrical stimulus is measured (normal, weak, strong, or chronically weak) with a probe placed on specific EAV points on hands and feet, some of which are the same and some different than in traditional acupuncture.

The discoverers of this method were German M.D.s, surgeons, and medical DDSs. They found that **Gong Sun/Sp-4/Yellow Emperor- Grandfather Grandchild** on the right foot corresponded to the pancreas producing lipase to break down fats, while the corresponding point on the left foot relates to the spleen, white blood cells, and immunity.

This is in alignment with the traditional action of **Sp-4** dealing with both digestion and immunity. Symptoms of poor digestion, menstrual problems, thoracic cardiovascular impairment, damage from environmental toxins, genetic illness, birth defects, low-back pain, habitual responses, social conditioning, and exhaustion of resources are noted therapeutics of this Vessel.

Cure: I appreciate and love who I am, no matter my genetics/fate.

Herbs:

- **Wu Wei Zi/Schizandra** enters all twelve channels to benefit and boosts Qi/energy, as an adaptogenic that improves taxation syndrome, purifies the liver, sharpens the mind, and is an aphrodisiac.

- **Yu Zhu/Polygonatum Solomon's Seal** augments the lung's ability to *let go of grief, sorrow, and despair,* assisting alchemical redemption of self from materiality for those who are willing to put in the time and energy. Polygonatum strengthens the kidneys, ova/testicles/sperm count, lower back and tendons, so it is also valued by athletes.

- **Xuan Shen/Scrophularia** clears phlegm and dispels accumulations and consolidations in the abdomen from undigested food, benefiting kidney Qi.

2. **Dai Mai/Belt Vessel** is for storage of excesses, whether emotional, biological, or traumatic. Belt Vessel issues reveal a world we do not comprehend or issues with which we had trouble dealing and have swept under the rug. Repeatedly pushing against immovable obstacles can result in frustration, inaction, or giving up. This channel aids in making good decisions to find a clear path around apparent obstacles, like the plant that pushes its way through cracks in a footpath. Here we rid ourselves of what we do not like about ourselves or what others do not like about us, if we decide that other people are evaluating us accurately and changing is to our advancement.

Zu Ling Qi/GB-41/Foot Overlooking Tears is the opening point and deals with being overly sensitive to man-made toxins, allergies, heavy metals, etc., and it regulates the

Gall Bladder's decision-making process and our horizontal balance in space through rapid adjusting of the tendons and ligaments.

Symptoms are of a gynecological or genital nature. Cystitis, diaphragm spasms, heartburn, digestive troubles, abdominal muscles, or low-back pain are noted. Issues/emotions that have not been dealt with can leak out in the form of leukorrhea or spermotorrhea later in life.

Cure: Breathing through the diaphragm releases blockages.

Herb:
- **Long Dan Cao/Gentianna** works on the GB and diaphragm.

Next, we work on the Qiao Mai Channels/Heel Vessel Meridian, which gives us a snapshot of how we view and articulate ourselves toward the world in the present moment. Once we have a personal story or identity, by definition we have conflict/disparity with what is not included in our story. This dynamic of opposing qualities opens the opportunity for disagreement, judgment, and hostility, but also gives us the opportunity to strengthen qualities we like about ourselves or change out the ones we deem we want improved.

Since Qiao refers to tightening and loosening muscles, especially in the legs, the Qiao Mai address musculoskeletal, endocrinological, and kidney-bladder patterns. Sometimes translated as Heel Vessel Meridians, they innervate the ankle/foot zones, the domain of the kidney and bladder meridians, and are associated with agility and maintenance of balance in yin-yang see-saw muscle movement.

We notice the aging often have compromised balance and agility. It is easy to explain this away with physiology as lack of hyaluronic acid, injuries, impaired circulation, compromised gut, tight tendons/ligaments, muscle weakness etc., but the aging process is also a result of accumulated beliefs, emotions, and toxins. What we do not eliminate literally makes us sick. My bias is that our consciousness determines how effectively we eliminate outdated beliefs, emotions, and toxins. Qigong practitioners talk about breathing from the heels at Zhao Ha/Ki-6/Shining Sea and Bl-62/Shenmai/The Extending Vessel, referencing Taoist literature of fully inhabiting one's body and standing up on one's own.

3. **Yin Qiao Mai/Yin Heel Vessel** reflects the current timeframe. How do you see yourself right now? After separating from our mothers or caretakers, we stand up and explore the world, discovering what it means to be mortal. **Zhao Ha/Ki-6/Shining Sea** is the opening point and nourishes the kidney by reabsorbing minerals, and is involved with hormone production.

Symptoms may be absence of sexual pleasure, impotence, difficult delivery, frigidity, sterility, ovary/prostate problems. Also, addictions, escapism, and epilepsy can be treated with this methodology.

Cure: Understanding what suffering can teach us.

Herb:

- **Sheng Di Huang/Rehmannia/Marrow of the Earth** builds back the flesh, treats broken bones and injured sinews. It cools desires that produce heat/inflammation in the blood. Rehmannia is referred to as the kidney's own food and is common in anti-aging formulations for regeneration and longevity.

4. **Yang Qiao Mai/Yang Heel Vessel** is involved with how we perceive the world and how we articulate ourselves toward it. Does our skeletal structure and alignment allow us to engage the world in the ways we would like? Do we judge the world, not liking what we see? What is our identity? Do we suppress our feelings (boys don't cry) or mistrust the world? Schizophrenia is an extreme example of constantly searching but not finding an identity in the world.

Shenmai/Bl-62/The Extending Vessel is the opening point to the vessel and used to close openings/sensitivity to physical viruses, discarnate entities, or to be unduly influenced by another person.

Houxi/SI-3/Behind the Ravine/ Behind the Kidneys is used if we do not have the ability to connect with the world or are averse to change. Symptoms of insomnia, obsessions, paralysis, stroke, and problems with balance and coordination.

Cure: Coming to terms with our identity in the world.

Herbs:

- **Wei Ling Xian/Clematis/Awesome Spiritual Immortal** opens channels and relieves blockages and pain.
- **Shan Yao/Dioscorea/Mountain Medicine** transports water, supports muscle, and is an appetite suppressant.
- **Gan Jiang/Zingaberis Officinalis/Dried Ginger Root** aids digestion and clears phlegm.

Then we address the Conception and Governing Vessels:

5. **Ren Mai/Conception Vessel/Sea of Yin** is where Jing/hormones are produced and bonding takes place. It is referred to as the location of our resources, and it influences our ability to utilize the cards we have been dealt, identified as our fate. We can say this vessel is the basic format of our life and temperament. The Chinese word Ren means *direction, responsibility*. While breastfeeding, there is a bond between Conception Vessel of infant to Conception Vessel of mother as eyes meet and their cycles synchronize.

   At some future time, we break away from mother and search to bond with another in our quest to become spontaneous, sovereign individuals. Mothers must allow children to stand on their own or the child will look for protective relationships or will be too shy/timid to ask for what they need, and sadly, their needs likely will never be met. Over-bonding may produce asthma.

   With sex, one must move away from oneself and embrace another. The *Su Wen* describes the **Conception Vessel** and the **Chong Mai/Thrusting Vessel** together as controlling the Cycles of 7 and 8.

   Lieque/Lu-7/Lightening Strike is the opening point. Symptoms of the respiratory, digestive, reproductive and genital systems are accessed. Symptoms of a sexual nature could be because of co-dependence, feeling victimized, looking for a soul mate, or possibly having a demanding personality. Phlegm exists where we should have Jing/essence-hormones being produced, so, in extreme, bones are fragile, the brain is inflamed, or there is phlegm in the ears/eyes leading to lesions, spinal tumors, or cancer. When this vessel is not balanced, people may be addicted to getting high in searching for something to feel bonded or the safety they felt being in-utero.

   Cure: Working with the Basic Self is essential.

   Herbs:

   - **Tien Men Dong/Asparagus/Doorway to Heaven** rids dampness, nourishes kidney's ability to reabsorb minerals, and clears heat/inflammation. It helps us to overcome the Three Worms/karma that gnaw on our life force. It also quiets the Shen to bring peace to the soul.

   - **Chai Hu/Bupleurum** gets rid of the old and brings in the new by ridding obstructions in the head, heightening communication between little Shen within and the universal Shen. It harmonizes thoughts and emotions to relieve liver tension/stagnation virtually everywhere in the body.

- **Sheng Di Huang/Rehmannia/Marrow of the Earth** builds back damaged flesh and bones and injured sinews/tendons. It cools desires, which produce inflammation in the blood. Rehmannia is the kidney's own food and common in anti-aging formulations for regeneration and longevity.

6. **Du Mai/Governing Vessel/Sea of Yang** determines how we construct life. **Du Mai** speaks to our evolution as we hopefully walk upright and strong, independent and curious. The Governing Vessel's chief job is to support the postnatal Qi to protect us from external *aberrant Qi*, that which is physically or psychically incongruent. It nourishes the organs, spinal cord, and the brain.

   Houxi/SI-3/Behind the Ravine/Behind the Kidneys is used if we do not have the ability to connect to the world or are averse to change.

   Shenmai/Bl-62/The Extending Vessel is used to close openings to physical viruses, disincarnate entities, or our being unduly influenced by someone else. Notice these points are opposite order of #4 Yang Qiao Mai.

   Symptoms of nervous system, spine, brain, endocrine, and corresponding Zang/Fu organs (see list of organs in the Five Phases), vertigo, motor system trouble, dementia, neck, tightness of the spine, and lack of yang going to the extremities.

   Cure: Curiosity and desire to learn. Being able to walk away from what is not working. Working with the high self is indicated.

   Herb:
   - **Chuan Xiong/Ligustricum Wallichi** invigorates the blood and removes Qi stagnation, expels wind and relieves pain.

   Next are the **Wei Mai Vessels** which govern how we assimilate changes and growth, the process of maturing and aging. **Wei Mai** means *linking/connect/safeguard*, so these two vessels influence boundaries and self-protection, interpersonal problems, and immunology. Fulfilling one's destiny through the Cycles of 7 and 8 are referenced here.

7. **Yin Wei Mai/Yin Linking Vessel** shows how we assimilate changes over time. We take possession of our Ren/resources and attempt to harmoniously construct life. If deficient, **Yin Wei Mai** might manifest as not knowing how to move forward or having guilt and subsequent detrimental self-talk. Possibly we run from bonding with another or from fulfilling our destiny. The extreme would manifest as one who would rather be someone else or preferring not even to have been born.

Nei Guan/PC-6/Inner Pass is the opening point.

Symptoms of heart palpation, anxiety, emotional states, depression, addictions, psychosis, or loss of will are exhibited. This person may manipulate others in a childlike voice.

Cure: Harmonizing life, integrating past, present, and future decisions, and releasing the diaphragm.

Herbs:

- **Dang Gui/Chinese Angelica** is used when we do not know who we are or what to do. It tonifies blood for the heart and liver and moves the blood to alleviate pain.

- **Wu Wei Zi/Schizandra** is used for trauma or stress.

- **Chuan Xiong/Ligustricum Wallichi** invigorates blood and moves Qi stasis, expels wind, and relieves pain.

- **Wu Jia Pi/Acanthopanax** dispels wind and dampness, strengthens the tendons and bones, and promotes urination.

- **Dan Shen/Salvia** invigorates blood circulation and removes stagnation.

- **Xuan Shen/Scrophularia** clears phlegm and expels accumulations and consolidations in abdomen from undigested food, thereby benefiting kidney Qi.

8. **Yang Wei Mai/Yang Linking Vessel** reflects what may be needed in the future to complete one's curriculum. Are we independent of our parents and fulfilling our destiny? Do we want to change who we are going forward?

Weiguan/T-5/Outer Pass is the opening point.

Symptoms are of bones and joints and lack of circulation. This person is adversely affected by climate, which can lead to uncertainty.

Cure: Accept yourself, your life, what is, and release the diaphragm.

Herbs:

- **Xiang Fu/Rhizome Cyperi** opens all meridians and releases Liver Qi stagnation, including pain under the ribs, abdomen fullness, emotional disturbance, poor appetite, and frequent sighing.
- **Shan Yao/Dioscorea/Mountain Medicine** is responsible for transporting fluids to rid heat/inflammation and assists pancreatic digestion to engender the musculature.

* * *

★ Go through the Eight Extras and figure out which one(s) match your constitution/habitual responses. Set up a thirty-two-day re-programming to adjust unconscious choice behavior to a more conscious approach.

ALIGNING THE THREE TREASURES/THREE SELVES

Techniques to align the Three Treasures/Three Selves vary with lineages, teachers, and beliefs. Below is one approach.

★ Call in the Light for the highest good and intend that the Three Selves come into alignment. If convenient, ground yourself, putting bare feet on soil, grass, or sand.

★ With visualization, extend Qi/energy from the bottom of the foot at **Yongquan/Kidney-1/Gushing Spring** like a tree pushing roots into the earth. The earth will reciprocate. Feel Earth Qi come back into the lower Dantien/abdomen, approximately three finger widths below the naval. If it is not convenient to be outside in nature, extend your Qi down through whatever you are sitting or standing upon and down into the earth.

★ To locate where the Basic Self is residing at the moment, place your hand and attention at the umbilicus, **Shenque/CV-8/Spirit Gateway.** If you do not feel a connection, focus three finger widths below the umbilicus at **Qihai/CV-6/Sea of Qi** or two finger widths below that at **Shimen/CV-5/Stone Gate** or at **Guanyuan/CV-4/Gate of Origin.** If not there, place your hand two finger widths above the umbilicus at **Xiawan/CV-10/Lower Epigastrium.** The Basic

Self is dynamic and not locked into a specific point.

* Place your hand over the area in which you feel affinity. The body will likely relax, maybe taking a deep breath. Thank your Basic for doing such a marvelous job of keeping you alive and to the degree of health that you enjoy. Now is not the time to judge what you might consider to be ill-health. Perform either regular or reverse abdominal breathing.

* Place the hand on the heart center, at the sternum between the nipples at **Tanzhong/CV-17/Center Chest.** Change the breathing pattern to full lung breathing, getting air down into the bottom third of the lungs. Perhaps become aware while focusing here if the breath is not full.

* Inquire why you feel stress, or why you are not present in the body or wanting to do something else. Place whatever awareness you have in the Light. What belief or behavioral change might rectify any stress?

* If you become aware of a beneficial action step that needs another time frame, write it down. When you feel aligned, move to the next step.

* Place a finger on **Yin Tang/Third Eye/Hall of Impression** between and slightly above the eyebrows to access the High Self. Focus breathing in and out of the **Yin Tang/Third Eye** until it vibrates, or you feel an expansion of consciousness.

* Focus now on the intersection of the Third Eye and the tips of the ears, in the center of head, at the **Purple Palace.** Ideally, now you have access to your soul. Begin chanting Hu or Ani-Hu, either inwardly or out loud. Rather than meditating, become aware that you are being meditated.

* Experienced meditators will expand awareness and move out of the body. One way is to focus about twelve inches above the crown chakra/**Bai Wei/GV-20/Place of 100 Meetings** and breathe from there. Stay with your experience as long as it lasts.

If we are successful in moving from the physical body through the emotional and mental bodies, past the unconscious and into the soul, past and future do not exist, since we are not bound by time or space in the soul and above. The longer we stay in the soul body where everything is *here and now*, co-creating with the divine, life takes on an effortless quality. The trick is to hold this consciousness after meditation sessions as we move about and interacting in and with our daily lives. The sage will stay in his/her center and act rather than reacting to outside stimulus. Who they are does not change according to circumstance. Who we choose to be in any given moment is always up to us.

***

It is helpful, almost necessary, to view life in an objective, non-attached manner to keep the mind clear. It is said that the Gold Elixir is finally restored when the alchemist merges the human mind with the mind of Tao/Spirit, giving up doing and accomplishing to enter the state of being, or Wu Wei/non-doing/cooperating with spirit. When we cease efforting to increase or decrease, we experience freedom, as the false self takes a secondary position to the true self. When we allow Spirit to direct us, we do not create more karma. We give spirit the credit and spirit will get the karma, and we walk free.

Settling the consciousness coupled with relaxed breathing and chanting sacred words will burn away the mundanity of conditioning of the false self, leaving the pure True Self. People will notice our transformation when we realize, without fanfare, what has always been so. A Taoist saying is that we leap out of the cage of the ordinary to live as long as heaven and earth.

The *I Ching* teaches when we assume our proper position in the family, the community, and the world and we act sage-like, there is no wasted energy, no squabbles, no war. We keep a Light consciousness while walking, standing, eating, sitting, working, sleeping, and dreaming. We put the Light around us that filters all elements coming into us and going out from us. We bless our food and drink, our brothers and sisters, wherever our attention is drawn.

THREAD BREATHING FOR DAILY MICROCOSMIC ORBIT BALANCING AND EXTRAORDINARY VESSEL TREATMENT

To balance and align chakras during daily meditation practice, follow this arrangement. Note that the sequence is an extension of the Microcosmic Orbit presented previously.

There are multiple approaches to any outcome. These Eight Extra sequences are taken from *Taoist Yoga, Alchemy and Immortality* by Lu K'uan Yu. Additional explanations can also be found in Dr. Yang Jwing-Ming's *Qigong, the Secret of Youth*.

Notice the chart below identifying the Chinese chakra points and characteristics. A plus (+) sign indicates it's characteristic when that chakra is in balance, while a minus (–)

indicates deficiency or blockage. Breathe in when going from one point to another on the Governing Vessel on the back. Breathe out as you go down the Conception Vessel on the front.

As you transit through the Vessels and find a deficiency or blockage, place the light for healing into the point and breathe through that point. If it doesn't clear or balance within a few breaths, note which one it is, and when you are finished you can look up the attributes and do a deeper dive into what it might be, asking the energetic of that area, What do you want to communicate to me? What is my opportunity right now to balance this?

* Call in the light for the highest good for yourself. Remember, intention is more important than technique.

* With your creative imagination, start at the perineum area **CV-1/Gate of Life and Death**, with an inhalation and exhalation. If balanced, move Qi along the Governing Vessel with the next inhalation. With each breath, focus on another chakra point, each in order: **GV-1, GV-4, GV-6, GV-11, GV-14, GV-16** and the brain at **GV-20,** and then to the third eye. Stop for a breath or two at each point or longer, if you feel the Qi is not balanced. When there are no blocks and sufficient Qi at each point, move to the next with an inhalation. (See chart below.)

* Now, gently place your tongue on the roof of the mouth and on exhalation, move awareness down the Conception Vessel, stopping for a breath or two at each point, or longer, if you feel the Qi has not balanced. Move down from the third eye with exhalations through **CV-22, CV-17, CV-12, CV-8, CV-2**. Then, bring the Qi up to **CV-6/Sea of Qi Vitality,** and pack Qi/oxygen into the Basic Self area with concentrated breathing at that point.

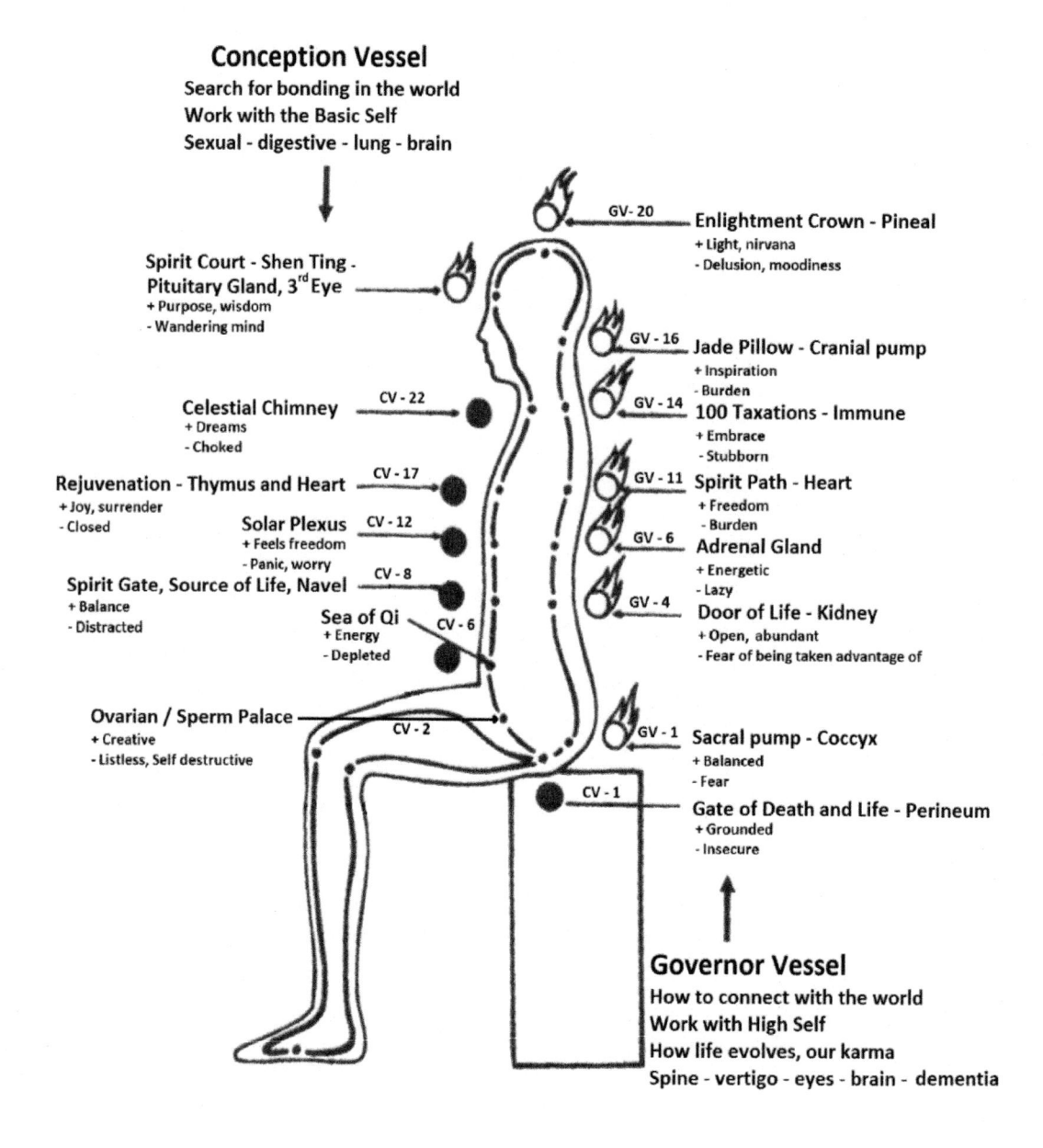

Conception Vessel
Search for bonding in the world
Work with the Basic Self
Sexual - digestive - lung - brain

**Spirit Court - Shen Ting -
Pituitary Gland, 3rd Eye**
+ Purpose, wisdom
- Wandering mind

Celestial Chimney — CV - 22
+ Dreams
- Choked

Rejuvenation - Thymus and Heart — CV - 17
+ Joy, surrender
- Closed

Solar Plexus — CV - 12
+ Feels freedom
- Panic, worry

Spirit Gate, Source of Life, Navel — CV - 8
+ Balance
- Distracted

Sea of Qi — CV - 6
+ Energy
- Depleted

Ovarian / Sperm Palace — CV - 2
+ Creative
- Listless, Self destructive

CV - 1

GV - 20 **Enlightment Crown - Pineal**
+ Light, nirvana
- Delusion, moodiness

GV - 16 **Jade Pillow - Cranial pump**
+ Inspiration
- Burden

GV - 14 **100 Taxations - Immune**
+ Embrace
- Stubborn

GV - 11 **Spirit Path - Heart**
+ Freedom
- Burden

GV - 6 **Adrenal Gland**
+ Energetic
- Lazy

GV - 4 **Door of Life - Kidney**
+ Open, abundant
- Fear of being taken advantage of

GV - 1 **Sacral pump - Coccyx**
+ Balanced
- Fear

Gate of Death and Life - Perineum
+ Grounded
- Insecure

Governor Vessel
How to connect with the world
Work with High Self
How life evolves, our karma
Spine - vertigo - eyes - brain - dementia

Original diagram copied from Universal Healing Tao *by Master Mantak Chia and altered to fit Workbook*

THE NINE TRANSFORMATIONS

The Microcosmic Orbit meditation is primary and can be done on its own. Once the alchemist has a knowledge of the chakras and some awareness of the BS/CS/HS, the complete Eight Extra Vessel meditation can be a great way to check if you are blocking Qi or are free flowing. As we match feelings and thoughts to our curriculum, we more easily complete what is incomplete and transform base personality traits into the gold of our true self. An ounce of prevention is worth a ton of cure.

The rest of the Eight Extras follows below.

* Breathe in and move Qi from **Qihai/CV-6/Sea of Qi** below the umbilicus, where you packed Qi through the **Dai Mai/Girdle Vessel** (storage area for what has not been dealt with), dividing into two branches encircling the belly to reach the small of the back. This might take two smaller in-breaths or one large in-breath to complete. Then move up to both shoulders.

  Note: As you perform the Thread Breathing, if you find a blockage on one or another of the Vessels, refer to the previous discussion of the Vessels, their attributes, cure, and herbal suggestions.

* Breathe out from both shoulders going down the **Yang Wei Mai/Yang Linking Vessel** (what may be needed in the future) on the outer side of both arms, wrists, and middle fingers before reaching the center of palms, where it stops. I recommend tracing through one arm at a time when vessels are bilateral. Once you get more adept, you can do both sides at the same time and be aware of any blockages.

* Breathe in to move vital Qi/oxygen from the center of the palms up the inside of the arms along the **Yin Wei Mai/Yin Linking Vessel** (assimilating changes over time), stopping at the chest.

* Breathe out, moving Qi/vitality down to the **Girdle Vessel** around the waist, where the two branches re-unite and return to the genital area at **CV-2**.

* Breathe in and lift Qi/vitality from the genital area up the **Chong Mai/Thrusting Vessel** (blueprint of life) in the middle of the body, stopping at the solar plexus (middle of the stomach) under the heart. Do not go above the heart.

* Breathe out, and send Qi/vitality from the solar plexus down to the genitals, where it divides into two branches on the outside of the thighs with the **Yang Qiao Mai Vessel/Yang Heel Vessel** (how we perceive the world) and goes through the little toes and to the soles of feet at **Ki-1**, where it stops.

Breathe in, raising Qi/vitality from soles of feet in the **Yin Qiao Mai Vessel/Yin Heel Vessel** (explore what it means to be mortal) on the inside of the legs to the genitals, and then go back to **Qihai/CV-6/Sea of Energy Vitality** below the umbilicus, approximate location of the Basic Self, and stop there.

Synopsis of Thread Breathing Clearing

Vessel and intent	Inhalation/Exhalation
Governing Vessel-spine: Governing yang	IN
Conception Vessel-front: Resources	OUT
Belt-waist: excess baggage	IN
Yang Wei Mai-external aspect arms: Fulfilling destiny/future	OUT
Yin Wei Mai-internal aspect arms: Harmoniously constructing life/Taking possession of body	IN
Down to **Belt Channel** and to genitals	OUT
Chong Mai-interior: Blueprint only go to area under heart	IN
Yang Qiao Mai-external aspect legs: How we perceive world	OUT
Yin Qiao Mai-internal aspect legs: Self-image/identity/exhibit free will	IN
Stop at **Qihai/CV-6/Sea of Energy:** Vitality	

We can also focus on specific Extraordinary Channels based on the season:

➢ **Spring** beginning around February 2: Work with **Yang Wei Mai** to view who we want to be going forward.

➢ **Summer** beginning around May 5: Stimulate **Yang Qiao Mai** to assist how we project ourselves in the world.

➢ **Late summer** beginning around July 25: Work with **Dai Mai** to deal with issues we do not comprehend before energies move inwardly for autumn and winter.

➢ **Autumn** beginning around August 8: Stimulate **Yin Wei Mai** to harmoniously integrate past and present.

➢ **Winter** beginning around November 11: Access **Yin Qiao Mai** to determine self-identity at that moment.

CLEARING THE LOWER PORTALS

Clearing toxins from the body equates to clearing past thoughts and dropping our personal story/identification. At this point in our alchemy, the bladder is the associated organ, eliminating waste products and excess fluid.

- **Yi Yi Ren/Coix-Plantago Seed** clears damp heat and cold that lingers in lower burner and deals with the Three Worms/karma. Coix-Plantago Seed is barley, so avoid if gluten sensitive.
- **Mu Xiang/Saussarea Vladimiriae - Peach Wood Fragrance** clears perverse Qi and obstacles in lower abdomen. Good if sensitive to psychic energies of groups or ghosts in any environment which may alter one's personality.
- Excessive grains/carbohydrates can lead to food stagnation, which encourages procrastination and physical accumulations. Break up food stagnation with tea made with either **Chen Pi/Mandarin Orange Peel** and/or **Ju Pi/Tangerine Peel.**

Foods to eat for moderate periods to enhance listening to internal dialogue and intense meditation could include:

- ✓ Mung beans and lentils treat hundreds of diseases and are an anecdote for toxins.
- ✓ Adzuki beans for blood production and diuresis.
- ✓ Raw soaked pumpkin, sunflower, brown and golden flax seeds.
- ✓ Soaked and cooked black and white sesame seeds are kidney tonics.
- ✓ Soaked pine, cypress, walnuts, filberts, and chestnuts.
- ✓ Small amount of soaked cereal grains such as millet.
- ✓ Small amount of animal protein. Wild birds are the animal product that comes closest to superior herbs. Cook with plum/apricot/cherry fruits to assist digestion.
- ✓ Jujube, grapes, berries, and avocado.
- ✓ Fermented soy/natto to assist gut flora.
- ✓ Soups, leafy greens, and seaweed.

Note: Beans, lentils, pumpkin, and sunflower seeds contain lectins and can cause mild abdominal upset.

SEEING THE PERFECTION AND BEING A SAGE

Tao lineage masters in the tenth and thirteenth centuries, the Sound Current masters of India and modern sages tell us that if we do not travel the Sound Current back to the true source then most likely whatever practices we do—celibacy, fasting, burning plants, drinking clouds and morning mist, absorbing sun and moonlight, breathing exercises, meditations and visualization, sticking to emptiness or clinging to form—have no connection with the true matter of fully completing our curriculum and having our name recorded in heaven.

We do not take our alchemy practice lightly, as it is the path to liberation and freedom. Since the quality of the *It of Itself/Source/Tao/God* (whatever name you like) is loving, whatever we do that enhances our ability to love unconditionally is a desired outcome of any approach or system.

Palaces Eight/Wisdom and Nine/Going Home focus on Zhuo/ascension and transcendence. The Taoist purview is that we meet another person inside of us; our little self meets the greater spiritual self. When meditating or doing spiritual exercises, one *sits so that he/she can forget* the individualized self, which is idealized for good or bad, in our personal story. As we let go, the weightiness of the body and consciousness lessens. Like levitation, we rise above excessive worldly concerns, meet our greater spiritual self, and ascend toward heaven. The Basic Self keeps the body alive and communicates life's curriculum that it received from the High Self to the Conscious Self, arbiter between High Self and Basic Self, deciding how to fulfill the spiritual destiny. As we expand our awareness and realize the perfection of what is so, we move from doing to *being*.

I Ching hexagram #8, Unity of Holding Together, says, *If bamboo breaks, repair it with bamboo. To learn sage-hood, seek the seed of sage-hood, which is real knowledge (Water Phase) and spiritual integration (Fire Phase), not just intellectual knowledge/sense of knowledge (Metal Phase).* Book knowledge has to be integrated and utilized.

The maxim is to see with the eyes of the master. Then, acting sage-like, we express our original nature, which is loving. Loving softens the hardness of the crystalized mind, and we become free of judgment. If we want loving, we love, and by doing so we create an internal terrain within which we heal.

When the Soul starts turning toward its true home, the grip of the lower levels is loosened and falls away. When we are in Soul, the spiritual energy starts radiating out, not as personality but from the center of lightness, which is your own Light. It radiates out and becomes the order of your universe.

(Excerpted from J-R quote)

- **Tu Si Zi/ Cuscuta Rapid Silk Seed** decoction processed in a wine and taken over a long time strengthens any weakness from injury or emotion.
- **Ba Ji Tian/Radix Morindae Officinalis** treats impotence, premature ejaculation, and soreness of the lower back and knees from long-term illnesses. Morindae increases mental power and keeps us strong and robust, and therefore it is valued by both athletes and alchemists.

* * *

Notes

8. WISDOM PALACE

UNDER THE AEGIS OF THE KIDNEY meridian encompassing Jing essence/hormones and our constitution, the Wisdom Palace sets the final scene for moving beyond the confines of society's normal patterns. Ruling the bone marrow, filling the brain, and guiding birth, growth, development, reproduction, water metabolism, and sexuality, it is referred to as the root of life and is the residence of Zhi/will power.

We now are more focused on Wu Wei/being than we are with doing and accomplishing. Laozi and many spiritual masters have stated, *Everything gets done because I don't do it*, meaning they do not react based on their personality/volition but act in cooperation with spirit's direction for them.

There is an enormous difference between acting and reacting. We act when in cooperation with the mind of Tao/Spirit. We react when we use the human mind, based on personality choices.

We attain liberation by seeing the unity in apparent opposites. We listen inwardly for direction from our spiritual heart. When we are spiritually aligned, our universe moves with us. The Wisdom Palace is the Palace of spirituality, of expressing the True Self.

The Cycles of 7 and 8 for the Wisdom Palace are ages 56-63 for women and 64-72 for men. We turn life experiences into knowledge and knowledge into wisdom, ultimately realizing we are *as one* with Tao/Source/God. We avoid entanglements that are not in accord with our nature and go back to original innocence. We endeavor not to be over-responsible for people or things, and we do not give our power and authority over to someone or something else.

A human being is more worthy than any man-made organization, movement, or government. Those in power often want citizens to give up individual sovereignty. The problem lies with who makes what decisions. If spirit decides it is for the highest good to sacrifice for a group, then wonderful. But the awareness and decision must be made individually, listening within, and not conscripted by an outside person or source.

Key: We use meditation and insight to transcend the rationality of the mind. We realize external information is useful, but we do not depend on it for happiness or fulfillment. We have fewer questions of why and focus more on, *How do I make this work?* which is what we seek when asking any question. We all want to feel good, so all questions ultimately are, *How do I get more loving into this situation that benefits me and others?* To do this, we focus on peace and contentment, as alchemy is a path of peace and contentment the measurement.

Lao Gong/PC-8/Palace of Weariness is the point in the center of the palm and used for relieving the Five Taxations when we have reached for too many experiences. In this Palace, we give up striving for achievement, results, excellence, material items, and even striving to become spiritual. *We relax into who we are*.

Qi can become stuck in the spine with extreme measures of becoming enlightened, such as ayahuasca, psychedelic drugs, some forms of kundalini yoga, some tantric sex practices, extreme fasting, etcetera. I had several patients who presented with this condition. They were agitated, crazed, somewhat psychotic, unable to get calm, and needed intensive therapy or prescription drugs to obtain a level of balance between the human consciousness and the spiritual consciousness. An extreme example is the person on the street corner, yelling virtues of some purported philosophy or religion at passersby who are not interested. **Lao Gong/PC-8/Palace of Weariness** is the acupoint for this condition as well as for mental exhaustion, deep despair, fear of death, and the need to balance action with wisdom. We relax into who we are, rather than attempting to pry open our consciousness.

Chinese medicine states that our experiences are stored in the blood, so an experienced doctor can see someone's personality temperament and subsequent repetitive choices reflected in blood laboratory testing. The blood is either a life-giver or life-destroyer, so, in this Palace we filter out and eliminate toxins accumulated in the blood. Practically, this may mean a more alkaline diet, or chelation of heavy metals and environmental toxins or accumulated plaque.

TONING AND CHANTING

Toning or chanting Chinese sounds can balance and tonify organs. Produce a tingling resonance as you focus on an organ that requires attention. Experiment with the pitch of your voice to produce a rich, sonorous tone that is pleasant to you. If you are attuned to musical notes or can obtain a pitch pipe, Tone/Chant the specific note indicated. Even better is chanting along with the associated instrument in the corresponding key.

Organ	Sound	Note	Instrument
Heart	HAAA	G	strings
Pericardium/endocrine	HEEE	G	strings
Pancreas-spleen	WHO	C	repetitive drumming
Lungs	SEEAHH	D	metallic bell
Kidney	CHEW	A	repetitive cymbals
Liver	SHOU	E	blowing into horn

- Relax and loosen the neck by rotating **Feng Men/Bl-12/Wind Gate** and become like the wind, going where you are needed.
- Have a practitioner moxa **Ling Tai/GV-10/Spiritual Tower** and look at the world from your Ling/soul.
- Also, moxa **Shen Dao/GV-11/Spirit Path** to assist becoming an ordinary person who acts like a sage by following spiritual direction.

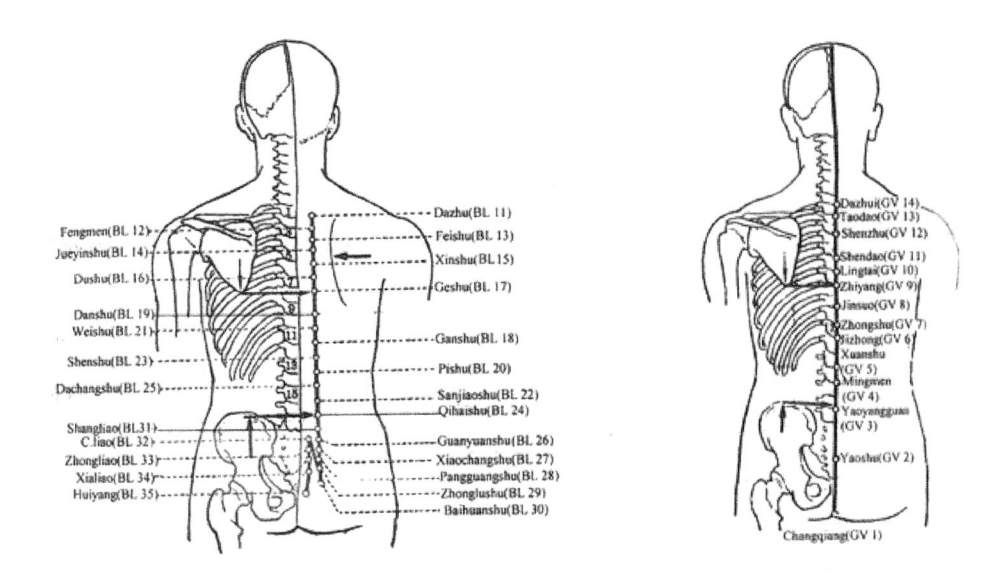

The purpose of the Nine Transformations is to have a viable plan to complete one's curriculum/karma. It is easier to introspect, cultivate, and focus on our main purpose/intention when we simplify life to essentials, supporting ourselves with correct eating (whatever that might be for us individually), exercise, breath regime, and chanting to keep the Five Zang organs, the sinews, the bones, and the brain strong and vital.

Once we are in a relaxed state of observation with enough Yi/intention and Zhi/Will, we lift above the Basic Self's identification of personal story and listen with our heart to

Spirit, that which has no curriculum. We are above the limited mind and emotions of yin/yang duality in a consciousness that surpasses understanding; know that the Father/Source/Tao does the work through us.

* * *

Taoist **Two Immortal Powder** strengthens the kidneys and increases Zhi/will-power, so we can take care of ourselves and take care of others. Three grams of powder of each in water in the morning as a daily formula is recommended. If you get the herbs in raw form, ask your herbalist for cooking directions.

- **Lu Rong/Deer Antler** replenishes yin essence, tonifies Qi, and tonifies yang.
- **Di Huang/Rehmannia** strengthens the kidneys and adrenals, builds blood, and heals injuries.
- **Go Ji/Lycium Berries** is a blood and circulatory tonic and used for longevity.
- **Ren Shen/Ginseng** is an adaptogen, an athletic and nerve tonic.

USING TREES TO TONIFY THE BODY AND ASSIST ASCENSION

Trees begin life with a firm foundation by rooting firmly in the earth before growing toward heaven, becoming the tallest of the plant kingdom. Similarly, we establish a firm foundation and during meditation, move consciousness up the spine and exit the body through the crown chakra at **Baihui/GV-20/One Hundred Meetings** as we reach for heaven.

Application of essential oils of trees can be utilized. Inquire with a practitioner as to location of application and dosage.

- Wood phase **Maple** adjusts one's temperament.
- Fire phase **Cinnamon** is a bridge between heart and kidney and brings Jing/essence to everything in life. Note that the essential oil is caustic and can burn the skin.
- Earth phase **Elm** is good for accommodating whatever is needed.
- Metal phase **Pine** is the tree of elders and connects us to past lives. It is a tree of permanence, as it is green year-round.
- Water phase **Sophora Cherokee Rose** rids perverse Qi in rooms that need fumigation for ghosts or feeling uncertain.

Herb-wise, we pick trees that give us the best feeling/nourishment through their taste: sour, sweet, bitter, spicy, and salty. Watch that you do not immediately think, Oh I like sweet taste... Which taste nourishes you most?

- Sour: **Suan Zao Ren/Zizyphus** clears the heart of agitation and relaxes the mind. It is good for insomnia and achiness in the four limbs.

- Bitter: **Rou Gui/Cinnamon Cortex** is a bridge between heart and kidney and brings Jing/essence to everything in life. Cinnamon has both a bitter and a spicy flavor. Exercise caution when using the essential oil.

- Sweet: **Fu Ling/Poria/Revelation of the Curriculum,** whose attribute is letting go, nourishing, and allowing the heart to be free. Fu Ling helps us resolve emotions by quieting the Hun/Basic Self, which is known as the collector of experiences. Fu Ling embraces all, knowing God is found in all things. Fu Ling rhymes with the Ling in Ganoderma, which means soul/mandate/command.

  Fu Ling is found at the base of willow, morus, mulberry, elm, and tremella trees; it is viewed as the root of hidden curriculum or aspirations. It is taken at bedtime to have prophecy dreams seeing into the future. It is also good for fear, worry, and fright, being insulted, or having one's honor challenged, as it releases distention in the diaphragm from emotional stress.

- Spicy: **Rou Gui/Cinnamon** treats hundreds of diseases by connecting the little Shen to big Shen and helps alleviate a congested heart. Cinnamon nurtures the Shen and Jing and assists our return back to Ming Men/source energy. The cosmetic industry has recognized cinnamon's qualities and includes it in many products. Chinese cinnamon bark is one of the most warming of all herbs and will strengthen aversion to cold, weak kidney/backache, and lack of sexual energy. Since the herbal quality of Chinese cinnamon is strong and potent, ask an herbalist for a proper dosage.

- Salty: **Du Zhong Eucommia** prevents our structure from breaking down, strengthening the bones, ligaments, and tendons.

Herbs can be purchased either as raw herb or powdered. Some companies that sell online may not distribute the highest quality herbs, so you may need to order from a licensed practitioner who buys directly from pharmaceutical quality distributors.

Anti-Aging

After years of cultivation, the eyes and face glow, the countenance is beatific and we realize the alchemical process is anti-aging. A halo above the head begins to develop as we access the greater Shen more and more. I saw a halo over my spiritual teacher, J-R, in the late 1970s, during a treatment, so for me this phenomenon is not just a representation depicted in Asian and European religious art.

Finish the herbs in the section above (or skip them) before embarking on the herbs depicted below. Pick one or two that sing to you. The most effective way is to have the intention to *take on* their attributes as you drink a decoction of the herb.

- To nourish the heart to make embracing everything easier, take **Nu Zhen Zi/Fructus Ligustricum**. Nu means receptive woman and Zhen means true femininity, so we can be reborn with childlike innocence. **Ligustricum** is said to rid hundreds of diseases because it supports the true self.

- **Sang Ji Sheng /Loranthus/Woman and Child/Boy and Girl.** When we see life as pleasant, rigidity in the neck and back relaxes, giving us the suppleness to move into new ventures. Most people are stiff in their upper back and neck. If so, also stretch and rotate the neck to allow pleasantness and a relaxed feeling into the body and mind.

- **Bai Zi Ren/Biota Seed/Platycodon/Seeds from the Tree of Life** is the most commonly prescribed tree in Chinese medicine. It has a soothing effect on the Five Zang organs and the Five Spirits: Hun/BS, Po/CS, Shen/HS, Yi/Intention, and Zhi/Will. It is often planted in cemeteries to appease both the aggrieved and deceased.

- **Mu Xiang/ Radix Aucklandia.** When we speak truthfully, people sometimes are annoyed, as it points out their schemes. They might react negatively, even violently. Aucklandia helps us deal with perversity from others, as well as pestilent Qi/epidemics.

- **Long Dan Cao/Gentianna** settles the 5 Zang organs so we are comfortable with who we are, and it assists us when afraid of change.

- **Yi Mu Cao/Leonorusi** has connections to the Eight Extra Vessels and our blueprint. Leonorusi brightens the eyes so, with heightened perception, we see into the mystery.

Consult with a qualified herbalist regarding the dosage, frequency, and combinations for tree herbs.

Co-Creating

> When you attempt to make your will the will of God, you are up against the impossible, because God's will resides in all things, while the body, being rather finite, cannot reside in all things. What you are really attempting is to make your will work for you in the best way possible. You're moving yourself into your own will, into those things you have put into motion from higher consciousness, those things you have said you would do. And when you have moved into that, when you have moved into the inner self and are following your blueprint, your life will flow so beautifully that you will feel your will and the Father's Will are one. But it is really that you are following the direction of your High Self and are fulfilling your destiny here on the planet. (Ref: J-R)

I was relieved to read this. I dropped anxiousness about having to change the world or accomplish something great and leave a legacy.

The Hun/Basic Self and Po/Conscious Self

My understanding of this topic has been framed by working with patients, from lectures by J-R and Jeffrey Yuen, and Elisabeth Rochet de la Vallée's lectures, recorded in *Aspects of Spirit*. The translations from the *Ling Shu* and the *Su Wen* chapters are taken directly from her book.

Liver Hun and Lung Po have the character Gui in common, which depicts the spirits of the earth. The Hun has a coming and going, likely referring to the Basic Self being brought forward each lifetime from a repository of basic selves to serve the soul's agenda and its direct participation in the déjà vu process. The Hun/Basic Self has multiple lifetimes assisting different souls but can serve a particular soul more than once.

The High Self gives a person's life plan/curriculum to the Basic Self. The Hun/Basic Self follows the dictates by getting a person involved in concepts and activities that provide experiences in which to learn. The Basic Self passes the curriculum up to the Conscious Self which makes supporting decisions about direction and participation.

The Hun/Basic Self is free and easy in its movement when healthy and is constrained/constricted when not. Its Thief is irritability and impatience, while its Virtue is receptivity and flexibility. A famous liver herbal formula is named Relaxed and Easy

Wanderer, supporting the receptive, flexible attribute.

We identify the Hun/Basic Self as having a consciousness of about a six-year-old youth, curious and active. Its main job is to keep us alive and healthy and thus, survival is a main focus. Huge and magnificent as it is, the Basic Self is not mature enough to see the whole of a situation as would a mature adult, represented by the Conscious Self, or as would a wise teacher, represented by the High Self. My experience is that the story we tell ourselves about how we are justified to act out, even defending our position to the death, comes from the Basic Self acting out through the personality temperament as described in a prior discussion.

Problematically, defending one's actions leads to confrontation. A wiser approach I learned, after defending my position for many years both to myself and others, is to acknowledge, Yes, I did that, whether I did or didn't, because then I don't have to *defend* my actions, even to myself, which saves blocking Qi/energy that leads to ill health. We all have experienced relaxation and a surge of energy once situations are resolved, which indicates *relaxed and easy wandering* is preferable to being rigid and blocked.

It is said that if we follow the natural order, modeling the way of Heaven, everything will be perfect. Most healthy individuals want to be free to act spontaneously, not reacting or responding to outside pressures to conform. We decide whether we benefit more by following the culture in which we find ourselves or the beat of our own drummer. Driving on the correct side of the road is not a hardship, since driving the wrong way can be fatal. Listening to family, politicians or media telling us what we should think or do can be fatal, such as being told to join an imperialistic army. Many generations of Chinese alchemists removed themselves from harm by going into the mountains to quietly cultivate and nourish their consciousness while society killed one another.

The Po/Conscious Self is associated with the body and cannot leave it, except upon death. The phonetic part of Po is the color white, relating to the Metal Phase lungs and breathing, and the color of bones in the ground. The Thief is misdirected feelings while the Virtue is doing the right thing because it is the right thing to do.

Ling Shu Ch. 8 tells us:

> *In treating a patient, one who wishes to use needles must examine attentively the way the patient presents themselves, to perceive the preservation or disappearance of the Jing Shen/vital spirits, the Hun and Po, and whether the Yi/intention/inner disposition is favorable or unfavorable. If those five spirits are injured, the needle cannot treat.*

It has taken me literally five decades to understand the wisdom of Chapter 8 and the interaction between Conscious Self and Basic Self and how they are informed by one's intention and will. I have had many patients who did not find satisfaction in my clinic, either because I didn't know how to work with the Five Spirits well enough, or they didn't have clear intention and sufficient will, or they had not yet extracted the lessons from the experience and needed more time.

I can give the most erudite, sophisticated treatment protocol to a patient but if the Basic Self is *not on board*, the treatment will not be successful. If the Basic Self likes a simple, generic approach, it can heal difficult illnesses. Survival and health are its job, and as such, because we do not utilize it adequately, the Basic Self is the least-utilized healing modality on the planet.

I have to add an addendum to this subject. We also have an *inner child* that is a repository for unfulfilled hurts, so when we do forgiveness and free-form writing, we are also relieving the inner child of its burdens. Because the Basic Self and inner child are entwined, it is not necessary to differentiate when placing situations in the Light, when doing clearing exercises with self or others, when re-framing, doing free-form writing, or the Forgiveness Meditation.

The Hun/Basic Self resides in the liver. The liver stores blood, and blood contains our experiences. The liver meridian is the last of twelve meridians in the daily twenty-four-hour cycle of Qi movement through the meridians, which begins at the source point for the lung at **Taiyuan/Lu-9/Great Abyss** at 3 a.m. and finishes at **Qi Men/Liver-14/Cycle Gate** at 3 a.m. Since it contains the element of time, **Qi Men/Liver-14/Cycle Gate** is used for treating unfinished business or ambitions. Laterally stretching the intercostal muscles while breathing deeply assists if we are beginning/ending a new cycle or out of emotional balance. Yoga postures are perfect and eating or juicing leafy greens is appropriate. **Long Yan Rou/Longan Fruit** helps to settle someone who is overly ambitious, stuck in the past, or cannot find completion and contentment because of lingering and unfinished business.

* * *

If one wants to change a busy city life to become somewhat of a recluse for alchemical cultivation, **Ren Shen/Ginseng** calms both the Hun and Po by helping one leave behind excessive ambition and to mind his/her own business. Problems are created when we start to mind other peoples' affairs. Modern texts would not agree that **Ren Shen/Ginseng** calms the Hun and Po, as Confucians altered Taoist vernacular and rewrote the medical books when they had Imperial decree. From earlier Taoist texts:

- **Ren Shen/Ginseng** calms both the Hun and Po.
- **Reishi/Ling Zhi** calms the Shen.
- **Fuling/Poria** quiets the Hun, Po and Shen.
- **Da Zao/Jujube** quiets the Yi/intention.
- **Huan Pi/Albizzia** quiets the Zhi/will.
- **Ba Ji Tian/Morinda** calms the five Zang organs of heart, spleen, lung, kidney, and liver.
- **Bai Zi Ren/Semen Platycondon** has same qualities as **Ba Ji Tian/Morinda**.
- **Nu Zhen Zi/Fructus Ligustri** quiets the Five Zang and treats hundreds of diseases.
- **Mu Dan Pi/Cortex Moutan** is a lower-grade herb that also will quiet all five organs, resulting in calming the Shen, Hun, Po, Zhi, and Yi.

These herbs help us find a degree of redemption from discomfort or disease or a sense of inadequacy. It is vitally important to have calm Shen, regardless of whether it is overly ambitious or deficient and fatigued. The *Ling Shu* chapter 8 tells us that when something takes charge of the being, that is called the heart. Going back to our Five Phase chart, the heart takes the uppermost position and is regarded as the emperor and the location of the integration of the Three Treasures/Three Selves.

It is common knowledge that, as the Emperor goes, so goes the country. In companies, the culture is set by the owner/CEO, and company attitudes will reflect that person. In people, as the heart Shen goes, so goes the body.

Yi/Intention and Zhi/Will

Both Yi and Zhi contain the radical for heart, pointing us back to our Shen/spirit. Yi intention/inner disposition is located in the Earth Phase and has the radical for heart below and a modulated sound coming from the mouth as the upper radical. The Yi character is also used for the five musical sounds. Our voice changes according to circumstances, based on what is in our hearts. If we are happy, we sing, but during war, our tone is more like a dirge.

Zhi/will's inner orientation is located in the Water Phase. The lower radical also depicts the heart while the upper radical is a small shoot representing something that can grow and develop correctly, if following the natural order. With Zhi/will, we do not just talk but must be willing to live for something, backing intention with action, hopefully in accord with the natural order.

Ling Shu Ch. 8 says:

> *That which takes charge of the being is the heart. When the heart applies itself (Zhi), we speak of intent (yi). When intent become permanent, we speak of will. Yi/intention and Zhi/will are so closely related, they are almost interchangeable.*

Huangdi Neijing, The Book of Yellow Emperor (475-225 BC), written by enlightened beings as a dialogue between the mythical Emperor Huangdi and his physicians, is a dissertation on treatment and preventive medicine that is still venerated today.

> The Yellow Emperor Huangdi: *What makes the spirits?*
>
> Chief Physician Qi Bo: *When blood and Qi are in harmony, when nutrition and defense commune and circulate freely, when the five Zang (organs) are perfectly achieved, then the Shen Qi dwells in the heart. Hun/Basic Self and Po/Conscious Self complete with all their capacities, and this perfect achievement is a human being.*
>
> *When you practice the way of the needles, if the vital spirits cannot more forward, if the will and intent do not rule, then the illness cannot be cured. (Ling Shu, Ch. 54)*
>
> *Link up with the patient: ask methodical and numerous questions on the patient's emotional state, their qing/disposition so as to follow the Yi/intent. To possess the spirits is radiant splendor. To lose the spirits is to be entirely lost. (Su Wen, Ch. 13)*
>
> *In all methods of puncture, it is necessary to observe what is below, to follow the pulses, to examine the will and intent and the characteristics of the illness. (Su Wen, Ch. 11)*

When I was in hospitals and clinics in Hong Kong, Taiwan, Beijing, and Kyoto, rarely did I hear a doctor ask their patient about emotional states or their inner disposition... even though this is the acknowledged main cause of disease in Oriental medicine. Why? Probably because it takes too much time, and the doctors are skilled at performing acupuncture and prescribing therapeutic herbs for physical conditions, but less so with intention and will as they are more obtuse. Additionally, my experience of Asian culture is that one's inner disposition is kept tight to the chest and not easily spoken about or shared.

What I have found over the years is a person's Yi/intention and Zhi/will show up in blood test results, so this ancient observation should not be viewed as antiquated and cute, but as useful and necessary. Otherwise we are treating human beings like a physiological machine, which we definitely are not.

> ➢ A non-grounded person with low-blood-glucose hypoglycemia can easily be one who finds it difficult to find their overarching intention of the Earth Phase. They tend to flit from interest to interest without finishing.

> ➢ A person with exhausted adrenals (systolic blood pressure drops precipitously as they stand in comparison to their seated blood pressure and/or blood cortisol and or DHEA levels are low) have a difficult time moving forward, completing, and living their ideals, since they do not have the Will/energy found in the Water Phase.

> ➢ A person with auto immune disease showing low WBCs and/or lymphocytes often find themselves too sensitive around others and have difficulty integrating into the rigors of normal society and environments. Since immunity is in the Metal Phase between the Earth Yi/intention and the Water Zhi/Will, this person will exert much Qi/energy toward being normal, which affects both intention and will, though the Zhi/Will is affected more because of the Taxation effect. In reflecting back on my difficult cases, most were auto immune and their will was deficient because of Taxation exhaustion.

Referring back to the cure listed in the Health Palace, and since health affects all other Palaces, we realize for all illnesses or disease, or any situation, if behooves us to start with Grace, opening the chest to allow the heart to lead our decisions and actions. Then we eliminate Taxations through smart choices and balancing the Three Treasures/Three Selves. Then we address the Yi/intention and Zhi/will. Then we address laboratory tests, physical exams, etc. This is not easy. It is a blessing for a patient to find a practitioner who will treat them, and not symptomatically treat signs and symptoms and disease categories.

> *Will and intent are what direct the vital spirit, gather Hun/Basic Self and Po/Conscious Self, regulate hot and cold, harmoniously blend elation and anger (the E-motions). When will/(kidney-adrenals) and intent (pancreas-spleen) are in harmony, the vital spirit is concentrated and correct, Hun and Po are not dissipated, regret and anger do not arise and so the five Zang do not receive perverse influences. (Ling Shu, Ch. 47)*

I have conversations with my Basic Self, thanking it for its good works, and make sure I have a positive image in my mind of my intention/desired outcome so it can help bring into manifestation that which I am focused upon.

As I am writing this, a patient texted me saying her friend was just diagnosed with ALS. She was wondering whether ALS is easy or hard to treat. Also, she did not know what to say to her friend.

I wrote back: No, not easy to treat. Just be there for her as a friend and let her go through the process of finding which therapies she wants to pursue, since it's an individual process, depending upon conditioning, availability, beliefs, and prior experiences. Ask her if there is anything you can do for her, and she will get your caring. This is a far greater benefit than suggesting or telling her things she needs to do.

My patient responded back, Thank you… That really helps!

Both women will get the benefit of this approach as it elicits support, respect, and caring.

CHENG XIAN/THE ART OF PROLONGING LIFE AND ACHIEVING IMMORTALITY

In medicine, the next big thing is always being sold to the public: possible cancer cures, gluten-free, neurotransmitters, ten different styles of fasting, eat eggs, don't eat eggs, coffee good, coffee bad, coconut oil, diets, fifty kinds of exercises, etc. etc. There is no magic bullet. A cure depends on many different factors. I use the word *multi-factorial* in explaining to patients why they have certain symptoms and how to achieve health, meaning there are multitudes of reasons, and they differ from person to person.

Habituation can be defined as an accumulated experience and can be equated to *aging*, creating a loss of potential, to have less choice, losing one's sovereignty. Clearing habituation is beneficial:

- ➤ Activities
- ➤ Actions
- ➤ Feelings
- ➤ Thoughts
- ➤ Beliefs
- ➤ Unconscious senses
- ➤ Reactions we repeat without awareness
- ➤ Brushing our teeth the same way every day

- Unconsciously reacting to the political news
- Eating the same foods
- Crystallized beliefs about ourselves, life, our relation to others, to God
- Diet without consideration of the seasons
- Same exercise throughout different seasons

Habituation is a form of procrastination, lessening our opportunities to learn and grow. Procrastination is wasteful, sloppy, and depletes energy. We can free locked energy of incompletion by moving the body into action. Energy comes loose, and aches and pains release. We all have experienced the elation after finishing a difficult project or getting something off our backs.

***

A definition of alchemy is to redeem one's spirit from materiality. The two last stages of the Nine Transformations involve ascension and transcendence. Zuo/ascension has the radical Tu/earth in it. There is a Ren/person in the top radical, depicting another person inside of us, referencing our higher spiritual self. When we meditate, we Zhuo Wang/sit, so we can forget our attachments and redeem our soul from the solid material quality of the physical plane.

Ascension comes when we leave behind the attachments of who the Basic Self purports us to be. This is important, since the Basic Self wants to be like a god, while its decisions from its position of survival many times do not include the altruistic High Self's *for the highest good of all concerned.* When we relegate the Basic self to its proper place of keeping the body healthy and alive and taking direction from the wise High Self, we realize our true nature. By dropping the weightiness of materiality, the body and consciousness feels lighter, and hence references in the Asian literature to adepts *flying*.

OBSERVING, ACCEPTING, AND COOPERATING WITH WHAT IS

The True Self is content observing. Observing informs us about what is taking place, giving us feedback whether what we are doing is beneficial or detrimental. By observing, we are relaxed without a position to defend. If we move from a state of tension, we block ourselves, but if we are relaxed, we are free.

Indian Naval Commander Abhilash Tomy sailed 23,000 nautical miles during a 151-day solo, nonstop and unassisted voyage. Without the extraneous thoughts/activities of normal life, Tomy said he came back completely wiped clean, deconstructed, without memory or guilt or morality or cravings. He said what was critical for him was that his self was so distilled, he became like a no thing. *I became very clairvoyant. I could see far into the future, far into the past. Many, many things. I saw everything.*

THE CAULDRON, THE FURNACE, AND THE FIRING PROCESS

The mind of Tao, to which we have access if we listen within, is considered strong, while the human mind is capable only of conscious knowledge and is considered weak. In the Five Phase chart, fire/spirit controls metal/conscious mind. (Follow the arrow from the fire element to the metal element. This indicates the control cycle, controlling the element two phases ahead). There is an alchemical admonition to *make the mind of Tao great and minimize the human mind.* Sages have a human mind and ordinary people have a sagely, spiritual mind. The human mind sees objects and leaves the center as it goes to that object. The reason why sages are different is they remain at home in a state of observation.

Ancients drew a circle and called it Tao, infinite Source, the great ultimate, the Effortless Way. Li Daochun (1290 AD), a great Taoist master during the Mongol Yuan Dynasty, wrote in his book, *Balance and Harmony* that

> *The outer medicine is perfecting life, curing illness, and prolonging life through the energy of breath, the thinking spirit, and sexual vitality. Do this with the Microcosmic Circulation (explained in Palace Six). The inner medicine is perfecting essence so that one can transcend being and enter into non-being Wu Wei.*

Li explains the precise details of the inner medicine must be passed on personally, face-to-face.

The *Tao Te Ching* chapter 56, Gaining Oneness says: (I added the words in parentheses to represent my understanding).

> *Those who know do not speak* (truth is far subtler than we can convey with words)
> *Those who speak do not know* (intellectual knowledge is not real knowledge)
> *Block the passages* (the 9 orifices)
> *Close the door* (of desire)
> *Blunt the sharpness* (of the critical mind)
> *Untie the tangles* (of one's emotions/karma/attachments)
> *Harmonize the brightness* (of the Light/Spirit)
> *This is called Profound Identification* (with the Spirit)
> *It cannot be gained through attachment*
> *It cannot be gained through detachment*
> *It cannot be gained through advantage*
> *It cannot be gained through disadvantage*
> *It cannot be gained through esteem*
> *It cannot be gained through humility*
> *Hence it is the treasure of the world*

Embrace the whole Spirit… Stand in it, *be* with it and the inner medicine is complete.

I Ching Meditation

I excerpted ideas from the *Taoist I Ching,* translated by Thomas Cleary, leaving out what I have not experienced and changing phrases that those of us in a Western culture find easier to understand.

Read through these ideas slowly, meditatively. If one resonates, stop and contemplate. Call in the Light for your highest good before beginning.

- There are 9 transformations in the alchemical process. We use single-minded devotion, dedication, and consecration to and of our spiritual self to transform ourselves. Acknowledge that you have all the tools necessary within.
- Embrace the Spiritual Light.
- In the beginning of our alchemical journey, many elements struggle to take form.
- An issue or situation by itself is not important. How we chose to respond is what is important.
- We start with sincere intention. We decide what is our singular and highest intention and align our lives around this Yi/intention.
- Breathing and exercising is for the body. When we have the true elixir/initiation into a mystery school, real evolution can occur. Otherwise, it is like boiling an empty pot.
- To which voice are you listening? The Basic Self voice often argues for the Five Thieves that steal our life force. We embrace Five Virtues over the Five Thieves.
- We seek real knowledge by emptying the mind, chanting sacred tones, and listening to spirit.
- We combine the firm strength of the High Self with the flexible receptive Basic Self and travel nine times around the triangle into realms above soul into higher realms of Light.
- We have fellowship with a community of seekers and initiates.
- We know that ordinariness is a prior step to realizing we are as God since all humans emanate from the same source. Feigning specialness is a function of the false self and blocks clarity. What aspect of specialness are you willing to give up or sacrifice?
- We integrate the Three Selves to burn away the dross of the Basic Self's demands.

- ❖ We examine how we lie to ourselves and release position, pollution, and poisons.
- ❖ We grow up and become responsible in a balanced and self-disciplined manner to ourselves, our intention, and to others.
- ❖ We restore, rejuvenate, and regenerate our body, mind, and spirit with spiritual exercises/meditation. We take care of ourselves on all levels.
- ❖ We transmute problems by getting above them and dissolving them from on high.
- ❖ We emphasize the positive aspects of our own divinity, the benefits of a calm mind, and endure to the end.
- ❖ We know progress is gradual and do not take habituation lightly. We keep returning to the Spirit/Light.
- ❖ What small thought is the parent of unnecessary action? Merge the wisdom of the discriminating mind with the flexibility of the Hun/Basic Self. Check the results with the knowing heart and Three Selves' alignment. Produce innocence by avoiding unnecessary entanglements and missing the mark by giving the Hun/Basic Self mature guidance.
- ❖ Great opportunity and nourishment await us after nine months of internal gestation/awareness as we touch to others in the Tenth Palace.
- ❖ There are many techniques. Carefully select what knowledge to absorb.
- ❖ Study directly with a spiritual master.
- ❖ Spirit is hard to find and easy to lose. Learn how to follow closely.
- ❖ Lessen the human Conscious Self and increase the spiritual High Self mind by going to the spiritual heart again and again and again.
- ❖ After *loving it all* for multiples of ten lunar months, our work is done in the material world and our name is recorded in Heaven.
- ❖ Listen to the spiritual heart and its enduring values.
- ❖ The Tao/The Way can hardly be known without a Way-shower.
- ❖ Realize and cooperate with *That Which Is*.
- ❖ As we merge duality into unity, we spiritualize materiality, rid illness, extend life, nullify calamity, and avoid problems.
- ❖ We assume our proper role in the family, at work, and in society.

- Everything is in its own time. It was etched in our bones before inception when we would meet a Way-shower.
- When we ingest the Golden Elixir, we know our destiny. Afterward, it is difficult to deny the Spirit.
- Those who know Light and Sound are liberated.
- Once we ascend through our own kingdoms, we restore life from death. Is this not the most marvelous?
- On doing and non-doing: we listen to the spiritual heart to see and cooperate with Spirit. This augments and benefits both us and others.
- We align the Three Treasures/Three Selves daily. We separate them to talk about them, but they are one vital energetic jewel when aligned.
- Gathering with others of like mind at a spiritual celebration elicits harmony and pleasantness and myriad diseases vanish.
- When the Basic Self is relaxed and not creating from its own volition, and Wu Wei/non-doing fills the belly, we are integrated with celestial design. Even if the oceans overrun the hills and the valleys shift, our spiritual body is permanently indestructible. However, we need to stay within the teachings.
- Adversity gives a chance for self-reflection.
- We empty the human mind, meditate, are of service, and return to Source.
- We peel away the false self.
- We awaken to the spiritual dimensions and are spiritually reborn.
- We use the sword of wisdom to cut away that which is not needed and to discern and embrace that which is of value.
- When we transform our self by minimizing self-identity, the next steps to our destiny are revealed.
- There is ease in finding the True Self, but it takes time.
- We do not take our meditations lightly and nurture the process daily.
- Greed and folly steal our vital Qi/energy. Things come to fruition through care and cultivation. When the time comes, we use things for everyone's benefit. We give thanks for all the people who have contributed to life's upliftment.

- ❖ We cannot be in the Light 24/7 or the fires of spirit will burn us up, so we are intelligent about advancing and withdrawing and giving the Basic Self proper attention.
- ❖ We see that things are perfectly imperfect.
- ❖ We have the fun of walking across the Golden Bridge.

* * *

Notes

9. COMING HOME TO THE SPIRITUAL FULFILLMENT PALACE

THE NINTH PALACE focuses on finding our way back home under the aegis of the spleen/stomach/pancreas channels, representing our physical center. We become Ko/still like a mountain (Earth Phase includes spleen/stomach/pancreas), trading our personal story about who/what we are for a more universal story, one with which we know there is only one energy, one Source, with many emanations and manifestations.

> You come into this world, attempting to fulfill certain qualities within yourself, and you go about it in many ways. But there is a prime directive that everyone works under: You are here to find out who you are, to find out where the Soul realm is and go there, and to have co-creative consciousness with God, the Supreme Father. This is your whole direction and purpose on this planet. This is where your satisfaction and your fulfillment lie. This is your spiritual promise. (Ref: J-R)

We have ingrained methods, techniques and strategies and it appears we exert little effort. We generate and project harmony, joy, and loving expressions of being and realize our oneness with all creation.

I am that I am. I am that. I am.

> We go to the celestial court/Soul Realm riding the back of a phoenix/the Sound Current flying aloft in broad daylight where nothing is hidden, and we become a celestial immortal. Would not that be pleasant?

> A spiritual master is in contact with both the world and the Spirit simultaneously. Most people are like apples that have fallen from the tree (the Source) onto the ground. The spiritual master is like an apple still connected to the tree, on a branch that has bent over and touched all the way to the ground. The apple is both on the ground with the other apples and still connected to the tree. (Ref: J-R)

THE NINE TRANSFORMATIONS

In becoming self-realized, we have expanded awareness. I am in touch with some of my Soul's journey in remembering past embodiments. What is important is bringing the learning forward in order to save us from having to learn the same lessons again and again. When in soul consciousness, it is hard to fathom how we forget that we are divine. Circumstances do not matter as much, as we gracefully ride above the dross. However, when we are not in the soul body, it is easy to forget, and we can get caught in muck and mire.

Cycles of 7 and 8 correspond to years 63-70 for women and 72-80 for men.

Key: We follow the inner guidance and achieve spiritual fulfillment.

- **Zhong Chong/PC-9/Balanced Friendliness** opens the sense organs in the head, the eyes, ears, nose, and mouth, so we can clearly perceive ourselves, others, and the world.

Additional points to assist PC-9 are:

- **San Yin Jiao/Sp-6/Three Yin Intersection** which mediates between going and staying in the body by tonifying the parasympathetic nervous system, relaxing, letting go, and letting God.
- **Yong Quan/Ki-1/Gushing Spring** grounds the physical/material body as we *exist in spirit and the material world simultaneously*. **Ki-1** is used for calming the Shen and tonifying Yin. It is a painful point to acupuncture, so I recommend either accessing through **Taichong/Lv-3/Great Surge** or acupressure.
- **Shang Xing/GV-23 Upper Star** dispels uneasiness with life changes.
- **Shen Ting/GV-24/Spirit Court** is used get out of the physical body during meditation. These points can be needled or in-direct moxibustion applied.

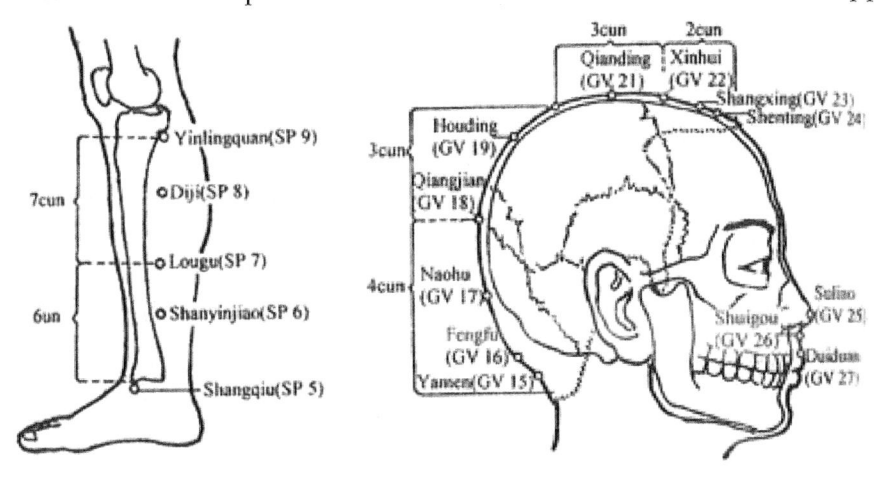

Chanting the Names of God

An effective technique to focus the mind and open to one's loving is chanting. Since the beginning of time, religious and spiritual groups have intoned sacred words, sounds, prayers, and songs. Chanting builds up a powerful field of spiritual energy that can change one's consciousness.

The key is your intention—bringing an attitude of reverence and love to whatever you are chanting. Mantras are specific sounds or syllables that invoke a spiritual essence. It is said, as you chant, you bring that essence or vibration into your own being.

I recommend the HU chant. HU (pronounced like the man's name, Hugh) is a name of God found in Pali and Sanskrit, ancient sacred languages of southern Asia. Chanting HU silently or aloud, alone or in a group, helps create attunement and bring you into spiritual alignment.

Call in the Light (just acknowledging that the Light is present) and ask to see spiritually. Begin meditating with a focus on the area behind the third eye, chanting the HU. Keep your attention steady with chanting and turning inward can break fixations. After five or fifteen minutes, stop and listen. Then go back to chanting. Then back to listening. (Ref: MSIA.org)

Chuang Tzu defined a sage as one who hears.

People have often asked me how I can know what is going on in a certain place. This is how: I step into the Soul, and in the Soul consciousness, my Soul can communicate with any other Soul. It is instantaneous knowledge, faster than the speed of light. In the spiritual Light, everything is instantaneous and exists now. (Ref: J-R)

As we complete our earthly karma, there is the potential for advanced cultivation, a new beginning. This takes commitment and unconditionality. Spirit is depicted as the wind—elusive and unpredictable, Fu/hidden-invisible and then reappearing. It is not static. If we pay attention and follow where it goes, we are formless, not bound by false criteria, and people will say we are not predictable. Where the Spirit comes from and where the Spirit goes is not predictable, and as we follow closely to Spirit, we also appear unpredictable.

During our alchemical journey, we take part in society in many ways. Now hidden, now leading; now quiet, now active. Everyone can talk about the ordinary world, but discussing Spirit is difficult, unless we have had direct experience. We do not reject the world because, if we did, we would not have a mechanism with which to grow.

There is a saying that I know well: *The hermit in the city is worthier than the hermit in the mountain.* I have lived as a recluse in the mountains for months, and while it is easier to stay balanced when only dealing with myself, more growth is possible when we live within society's demands and confusing scenarios.

Chang Po-tuan's *Understanding Reality, a Taoist Alchemical Classic,* translated by Thomas Cleary, tells us to seek the infinite, because one hundred years is like a spark.

> *Because the spiritual root of innate knowledge and innate capacity has been buried for a long time, it cannot emerge of itself. One must be diligent. What Confucianism calls the Great Ultimate; Buddhism calls complete awareness.*
>
> *Taoists say: When you get the One, the myriad is all done, and there is no need to distinguish south, north, east, and west. Alchemists use the mind of Tao to ward off human mentality, reducing and reducing, and eventually the acquired influence of the human mind vanishes. The discriminating human mind, along with acquired habits and aberrations of temperament, act up, and as long as there is any negative energy left, one does not become immortal. Therefore, after obtaining the elixir, it is necessary to eradicate entirely the seeds of the vicious circles that have been going on since time immemorial.*

Chang continues:

> *The elixir is the most precious treasure of the physical body; when cultivated to perfection the transmutations are endless. One can investigate the true source in the realm of essence and ascertain the ineffable function of the birth-less without awaiting another body in the next life, attaining the spiritual capacities of a Buddha in the present.*

It came into my awareness during introspection a few years ago that the reason we have such difficulty to *eradicate entirely the seeds of the vicious circles that have been going on since time immemorial* is, before Jesus, we were on The Great Path of Becoming, efforting to survive and striving to get ahead. The laws of the land dictated the balancing of karma/action as an eye for an eye, a tooth for a tooth… So, our go-to habitual response was one of struggle, determination, and endurance.

After Jesus overcame the world, resurrected, and went into the darkness and released bound souls, the Great Path of Becoming was no longer a necessity, as long as we embraced the new action of Grace, asking for the highest good of all concerned and following Spirit's dictates. As the gates to Heaven open outwardly and cannot be stormed, we ask for Grace and embrace Wu Wei/Thy will be done. The appropriate time to cross the great river into undifferentiated consciousness is a non-predictive state, decided in Spirit, so we prepare ourselves and are ready when our spiritual name is called.

THE GOLDEN BRIDGE

The Golden Bridge is a symbolic expression of God consciousness, Christ Consciousness, the Living Love. To move across, there are precepts:

- ❖ Acceptance
- ❖ Cooperating with what is accepted
- ❖ Gaining understanding with the cooperation, and then
- ❖ Building enthusiasm

Enlightenment is gaining knowledge, and illumination is having total spiritual flow. An illuminated one can illuminate the bridge but will not walk it for another. Too many will want to walk it for others. The fun of the whole thing is walking it.

The Golden Bridge has been called the true self, cosmic consciousness, the oneness, or all-ness. In moving across the Golden Bridge, one must have reference points of his or her progress—inside and outside, to help bypass the inner and outer illusions. The one who is the reference point outside must be relatively free of illusions. He can't be totally free, because he has a physical body, which is an illusion. The inner must be able to function both as an Inner Master and as an outer Mystical Traveler, or whatever term is used.

Do everything perfectly today. When done perfectly, the past reflects into the present. The Bridge is infinite; it goes from being to beginning, or from ending to ending, or from alpha to omega. Travelers crossing the bridge always lift to new levels, though at different points on the same bridge.

As above, so below; as below, so above applies up to soul realm. From soul realm and above, there are no reference points, because it just is. (Ref: John-

Roger, in the preface to *Across the Golden Bridge* (1974), co-edited by Sanderson Beck and Mark Holmes. A free copy can be found on my website, www.drmarkholmes.com.)

After Sanderson and I had finished editing and I was wondering about the cover, I dreamt the following, which I had an artist friend draw:

Alchemical Formulas

- We know there are no incurable diseases, only incurable people. We treat ourselves, rather than treating a disease. We know all disease is caused by a blockage of energy or not efficient utilization of energy. Find blockages, clear them, and do the Forgiveness process.
- We know the importance of the Basic Self and how underutilized it is in healing and curing. Amplify your relationship with the Basic Self.
- When was the earliest time you are aware of making up a story to support a limiting belief?
- If this story is anchored in your body, where is it? Place your hands on that place and ask the belief to speak to you. Give it a voice or sound.
- Put one hand on your heart and the other where the limiting belief resides and make statements of forgiveness out loud to release your story. Include forgiving yourself for buying into the misunderstanding.
- Take a deep breath and release that limiting belief/story to Spirit. Ask that the places that were emptied be filled with Light. Receive from Spirit what is authentic about your True Self.

* * *

Notes

10. LIBERATION-IMMORTALITY

THE LIGHT OF OUR CONSCIOUSNESS is the most magnificent gift we can give anyone. In the Tenth Palace, we touch to others with what we learned transcending through the Nine Palaces. We accept and give love, ideally unconditionally, returning back into society from the wilderness of our travails to assist others as Spirit directs.

Cycles of 7 and 8 are assigned to the years after ages 70+ until end of life for women and 80+ for men. We keep turning to the Light, and the Spirit will move through us to affect others, however Spirit chooses. It is the Light's job to deburr the planet, so we do not need an agenda or keep track of the results of our interactions.

An aspect of suffering happens when we do not honor our true nature, our reason for being. In the outer world, nature puts things in order. If man pollutes, nature will find a way to accept, cooperate, and institute balancing. We can apply this teaching of acceptance during our inner journey.

Key: We cultivate our true nature. The result is we have a life with heart. In loving others, we give them respect, care, and support.

***

The Evolved Way
Tao Te Ching, Ch. 81

Sincere words are not embellished
Embellished words are not sincere.
Those who are good are not defensive
Those who are defensive are not good.
Those who know are not erudite
Those who are erudite do not know.

Evolved Individuals do not accumulate
The more they do for others, the more they Tain.
The more they give to others, the more they possess.
The Tao of Nature
Is to serve without spoiling.
The Tao of Evolved Individuals
Is to act without contending.

* * *

To find out if I'm listening to the voice of love, I ask myself two questions:

Does the guidance I'm receiving promote or enhance at least one of the following qualities: health, wealth, happiness, loving, caring, or sharing?

Does the guidance serve or assist others in some way? If the answer to both questions is yes, then I am comfortable acting on my intuition. (Ref: J-R)

You are the source of what is happening around you in your world. If you change your behavior, people around you will start changing their behavior also. Be an example of what you want in your life. It is better to allow this formless Spirit of God to move through you, unconditionally, in all situations and at all times. Let it move as the wind from Heaven, of which you know neither the source nor the destination. As you open yourself to God's loving presence within you, share yourself fully with the Beloved. Hold nothing back. Be vulnerable, open, as you rest in the arms of the Beloved, for your perfect vulnerability will be your perfect protection. (Ref: J-R)

RESPECT, CARING, AND SUPPORT

When I look at you physically, I really don't see you. You are the Soul. The things around you that I see physically are what you have placed out into the world for the Soul to live here. So, if I want to relate to you, I must relate to you on a Soul level.

That's very easy to do. The first thing to do is to have respect, the second is to care for the person, and the third is to support the person. That is called loving. So, if we maintain the dignity of the human being, then we have respected, supported, and cared for them. It may do nothing for anything out there when we do that, but we're not trying to save the world. We evolve ourselves because of that goodness in our nature. (Ref: J-R)

To live with vitality to one hundred years, the sages have emphasized acceptance and tranquility, keeping our thoughts and spirit inside by observing. When we fill ourselves with Spirit, there is no room for pathogenic factors. If we do get sick, we can view it as a situation our soul has created, promoted, or allowed for our learning and growth. It may be a clearing action. My clinical experience is that it takes ten to fourteen days after an emotional trauma for the symptoms to show up in the physical body. We endeavor to become congruent by accepting and cooperating with what is. *Once we have the wisdom inherent in the lesson, we do not need the experience.* The dis-ease disappears, and we are cured.

It is said that our bodies belong to nature, so its fate is not as important as we commonly think. We drop attachment to our personal story and realize the oneness inherent in apparent duality.

> When you get high enough in the consciousness, everyone has the same name. That name is love. To see the face of God, you must see the face of God in all people. And that takes a lot of courage, because you have to continually move yourself past your personality, prejudices, and points of view until you recognize your oneness with those other personalities out there. Everyone lives inside you. (Ref: J-R)

> To transform the world
>
> You must accept the people around you.
>
> You must accept the people out in the world.
>
> You must accept the people who are killing other people
>
> Must.
>
> For in this acceptance, you can control their slaughtering.
>
> In your understanding, you can show them the way.
>
> In your cooperation, you can lift the world.
>
> And by your enthusiasm, the Soul walks alive in the human form.
>
> You have then fulfilled the spiritual consciousness present. (Ref: J-R)

HO'OPONOPONO

Ho'oponopono is an ancient Hawaiian practice of forgiveness and reconciliation. Traditionally, Ho'oponopono is practiced by healing priests and family members of a person who is ill. Modern versions are performed within the family by a family elder or by the individual. Similar practices are performed throughout the South Pacific, including Samoa, Tahiti, and New Zealand.

> *How Dr. Hew Len Healed a Ward of Mentally Ill Criminals with Ho'Oponopono*
> adapted from an article by Rosario Montenegro
>
> Ho'oponopono is the Hawaiian system that heals oneself and the world. More than thirty years ago, at the Hawaii State Hospital, there was a special ward, a clinic for mentally ill criminals. People who had committed serious crimes were assigned there, either because they had mental disorders, or they were checked to see if they were sane enough to stand trial. They had committed murder, rape, kidnapping, or other violent crimes. According to a nurse who worked there, the place was so bleak, "not even the paint could stick to the walls; everything was decaying, terrifying, and repulsive. Not day would pass without a patient-inmate attacking another inmate or a member of the staff."
>
> The staff was so frightened, they would walk close to the walls, if they saw an inmate coming their way in a corridor, even though inmates were shackled all the time—even being shackled wouldn't stop the aggression. The inmates would never be brought outside to get fresh air because of their relentlessly threatening attitude. Nurses, wardens, and employees preferred sick leave most of the time.
>
> One day, a newly appointed clinical psychologist, Dr. Stanley Hew Len, arrived at the ward. The nurses braced themselves for one more guy who was going to bug them with new theories and proposals to fix the horrid situation, someone who would walk away as soon as things became unpleasant. However, this new doctor didn't do anything like that. He didn't seem to be doing anything, except just coming in and being always cheerful and smiling, in a very natural, relaxed way. He wasn't even particularly early in arriving every morning. From time to time, he would ask for the files of the inmates.

He never tried to see them personally. He just sat in an office and looked at their files; to members of the staff who showed an interest, he would tell them about a weird thing called Ho'oponopono.

Little by little, things started to change in the hospital. One day, when somebody again tried to paint the walls, they stayed painted, making the environment more palatable. The gardens started being taken care of. Some tennis courts were repaired, and some prisoners started playing tennis with the staff. Other prisoners were allowed to be unshackled and received less-heavy pharmacological drugs. More and more patients obtained permission to go outside unshackled, and they did not cause trouble to the hospital's employees.

In the end, the atmosphere changed so much, the staff was not on sick leave anymore. More people than needed now wished to work there. Prisoners started to be released. Dr. Hew Len worked there close to four years. In the end, there remained only a couple of inmates, who were soon relocated somewhere else, and the clinic for mentally insane criminals closed.

How to Practice Ho'oponopono in Four Simple Steps

From Laughter Online University

Have you heard of the Hawaiian therapist who cured an entire ward of criminally insane patients without ever meeting any of them or spending a moment in the same room? It's not a joke. The therapist was Dr. Ihaleakala Hew Len. He reviewed each of the patients' files, and then he healed them by healing himself. The amazing results seem like a miracle, but then miracles do happen when you use Ho'oponopono or Dr. Len's updated version, called Self I-Dentity Through Ho'oponopono (SITH).

I had the pleasure of attending one of his lectures a few years ago and started practicing Ho'oponopono immediately. The results are often astounding.

Do you need a miracle?

What you might wish to understand is how this can possibly work. How can you heal yourself and heal others?

Why would it affect anything "out there"? The secret is there is no such thing as "out there"—everything happens to you in your mind. Everything you see, everything you hear, every person you meet, you experience in your mind. In fact, it is quite the opposite: you are responsible for everything you think and everything that comes to your attention. If you watch the news, everything you hear on the news is your responsibility. That sounds harsh, but it means you are also able to clear it, clean it, and, through forgiveness, change it.

(MH note: I have been taught we are not responsible for what comes into the mind, but what we hold in the mind. So, if we say deflect within a minute to expunge thoughts that come into the mind, we are able to release them. The conscious mind can hold less than ten thoughts for about ten seconds at any one time, so unresolved thoughts will get dumped into the subconscious, only to resurface later. It is best to be judicious about what thoughts we keep around.)

There are four simple steps to this method, and the order is not that important. Repentance, Forgiveness, Gratitude and Love are the only forces at work—these forces have amazing power.

The best part of the updated version of Ho'oponopono is you can do it yourself. You don't need anyone else to be there, you don't need anyone to hear you. You can say the words in your head. The power is in the feeling and in the willingness of the Universe to forgive and love.

> **Step 1: Love – I LOVE YOU**

This can also be step 4. Say *I LOVE YOU*. Say it to your body, say it to God. Say *I LOVE YOU* to the air you breathe, to the house that shelters you. Say *I LOVE YOU* to your challenges. Say it over and over. Mean it. Feel it. There is nothing as powerful as Love.

> **Step 2: Repentance – I'M SORRY**

As I mention above, you are responsible for everything in your mind, even if it seems to be "out there." Once you realize that, it is very natural to feel sorry. I know I sure do. If I hear of a tornado, I am so full of remorse that something in my consciousness has created that idea. I'm so very sorry that someone I know has a broken bone that I realize I have caused.

This realization can be painful, and you will likely resist accepting responsibility for the "out there" kind of problems, until you start to practice this method on your more obvious "in here" problems and see results.

Choose something you already know you've caused for yourself. Overweight? Addicted to nicotine, alcohol, or some other substance? Do you have anger issues? Health problems? Start there and say you're sorry. That's the whole step: *I'M SORRY*. Although I think it is more powerful if you say it more clearly: "I realize I am responsible for the (issue) in my life, and I feel terrible remorse that something in my consciousness has caused this."

> **Step 3: Ask Forgiveness – PLEASE FORGIVE ME**

Don't worry about who you're asking. Just ask! *PLEASE FORGIVE ME*. Say it over and over. Mean it. Remember your remorse from Step 1 as you ask to be forgiven.

> **Step 4: Gratitude – THANK YOU**

Say "*THANK YOU*" — again, it doesn't really matter who or what you're thanking. Thank your body for all it does for you. Thank yourself for being the best you can be. Thank God. Thank the Universe. Thank whatever it was that just forgave you. Just keep saying *THANK YOU*.

That's it. Simple and amazingly effective. Thinking or acting negatively places us under the law. Repeating the Ho'oponopono or its equivalent, allows us to be in the consciousness of Grace.

A spiritual path is a path of peace. One way to measure how spiritual one is to measure the peace in one's life. When we walk down a street, the spiritual consciousness radiates off us and affects people we do not see who are blocks away. We listen to Spirit and follow its guidance as we participate in the world, we will flow into the one beingness called Tao/Source/God.

I love you, I am sorry, please forgive me, thank you.

On July 14, 2015, physicists at the Large Hadron Collider at the CERN in Switzerland announced the discovery of a new particle, the pentaquark.

"The pentaquark is not just any new particle," spokesperson Guy Wilkinson of the University of Oxford told *Symmetry Magazine*. "Studying its properties may allow us to understand better how ordinary matter, the protons and neutrons from which we're all made, is constituted."

First predicted by Nobel laureate Murray Gell-Mann in the mid-1960s, the particle is made up of five (penta) quarks, a special kind of subatomic particle that will help physicists better understand how matter was first made in the early universe.

To my eye, this looks eerily similar to the Five Phase Chart and seemingly identifies and verifies one aspect of the ancient *as above, so below* statement as the sub-atomic microcosm having an identical relationship to the macrocosm.

* * *

Notes

APPENDIXES

Forgiveness Process

There are two layers of forgiveness. First, the person we judged (ourselves or another); and second, ourselves for having judged in the first place. The technique? So simple that some people doubt its effectiveness and don't try it.

Say to yourself, "I forgive (name of the person, situation, or thing you judged, including yourself) for (the transgression). I forgive myself for judging (same person, situation, or thing, including yourself) for (what you judged)."

That's it. Simple, but amazingly effective. You can say it out loud or say it to yourself. That's all there is to forgiveness. Simple but powerful.

How powerful? Do five minutes of forgiveness. See what happens. (Per J-R, MSIA)

* * *

Q: Sometimes, I feel as if I have emotions, thoughts, or even physical sensations that are not mine, and I think I may be picking them up from others. Is there a way I can clear these?

A: There is a technique you can use to clear people, places, things, etc., from yourself.

- ✶ You put the palm of one hand over your forehead and say the name of the person (or whatever, let's call it X) and then say, "Anything from or through X. Clear, disengage, disconnect." (You can also say something like "cut off," or any other verb that gets across, to you, what you'd like to take place.)

- Then, while your hand is still on your forehead, you ask that this be done through the Traveler, Christ, and Holy Spirit, and have the intention that it will clear completely.

That's it. You might take in a deep breath or two, but you don't need to concentrate intently, because whatever is going to happen is going to be done through the Spirit.

After you have cleared something, immediately place the Light in and around you; then just let go of whatever it was you cleared and don't look to see if it is still there or not.

You may find that this clears whatever it is, or you may find, after about five or ten minutes or so, you feel you need to do it again, at which time you can just repeat it. Sometimes these essences clear one at a time, so you might be doing it until all of them are gone. In addition, sometimes it may take quite a few times to clear some of these things; they come off like a peeled onion.

One other thing: when clearing a person, you may have to say the person's name backwards. In other words, say you are clearing "John Smith." You may also need to say "Smith John" when you do it, because the name has gone in "backwards."

(From the article, "Dealing with Black Magic and a Technique for Protection," by John-Roger, published in the print *New Day Herald*, Volume 10, Issue 1.)

**

Eight-Foot Cube of Light

You can ask for "the eight-foot cube of Light," and it will be there for spiritual protection in the physical world. It will be there. You can also just ask for "the cube of light." This is how to protect yourself before the event occurs. To protect yourself after the event has occurred is like closing a barn door after the horse has run out. It's called dumb time.

You protect yourself every time before you go out anywhere. When you go out your door, you just say, "Cube of Light." You may see it in your mind (but you don't have to see it); it's like a big box putting you in the light. If you're going toward a large group of people, then you may say, "I want a hundred-foot light barrier." The Spirit knows how to do this. You don't, but the Spirit does. What we do is inform the Spirit that we'd like it.

Whenever you hear of any negativity, don't condemn the people involved. Just send Light and love to everyone, even to those who have "messed up." Everyone messes up, so it's no big deal. We send Light and love to them and to the mess-up.

And send your Light and love to things you support, too. (Ref: MSIA.org)

Calling in the Light

There are many techniques for asking for the Light, and the main idea is along these lines: If this is for my highest good and for theirs, then I would like the Light to be placed with me, with them, and with this situation. If your intention is clear that you are asking for the spiritual Light for the highest good, you can also just say, "Light." This is the first thought in some people's minds when they hear a siren or hear about a situation that is distressing or challenging in some way. Some people read the newspaper and listen to news on TV and in their consciousness is "Light" for all they read, hear, or see. After Calling in the Light, you may want to chant a few times the Hu or Ani-Hu.

When you chant, you can pronounce Hu like the name Hugh or say the sounds of the individual letters H and U.

Ani-Hu is a variation of the Hu chant. Pronounced "ahn-eye-hu," it is also an invocation to God with an added dimension that brings in the quality of empathy and oneness with others.

These tones open the centers in the head. In MSIA, we do not work in any level below the upper part of the third eye. This is not because the energy of the centers below that is "bad" but because the most direct path to Soul Transcendence is through the top two centers. (Ref: MSIA.org)

Planting a Light Column

For the highest good, envision or intend a funnel or pillar of Light from the highest place you can imagine going right through you and into the very core of the Earth. That is all you need to do.

The Light column you place may be effective for two days, thirty minutes, or fifteen years. Its duration does not matter, and you do not even need to concern yourself with that, since Spirit is actually doing it. Perhaps a Light column will hold for two hours, which may be the exact amount of time it was needed in that area.

If you are in one area day after day, continue to place Light columns there. People who have used this technique in their homes and offices have noticed positive results. It is a beautiful and effective way to clean up your immediate environment. You can also do this throughout the city you live.

Placing Light columns is a way to integrate into your daily life and routine a specific awareness of Spirit. When you do this, you are using your spiritual energy in positive action that can bring positive results to the physical level. It is wonderful when more and more people are willing to say, "I'm a Light-bearer. I'll bear Light wherever I go." As a spiritual being, you have inside the ability to call forth and bring forth the Light of God into any environmental situation and to transmute the negativity into a positive gain.

As just one example of this, to help stabilize the Earth, you can ask that a column of Light be placed into the center of the Earth and then radiate to the North and South Poles. This can help areas that are prone to earthquake.

Light columns can be as big as a drinking glass, as thin as a pencil, as large as a house, as huge as an entire city, or like the Washington Monument. Have you ever seen the sun shining through a window and seen dust particles floating in the air? A Light column will sometimes look very much like that.

When you see that kind of Light energy or force, you may think your vision is a little disturbed, but it may be that you are tuning in to higher frequencies and seeing a little more than the physical realm. That is good news. Of course, you might not visually perceive the Light columns, and you certainly do not have to. Not seeing them does not lessen in any way your ability to create them. You will probably never know directly the benefit that such work has, the ways it touches to people, or the positive changes it brings about. It is a silent work, a silent ministry, and a powerful one. (Ref: MSIA.org)

Placing Light columns is a way to integrate into your daily life and routine a specific awareness of Spirit. When you do that, you are using your spiritual energy in positive action that can bring positive results to this level. (Ref: John-Roger, DSS)

Sound Current

The sound of the current that comes out of the heart of God we refer to as the Sound Current. And if we were using an acronym for that, we would say Speaking–Of–Ultimates–Now–Divine. It's a much higher quality than the Light. We see the Light when we are working in the realms of light in the physical, astral, causal, mental, and etheric realms, and it's very beautiful.

When you get in the Soul Realm, then you hear the Light, and that is the Sound Current. You hear it in a very special sound. Sometimes, it sounds like about four billion violins playing harmonious notes. It's a quality that can't be placed into words.

Once you hear the Sound Current or you have been connected to it, and you're traveling the inner levels of Light, you just keep the light in front of you and you listen to the sound. And you can follow it back through the levels into the ocean of love and mercy. Therefore, you're guiding yourself right back into the consciousness of this thing we call God.

That seems to be a word that doesn't really suffice either, but, for lack of a better word, let's say that's where it is. It's been called "Father-Mother-God," it's been called "it," it's been called a lot of things. But the essence is that it exists when everything else does not. It is that which we came from. And so, the value of the Sound Current becomes tremendously more important than the quality of Light, because you can live without the Light. Once you've seen it, you can turn from it. But once you have partaken of the Sound Current, you can never live without it. It fills your every beingness. It becomes the word made flesh within you. It becomes everything in totality. And you could live without food and water and air before you could live without this sound, this stream of the Sound Current that comes down to us. (Ref: MSIA.org)

* * *

Using Herbs as Teachers

To effect change, we can use herbs. Herbs have a chemical composition, an electrical frequency, and like all things living, consciousness. Since herbs originate outside of our bodies, they can be viewed as possible teachers.

We can take herbal qualities into our consciousness when taking them orally or during contemplation of their attributes. If you buy the herbs listed for the Palace within which you are working, tuning into their frequency while taking them as a tea can yield powerful results. Full descriptions of the herbs are found in the text. Descriptions here are edited for brevity.

Herbs can be ordered from my website in powder form: www.drmarkholmes.com/shop

1. HEALTH PALACE

   - **Shi Chang Pu/Acorus Root** opens the heart portal and promotes emotional balance for those who do not trust themselves, so they can make good choices. It is good for people who are unhappy with their lives. It opens the senses, clears the mind, overcomes illusion, develops intuition, and elevates the Spirit.

   - **Yuan Zhi/Polygala/Everlasting Will** returns willpower to its pristine state as extra strength is needed in a crisis to overcome dampness/resistance and to break through blocks.

   - **Fu Ling/Hoelen/Guiding my Soul Destiny** assists releasing what is no longer working, so we are not stuck in the past.

   - **Rou Gui/Cinnamon Cortex** is a spiritual plant with much Shen/spirit. Besides circulating Qi/blood in the chest area it protects against pernicious external energies of a toxic environment or psychic atmosphere.

   - **Ye Ju Hua/Chrysanthemum** helps guard against overthinking.

2. WEALTH PALACE

- **Ling Zhi/Reishi/Ganoderma/Guide the Soul** is the herb to which all other herbs and plants and vegetation evolve. It assists us to cultivate virtue while exploring the mysteries of life as we transcend the palace in which we are working. Reishi enhances our self-assigned meaning of life and lightens the body and consciousness so one feels like flying over the dross of life.

- **Tian Men Dong/Asparagus/Door to Heaven** flushes out stagnation and procrastination by purging turbid sticky phlegm that blocks cellular respiration. By extension, asparagus can break curses, psychic insults and lingering or outmoded thoughts/beliefs by increasing oxygen utilization.

- **Bai Zhu/Atractylodes/The Granary/The Great Harmonizer** conducts other herbs throughout the body. It also diffuses food stagnation and removes mucous that slows decision making.

- **Tian Ling Xian Tonic:** a more complex formula is the common Taoist Jade Purity School longevity herbal formula called **Tian Ling Xian**. It can be infused in rice wine by soaking four grams of each powdered herb together for at least two weeks. Take one ounce of liquid each evening to nourish the spleen/pancreas, which controls thoughts and memory and therefore is good for focused meditation.

- **Ling Zhi/Ganoderma** is a Lung Qi talisman.

- **Tian Men Dong/Asparagus** holds the lung Qi.

- **Mu Xiang/Saussarea** is a stomach and spleen Qi tonifier.

- **Sheng Ma/Cimicifuga** rids evils and parasites while tonifying the spleen-pancreas.

- **He Shou Wu/Polygonatum** tonifies liver/kidney yin.

- **Gou Qi Zi /Lycium berries** are good for the eyes and nervous system.

3. PROSPERITY-HONOR PALACE

No herbs used here. Moxibustion is utilized.

4. RELATIONSHIP PALACE

- **Yu Zhu/Polyganatum odoroti/Jade Bamboo** represents the evolution of one of our objectives: health and longevity through flexibility. This herb used to repair sinews, sprains, and tears.

- **Huang Jing/Polygonum/Solomon's Seal—Will Strengthener.** It has been said that will power/willingness is the fourth treasure in the Three Treasures system, being a necessary ingredient to breaking habits and holding through crises. Polygonum connects Kidney sexual energy with the loving heart, linking sexual function with good feelings, bringing new levels of happiness.

- **Di Huang/Rehmannia/The Marrow of Yellow Earth** is used here to build back the flesh, treating broken bones, torn sinews or tendons, and emotional rips or tears.

- **Sheng Ma/Cimicifuga** clears heat in head around **Touwei/St-8/Yin Yang House** at the side of the head and prevents our dying before we are destined. Sheng Ma draws out things hidden in deeper layers of subconscious and unconscious that can cause problems, such as ghosts, demons, toxins, obsessions, unfulfilled desires, and toxins inherited from parents. **Cimicifuga** assists our freeform writing exercise.

- **Chai Hu/Bupleurum** clears blocked Qi energy in the chest, abdomen, and throat, ridding obstructions in head that block communication between the Basic Self and spirit. **Bupleurum** impacts the liver, which deals with time, so it is good for acknowledging the past is past and to embrace the new.

5. CREATIVITY-CHILDREN-FRIENDSHIP PALACE

Notice that these herbs have "shen" in their name, indicating aspects of the Five Spirits.

- **Ku Shen/Sophora root** awakens us to the lessons inherent in suffering.

- **Xuan Shen/Scrophularia** After getting in touch with the cause of suffering, we reframe how we view the situation and which beliefs caused the suffering.

- **Dan Shen/Salvia** allows us to change who we think we are.

- **Ren Shen/Ginseng** re-orients how the consciousness will flow to the extremes of our lives. Ginseng tonifies yang Qi and gives us endurance.

- **Sang Ye/Morus** increases oxygen utilization.

- We add one more herb to move Qi into the pelvis, in alignment with large intestine's influence in this palace: **Niu Xi (Huai Niu Xi/Achrysanthis Root—100 Slops-Knees of the Ox** guides other herbs to the pelvis and consolidates energy for healing after stagnation has been addressed.

6. GLOBAL ADVENTURE-JOY-HAPPINESS PALACE

    - **Ren Shen/Ginseng** is known as the root of humanity. It works with the Three Treasures/Three Selves, opening the heart and quieting the Shen, and settling the Basic and Conscious Selves.

    - **Gan Cao/Liquorice** goes to all organs, making sure we remain physically strong, protects against adverse Qi, and addresses the uncertainty of whether to move quickly or hesitate.

7. CAREER-KNOWLEDGE PALACE

Chong Mo/ Thrusting Vessel

- **Wu Wei Zi/Schizandra** enters all twelve channels to benefit and boost Qi/energy, as an adaptogenic that improves taxation syndrome, purifies the liver, sharpens the mind, and is an aphrodisiac.

- **Yu Zhu/Polygonatum Solomon's Seal** augments the lung's ability to *let go of grief, sorrow, and despair,* assisting alchemical redemption of self from materiality for those who are willing to put in the time and energy. Polygonatum strengthens the kidneys, ova/testicles/sperm count, lower back and tendons, so it is also valued by athletes.

- **Xuan Shen/Scrophularia** clears phlegm and dispels accumulations and consolidations in the abdomen from undigested food, benefiting kidney Qi.

Dai Mai/Belt Vessel

- **Long Dan Cao/Gentianna** works on the GB and diaphragm.

Yin Qiao Mai/Yin Heel Vessel

- **Sheng Di Huang/Rehmannia/Marrow of the Earth** builds back the flesh, treats broken bones and injured sinews. It cools desires that produce heat/inflammation in the blood. Rehmannia is referred to as the kidney's own food and is common in anti-aging formulations for regeneration and longevity.

Yang Qiao Mai/Yang Heel Vessel

- **Wei Ling Xian/Clematis/Awesome Spiritual Immortal** opens channels and relieves blockages and pain.

- **Shan Yao/Dioscorea/Mountain Medicine** transports water, supports muscle, and is an appetite suppressant.

- **Gan Jiang/Zingaberis Officinalis/Dried Ginger Root** aids digestion and clears phlegm.

Ren Mai/Conception Vessel/Sea of Yin

- **Tien Men Dong/Asparagus/Doorway to Heaven** rids dampness, nourishes kidney's ability to reabsorb minerals, and clears heat/inflammation. It helps us to overcome the Three Worms/karma that gnaw on our life force. It quiets the Shen to bring peace to the soul.

- **Chai Hu/Bupleurum** gets rid of the old and brings in the new by ridding obstructions in the head, heightening communication between little Shen within and the universal Shen. It harmonizes thoughts and emotions to relieve tension/stagnation virtually everywhere in the body.

- **Sheng Di Huang/Rehmannia/Marrow of the Earth** builds back damaged flesh and bones and injured sinews/tendons. It cools desires, which produce inflammation in the blood. Rehmannia is the kidney's own food and common in anti-aging formulations for regeneration and longevity.

Du Mai/Governing Vessel/Sea of Yang

- **Chuan Xiong/Ligustricum Wallichi** invigorates the blood and removes Qi stagnation, expels wind and relieves pain.

Yin Wei Mai/Yin Linking Vessel

- **Dang Gui/Chinese Angelica** is used when we do not know who we are or what to do. It tonifies blood for the heart and liver and moves the blood to alleviate pain.

- **Wu Wei Zi/Schizandra** is used for trauma or stress.

- **Chuan Xiong/Ligustricum Wallichi** invigorates blood and moves Qi stasis, expels wind, and relieves pain.

- **Wu Jia Pi/Acanthopanax** dispels wind and dampness, strengthens the tendons and bones, and promotes urination.

- **Dan Shen/Salvia** invigorates blood circulation and removes stagnation.

- **Xuan Shen/Scrophularia** clears phlegm and expels accumulations and consolidations in abdomen from undigested food, thereby benefiting kidney Qi.

Yang Wei Mai/Yang Linking Vessel

- **Xiang Fu/Rhizome Cyperi** opens all meridians and releases Liver Qi stagnation, including pain under the ribs, abdomen fullness, emotional disturbance, poor appetite, and frequent sighing.

- **Shan Yao/Dioscorea/Mountain Medicine** is responsible for transporting fluids to rid heat/inflammation and assists pancreatic digestion to engender the musculature.

* * *

Clearing Lower Portals

- **Yi Yi Ren/Coix-Plantago Seed** clears damp heat and cold that lingers in lower burner and deals with the Three Worms/karma. Coix-Plantago Seed is barley, so avoid if gluten sensitive.

- **Mu Xiang/Saussarea Vladimiriae - Peach Wood Fragrance** clears perverse Qi and obstacles in lower abdomen. Good if sensitive to psychic energies of groups or ghosts in any environment which may alter one's personality.

Strengthening Weaknesses

- **Tu Si Zi/Cuscuta/Rapid Silk Seed** decoction processed in a wine and taken over a long time strengthens any weakness from injury or emotion.

- **Ba Ji Tian/Radix Morindae Officinalis** treats impotence, premature ejaculation, and soreness of the lower back and knees from long-term illnesses. Morindae increases mental power and keeps us strong and robust, and therefore it is valued by both athletes and alchemists.

8. WISDOM PALACE

    - **Taoist Two Immortal Powder** strengthens the kidneys and increases Zhi/willpower, so we can take care of ourselves and take care of others. Three grams of powder of each in warm or hot water in the morning as a daily formula is recommended.

    - **Lu Rong/Deer Antler** replenishes yin essence, tonifies Qi, and tonifies yang.

    - **Di Huang/Rehmannia** strengthens the kidneys and adrenals, builds blood, and heals injuries.

    - **Go Ji/Lycium Berries** is a blood and circulatory tonic and used for longevity.

    - **Ren Shen/Ginseng** is an adaptogen, an athletic and nerve tonic.

Herb-wise, we pick trees that give us the best feeling/nourishment through their taste: sour, sweet, bitter, spicy, and salty. Watch that you do not immediately think, Oh I like sweet taste... Which taste nourishes you most?

> Sour: **Suan Zao Ren/Zizyphus** clears the heart of agitation and relaxes the mind. It is good for insomnia and achiness in the four limbs.

> Bitter: **Rou Gui/Cinnamon Cortex** is a bridge between heart and kidney and brings Jing/essence to everything in life. Cinnamon has both a bitter and a spicy flavor. Exercise caution when using the essential oil.

> Sweet: **Fu Ling/Poria/Revelation of the Curriculum,** whose attribute is letting go, nourishing, and allowing the heart to be free. Fu Ling helps us resolve emotions by quieting the Hun/Basic Self, which is known as the collector of experiences. Fu Ling embraces all, knowing God is found in all things. Fu Ling rhymes with the Ling in Ganoderma, which means soul/mandate/command.

Fu Ling is found at the base of trees; it is viewed as the root of hidden curriculum or aspirations. It is taken at bedtime to have prophecy dreams seeing into the future. It is also good for fear, worry, and fright, being insulted, or having one's honor challenged, as it releases distention in the diaphragm from emotional stress.

➢ Spicy: **Rou Gui/Cinnamon** treats hundreds of diseases by connecting the little Shen to big Shen and helps alleviate a congested heart. Cinnamon nurtures the Shen and Jing and assists our return back to Ming Men/source energy. Chinese cinnamon bark is one of the most warming of all herbs and will strengthen aversion to cold, weak kidney/backache, and lack of sexual energy. Since the herbal quality of Chinese cinnamon is strong and potent, ask an herbalist for a proper dosage.

➢ Salty: **Du Zhong/Eucommia** prevents our structure from breaking down, strengthening the bones, ligaments, and tendons.

Finish the herbs in the section above (or skip them) before embarking on the herbs depicted below. Pick one or two that sing to you. The most effective way is to have the intention to *take on* attributes as you drink a decoction of the herb.

- To nourish the heart to make embracing everything easier, take **Nu Zhen Zi/Fructus Ligustricum**. Nu means receptive woman and Zhen means true femininity, so we can be reborn with childlike innocence. **Ligustricum** is said to rid hundreds of diseases because it supports the true self.

- **Sang Ji Sheng /Loranthus/Woman and Child/Boy and Girl.** When we see life as pleasant, rigidity in the neck and back relaxes, giving us the suppleness to move into new ventures. Most people are stiff in their upper back and neck. If so, also stretch and rotate the neck to allow pleasantness and a relaxed feeling into the body and mind.

- **Bai Zi Ren/Biota Seed/Platycodon/Seeds from the Tree of Life** is the most commonly prescribed tree in Chinese medicine. It has a soothing effect on the Five Zang organs and the Five Spirits: Hun/BS, Po/CS, Shen/HS, Yi/Intention, and Zhi/Will. It is often planted in cemeteries to appease both the aggrieved and deceased.

- **Mu Xiang/Radix Aucklandia.** When we speak truthfully, people sometimes are annoyed, as it points out their schemes. They might react negatively, even violently. Aucklandia helps us deal with perversity from others, as well as pestilent Qi/epidemics.

- **Long Dan Cao/Gentianna** settles the 5 Zang organs so we are comfortable with who we are, and it assists us when afraid of change.

- **Yi Mu Cao/Leonorusi** has connections to the Eight Extra Vessel and our blueprint. Leonorusi brightens the eyes so, with heightened perception, we see into the mystery.

Consult with a qualified herbalist regarding the dosage, frequency, and combinations for tree herbs. Recommendations are found on my website.

9. COMING HOME TO THE SPIRITUAL FULFILLMENT PALACE

No herbs, as this Palace is the arena of introspection, contemplation, and meditation.

NOTES

REFERENCES

Across the Golden Bridge co-edited by Sanderson Beck and Mark Holmes, 1974.

Acupuncture point location charts copied from www.acupuncture.com.

A Historical Perspective in Traditional Chinese Medicine by Paul L. Reller L.Ac.

Advanced Acupuncture, A Clinical Manual: Protocols for the Complement Channels by Ann Cecil-Sterman.

Aspects of Spirit and *Five Aspects of Spirit* book and seminar, Elisabeth Rochat de la Vallée.

www.Awaketolove.com. Michael Hayes and Alisha Das.

Ban Cao Jing, The Divine Farmer's Materia Medica by Shen Nong.

The Biology of Perception, The Psychology of Change by Bruce Lipton, PhD and Rob Williams.

Blood Stasis: China's Classical Concept in Modern Medicine by Gunter R. Neeb.

System of Self-Healing: Internal Exercise by Dr. Stephen T. Chang. San Francisco: Tao Publishing, 1986. p. 200.

Destiny, Vital Force, or Existence? On the Meanings of Ming in Daoist Internal Alchemy and Its Relation to Xing or Human Nature by Fabrizio Pregadio.

Encyclopedia of Taoism (2-volume set), Fabrizio Pregadio, editor

Book of Balance and Harmony by Li Daoqun, translated by Thomas Cleary.

Book of Heart Teachings by Bian Que.

The Complete Foundations of Internal Alchemy: The Taoist Practice of Neidan by Fabrizio Pregadio.
The Founding of Northern and Southern Schools, commentary by Lui I-ming, Thomas Cleary translation in *Vitality, Energy, Spirit.*

How Dr. Hew Len healed a ward of mentally ill criminals with Ho'Oponopono, Rosario Montenegro.

How to Practice Ho'oponopono in Four Simple Steps, Laughter Online University.

Inner Worlds of Meditation booklet, www.MSIA.org.

I Ching translations from The I Ching Workbook, R. L. Wing.

MSIA.org

The Mystery of Longevity, Liu Zhengcai.

Nature, Motion, and Stillness: Li Daochun's Vision of the Three Teachings, Paul Crowe. *Journal of Daoist Studies* 5:51-88. 2012.

The Nine Supreme Inner Alchemy Formulas of Grand Master One Cloud, Grand Master Mantak Chia & Al Dirk.

Neuro Emotional Technique (NET) developed by Scott Walker, D.C. A psychosomatic stress reduction intervention based on the Five Phases of Oriental medicine.

The (Only) 5 Fears We All Share, Karl Albrecht Ph.D. *Psychology Today.*

Original Tao: Inward Training (Nei-yeh) and the Foundations of Taoist Mysticism, Harold Roth.

"The Placebo Effect: How It Works." Faith Brynie, Ph.D. *Psychology Today.*

"Psychoneurogastroenterology: The abdominal brain, the microbiome, and psychiatry." Henry A. Nasrallah, MD. *Current Psychiatry.*

Seasons of a Man's Life, Daniel J Levinson.

The Seal of the Unity of the Three (Cantong qi), Fabrizio Pregadio.

The Seven Basic Plots: Why We Tell Stories, Christopher Booker.

Su Wen and *Ling Shu:* references framed by lectures by Jeffrey Yuen.

Translations of Taoist texts by Thomas Cleary provide background information.

Traditions of Divine Transcendents, Ge Hong. Translated by Robert Ford Company as *To Live as Long as Heaven and Earth.*

Treatise on Febrile Diseases Chinese Acupuncture and Moxibustion, Vol. 2

Understanding Reality, a Taoist Alchemical Classic, Chang Po-tuan, Fabrizio Pregadio, translated by Thomas Cleary.

Why Our Brains are Biased Toward Optimism, Tali Sharot. www.ted.com. Feb. 2012

The World Upside Down Essays on Taoist Internal Alchemy, Isabelle Robinet, edited and translated by Fabrizio Pregadio.

Zhou Dunyi's Diagram of the Supreme Ultimate Explained (Taijitu shuo): A Construction of the Confucian Metaphysics, Robin R. Wang. *Journal of the History of Ideas.*

ACKNOWLEDGMENTS

THE NINE TRANSFORMATIONS is a product of fifty years of personal alchemical work and learning through attending patients in a clinical setting. I hold in deep respect my primary way-showing mentors who represent an eclectic world approach: John-Roger-USA, Masaru Toguchi-Japan, Dr. Lee-Shing Sheng-Taiwan, Se Han Kim-Korea, Helmut Schimmel-Germany, and Jeffrey Yuen-China.

I appreciate and thank my editor, Kathryn F Galán, and her discerning eye and attention to detail. Thank you to Alisha Das Hayes, who proofread for accuracy and gave valuable suggestions in the sections detailing with karma as well as the Three Selves and their interactions; our understanding of these two aspects is critical to health, healing, longevity, and the attainment of "immortality."

I thank my patients, who trusted me with their health. I am grateful for our interactions as I learned as much from you as you did from me.

ABOUT THE AUTHOR

Dr. Mark Holmes, OMD, L.Ac, Dipl. Chinese Herbology (NCCAOM) and Dipl. Acupuncture (NCCAOM) began his alchemy journey as an oriental philosophy major in the late 1960s. He graduated from formal Oriental medicine studies in Hong Kong in 1974 and developed a high-profile practice at his Center for Regeneration in Beverly Hills, which included such notables as Nobel Laureate Bishop Desmond Tutu, R. Buckminster Fuller, and many executives and actors in the entertainment industry. Dr. Holmes now facilitates Chinese alchemy seminars.

Visit the author's web page at:

www.DrMarkHolmes.com